A primary function of any Bible commentary is to bring out, clearly and plainly, the essential meaning of every verse of the text without losing sight of the great theme or themes which are its main focus. This function is admirably fulfilled in the present volume. Allan Harman's exposition is as clear as crystal and he highlights the special importance of the covenant and the law, showing how formative they are in the whole structure of the book. This is a work of fine scholarship lightly worn.

Geoffrey Grogan
International Christian College, Glasgow

Allan M. Harman is Professor of Old Testament and Principal of the Presbyterian Theological College, Melbourne, Australia. Previously he was Professor of Old Testament at the Free Church College, Edinburgh, Scotland. For Christian Focus he has written a commentary on the Psalms as well as a short book called *Learning About the Old Testament*. In addition he edited a re-issue of the account of their visit to Palestine in the mid-nineteenth century by Robert Murray McCheyne and Andrew Bonar (also published by Christian Focus under the title, *A Mission of Discovery*). Currently he is writing a commentary on Isaiah for the Focus on the Bible series. Dr Harman was one of the translators of the New King James Version of the Bible.

Commentary on Deuteronomy

Allan M. Harman

Christian Focus

ABBREVIATIONS

AV	Authorised (King James) Version
LXX	The Septuagint, the oldest and most important Greek translation of the OT made in Egypt about 250 B.C.
MT	Massoretic Text, the Hebrew text of the Old Testament that became recognised as authoritative after the fall of Jerusalem in A.D. 70.
ms(s)	manuscript(s)
NASB	New American Standard Bible
NEB	New English Bible
NIV	New International Version
NKJV	New King James Version
NRSV	New Revised Standard Version

Note: When referring to passages in the Old Testament in which the covenant name of God occurs (*yhwh*), the form 'Lord' is used. This is in accordance with the practice of English versions, the form 'Lord' being reserved for the translation of words other than *yhwh*.

Published in 2001 by
Christian Focus Publications
Geanies House, Fearn, Ross-shire
IV20 1TW, Great Britain

Cover design by Alister MacInnes

For a free catalogue of all our titles, please write to
Christian Focus Publications,
Geanies House, Fearn,
Ross-shire, IV20 1TW, Great Britain

For details of our titles visit us on our web site
http://www.christianfocus.com

Printed and bound in Great Britain by
The Guernsey Press Co. Ltd., Guernsey, Channel Islands

Contents

PREFACE

Over twenty years ago I developed a particular interest in the book of Deuteronomy as I worked on translating it for the New King James Version. Since then I have come back to it repeatedly while lecturing on the Pentateuch. In addition, I had the opportunity to teach graduate courses on Deuteronomy at both Ontario Theological Seminary, Toronto, and the Reformed Theological Seminary, Jackson, Mississippi.

I acknowledge with great thankfulness all those who have written on Deuteronomy and from whose writings I have greatly benefited. In particular I acknowledge the tremendous stimulus of one of my own teachers, Meredith G. Kline, for his pioneering work on the covenant structure of Deuteronomy. In relation to Deuteronomy and the Decalogue I consider the work of Professor B. Holwerda of Kampen as outstanding, and it is a great pity his writings are not widely known in the English speaking world.

Once again my friends Bernard Secombe and Mark Tonkin have given great assistance in reading my manuscript, and their diligence and accuracy is much appreciated.

My wife Mairi has encouraged me when other commitments seemed to occupy all my time to the exclusion of continuing work on this commentary on Deuteronomy. She has read the whole manuscript and made very helpful suggestions.

Allan M. Harman

INTRODUCTION

1. Title

In the Hebrew Bible no titles are attached to the various books. For centuries the Jewish custom has been to name each book by its opening words. Deuteronomy starts with the words *'elleh hadᵉvarim*, 'these are the words', and hence it was called 'the words'. Our English title has come via Latin and Greek and means the second law. The expression is drawn from Deuteronomy 17:18. However, there it clearly refers to the king having a *copy* of the law for himself and not to a second law.

The contents of Deuteronomy show clearly that the book is not a second law, but a renewal of the covenant made on Mount Sinai (called Horeb throughout Deuteronomy except in 33:2). It is also linked expressly with the gracious promises God gave to Abraham, Isaac and Jacob (see e.g., 6:10-11 and 7:7-9). The children of Israel have come through their years in the wilderness. Now, on the brink of entering into the land promised to Abraham their forefather, they again acknowledge the LORD's rule over them.

2. Deuteronomy and the Pentateuch

Like all biblical books Deuteronomy can be studied separately, yet it forms part of God's total revelation. While it has to be viewed in its particular setting in the Mosaic period of Israel's history, yet it has also to be seen as providing foundational material for so much of later biblical teaching.

The Pentateuch is the name given to the first five books of the Old Testament. It is derived from the Greek word *pentateuchos* which means 'the five-volumed [book]'. Deuteronomy comes as the last of these five, and forms a fitting climax to this opening section of the Old Testament. The central ideas of Deuteronomy are not peculiar to it alone, but are common to all the books of the Pentateuch.

Genesis 1-11 is foundational for the rest of the Pentateuch and indeed for the rest of the Bible. *It details the nature of God's created world that overcomes the consequences of sin.* From

Genesis 12 the covenant blessings become dominant. In the covenant with Abraham God promised three things:

a large family (Gen. 12:2)
a land (Gen. 12:1, 7)
blessing to the nations (Gen. 12:3).

In each case the promise was confirmed by God to Isaac and to Jacob, but then jeopardised by human sin. At the time of Abraham's death only the promise of the large family was evidently being fulfilled.

The remaining four books of the Pentateuch reiterate the essential features of the Abrahamic covenant, and there is constant recall of the basic promises. The promise of a large family having been fulfilled, attention turns to the land. The emphasis in the last two books of the Pentateuch (Numbers and Deuteronomy) is on the aspect of the land. Israel is moving towards the land of promise, and on its border renews its allegiance to the God of the covenant. Even at this stage the promises are only partially realised, and the hope of the fullness of God's blessing has to lie in the future. Of all God's gifts to Israel, the land takes pre-eminence, and so Moses constantly reminds Israel that God was about to fulfil his word. It is solely because of his grace that the gift will become theirs (cf. 4:40; 5:16; 7:13; 11:9, 21; 21:1, 23; 25:15; 26:10, 15; 28:11, 63; 30:18, 20; 31:13, 20; 32:47). Deuteronomy ends with the death of Moses, but points ahead to the impending realisation of the possession of the land. While the opening of Deuteronomy is looking backward, the conclusion of the book is looking forward.

3. Deuteronomy and the Remainder of the Old Testament
The sequel in Joshua shows how the land came into Israel's possession, and the narrative indicates how the provisions given in Deuteronomy were known and applied. Both in warfare and in worship adherence was given to the requirements of Deuteronomy. Thus, for example, the principle of the devoted objects was obeyed in the case of Jericho (Jos. 6:21, 24) in accordance with Deuteronomy 7:1-6 (cf. also Deut. 13:12-18). Similarly, the

covenant ceremony between Ebal and Gerizim (Jos. 8:30-35) implemented the provisions of Deuteronomy 11:29 and 27:1-26.

Later Old Testament history shows how influential the covenant renewal in the plains of Moab was for Israel. Many detailed incidents recorded in the biblical record clearly relate back to Deuteronomic provisions, while drastic reforms initiated by Hezekiah (2 Kings 18:1ff.) and especially by Josiah (2 Kings 22:1ff.) were to bring Israel back into conformity with the laws of Deuteronomy. So much of the prophetical teaching is couched in terms reminiscent of Deuteronomy's language and in accordance with the covenantal principles set out in it.

The influence of Deuteronomy is also apparent in the primary history of Israel, the so-called 'former prophets' (Joshua, Judges, 1 and 2 Samuel, 1 and 2 Kings). The writers of these books were clearly influenced by Deuteronomy, because its teaching became the standard by which actions were judged (cf. the reasons given in 2 Kings 17:7-23 for the fall of the northern kingdom of Israel). The selection, use and commentary on historical incidents and personalities betray a prophetic background with a deep appreciation of the teaching in Deuteronomy. This history is 'deuteronomic' in the sense that it reflects the same standpoint in regard to the covenant relationship as does the book of Deuteronomy.

4. Structure

The relationship between God and his people is expressed in both the Old and New Testaments as a covenant relationship. A covenant was a bond graciously entered into by God. It denoted his sovereign rule over his people and their acceptance of that rule, with its implications for the totality of their lives. In some parts of the Old Testament the actual word covenant does not occur, yet the presence of associated vocabulary points clearly to the presence of the covenant idea.

In recent years, much helpful light has been shed on Old Testament covenants in general by the study of extra-biblical treaties. It is clear that there was a formal pattern to these treaties, and various Old Testament covenants reflect it. This is particularly so with features of the covenant with Abraham, covenant at Sinai and its renewal in the plains of Moab.

Between fifty and sixty of these extra-biblical covenants are now known, many from around 1400 B.C. (with some earlier still), while others come from the later Assyrian period (around 800 B.C.). Not surprisingly, echoes of their structure are found in the Old Testament. This is because God's revelation came in a precise historical setting, and he couched that revelation in terms that the people could readily understand. In this way they could more easily grasp its significance and show obedience to its demands.

The pattern of the Hittite Treaties from the second millennium B.C. has greater similarity to the pattern in Exodus and Deuteronomy than the Assyrian texts from the first millennium B.C. The pattern is as follows:

1. Preamble, identifying the King making the treaty.
2. Historical survey, outlining the events leading up to the treaty.
3. Stipulations required of those giving allegiance to the covenant.
4. Curses and blessings pronounced for either disobedience or obedience respectively.
5. Arrangements for seeing that the covenant was continued in succeeding generations.

There are also Near Eastern legal collections from the second millennium B.C. of which the laws of Hammurabi (from around 1750 B.C.) are the best known. They follow a standard pattern of history, laws, document clauses, curses and blessings, and differ markedly from later lists of laws.

When the covenant made at Sinai (see Exod. 20-24) is compared with these treaty and legal patterns the resemblance in order is remarkable. Even more striking is the way in which the structure of the book of Deuteronomy reflects this whole pattern. The preamble and historical survey occupy chapters 1-4. Then the basic core of the covenant is given in chapter 5, followed by expansion of it in chapters 6-26. The curses and blessings come in chapters 27-30, while the final chapters (31-34) deal with the provisions for the on-going covenant life under Moses' successor, Joshua.

This structure helps to highlight the uniqueness of the relationship between God and his people Israel. God had chosen Israel in love (Deut. 7:9) and now, as the covenant is renewed after forty years and as the people are on the point of invading Canaan, he re-affirms his demands upon them. A holy God required his people to reflect his holiness and to respond in obedience to his love.

The style of the book is also important. It purports to be words that Moses addressed to the children of Israel, and only in the opening words of chapter 1 (verses 1-5) and parts of chapters 29, 31-34 does narrative occur. The purpose of Moses' speeches is to encourage the people and to explain to them (see 1:5) the demands of their covenant God. Ultimately the speeches will bring the people, when confronted with God's demands, to take these demands that were already near them (30:11-14) and pledge themselves to obey them. Others, later in Israelite history (e.g., Joshua or the prophets Jeremiah and Ezekiel), also employed the same sermonic style in their appeal to their own generations.

The whole purpose of the book determines the contents. Thus, no attempt is made to repeat all the laws already given in the earlier books. There is no mention of circumcision, or the Day of the Atonement. Rarely does Moses give extensive treatment of the individual laws. Chapter 14, with its detailed laws about food, is an exception to the general method of stating the law briefly, sometimes with specific illustrative examples. In many cases the time and place of the covenant renewal governed the material included. Provision is therefore made for matters that will apply as soon as Canaan is entered (e.g., laws regarding warfare), or later, when a people, who had consolidated their position in the land, seek new institutions (e.g., kingship).

The book is entirely in keeping with its setting across the Jordan. The aged Moses looks back on all that happened since the people left Mount Sinai. There are also recollections which go back further to their sojourn in Egypt (see e.g., 5:6; 7:15; 11:10; 15:15; 16:12; 24:18; 28:27, 60). Moses not only sets out the major requirements but repeatedly urges the people to listen to their dying 'father' and obey the LORD's requirements. He knows that the past cycle of apostasy, punishment and pardon will occur again. However, his aim is not to stimulate Israel to delve into God's secret purposes, but rather to obey his revealed will (29:29). The encouragements and warnings of Moses to his 'children' play an important role throughout the whole book. It ends fittingly with the account of his death and burial (chap. 34).

5. Significant Teaching of Deuteronomy

5.1 Its Exposition of the Decalogue
Apart from the Book of the Covenant in Exodus 21-23, the book of Deuteronomy contains the fullest exposition of the Decalogue found in the Bible. Reference to the Decalogue and quotations of several of the commandments occurs quite often, but there is little exposition of its intent. Deuteronomy, from 6:1 through to the end of chapter 26, spells out the intent of the Decalogue and challenges the people of Israel to display, by their wholehearted obedience to his decrees and laws (Deut. 26:16-19), that they are his treasured possession and his holy people. Under the New Covenant the same pattern of obedient response to Christ's commands is expected (Matt. 28:20; Jn. 14:23).

The Decalogue is set apart as the basic core of the covenant. It is not to be equated with statute law for Israel, for no human penalties are specified. Instead, divine curses and blessings are included. That the Decalogue cannot be equated with criminal law is also shown by the presence of the Tenth Commandment, which deals with the sin of covetousness, which could not come within the scope of a human court. The Decalogue was applicable to all Israelites and every member of the society had the responsibility of observing the law. In addition there was a national responsibility of adhering to the sovereign's demands (Deut. 29:18-29).

The contrast between the Decalogue and the exposition (Deut. 6-26) is not between divine and human laws. Rather, the contrast is between the basic core of the covenant in the Decalogue and the exposition which sets out various applications of the Decalogue and which also impresses it on the consciences of the listeners. While the Decalogue was written by the finger of God (Deut. 5:22 'he wrote them'; Deut. 9:10 'written by the finger of God'; Deut. 10:2 'I will write on the tablets'; Deut 10:4 'The LORD wrote on these tablets'), yet it is expressly said that the decrees and statutes were given to Israel by a direction to Moses (Deut. 6:6), and Moses claimed that they were really the commands of the LORD (Deut. 11:26). The basic intent of the Decalogue is further maintained and illustrated in the exposition. The stipulations of the covenant are related to typical situations to which they will apply when Israel comes into the sworn land.

The order in which the exposition of the commandments takes place is striking. In the Book of the Covenant in Exodus 21–23 several of the commandments are covered, but not in the order in which they appear in Exodus 20. However, in Deuteronomy the commandments are dealt with in the same order. The prescriptive form of the commands comes in chapter 5 (the Decalogue), while the descriptive form occupies chapters 6 to 26. Since the middle of the nineteenth century various studies have shown that the Decalogue governs the ordering of the material in Deuteronomy 6-25 (or 6-26). While there is continuing discussion on this, yet it is clear that the stipulations section of the covenant document that makes up Deuteronomy is basically an unfolding of the significance of the Ten Commandments *in the order* in which they are set out in Exodus 20 and Deuteronomy 5. These chapters *expound* or *elaborate* the essential thrust of the Decalogue, but also show the *trajectory* for each commandment. That is to say, the implications of each commandment are set out, and these implications carry, for example, the sabbath principle much further than a first reading of the Fourth Commandment would suggest. So much of Israel's life was structured around this principle. Similarly with the Fifth Commandment, its trajectory included all the authority structures within Israel, not just the parent/child relationship.

Two further important points need to be made as well. First, the commandments are not as discrete in their meaning as we sometimes assume. There is overlap between them, and this is particularly clear with the final commandment, 'You shall not covet'. Hence it should not be surprising if the exposition of a particular commandment in Deuteronomy contains material that also relates to another of the commandments. Secondly, there is often a transitional passage between the exposition of individual commandments. These are the seams that bind together the various pieces that make up this sermonic elaboration and application of the Decalogue. They form a bridge between the discussion on individual commandments.

5.2 Its Teaching on Covenant

Deuteronomy is concerned with the relationship between God and his people. This is expressed in terms of covenant. As with other biblical covenants, the essential feature of it was God's act of gracious condescension in entering into such a relationship with his people. There was nothing in them which moved God, but it was solely his own love which impelled his choice of them as his people and their redemption by his outstretched hand of power (see especially 7:7-9, 9:5-6 and 14:2). The incomparable God of the covenant had stooped to meet them in their need. At Sinai and in many of the wilderness experiences he had shown them his glory and majesty.

The corollary of this was the special position afforded to Israel. Not only were they chosen by God as his people, but as adopted children they were to bear the family likeness (14:1-2). Holiness of life was to characterise them, and as devoted servants of the LORD they were to yield loving obedience to his covenant demands. The redeemer God demanded allegiance to his commands. Blessings for obedience, curses for disobedience – the choice was plain for Israel (11:26-28; 30:15-20).

Constantly throughout the book the reader is reminded that the covenant was not new. It was clearly a renewal of the covenant made forty years earlier at Horeb. But the link is made with earlier covenants still, in that there is repeated reference to God's promises to Abraham, Isaac and Jacob (see 1:8; 6:10; 9:5, 27; 29:13; 30:20; 34:4). The earlier covenants were not annulled by the later ones, but supplemented and expanded. God's revelation was cumulative, and at each stage of revelation additional teaching was given. There is continuity in Deuteronomy with the message of the earlier covenants and anticipation of the later ones.

What is unique about Deuteronomy is that the book itself is structured according to the pattern used in second millennium B.C. treaty documents. While many other books of the Bible have sections that show affinity with extra-biblical covenant patterns, Deuteronomy is the only one that displays *in toto* such a pattern. Its content and its structure are thus tied together by the common theme of 'covenant'.

Emphasis on the covenant structure should not divert attention away from the fact that the covenant was a *relationship* between God and his people. The covenant was an intensely personal matter, in which God drew near to people and promised, 'I will be your God and you shall be my people'. Hence a covenant was a bond between God and man, sovereignly imposed by God in his grace, whereby he and his people gave expression to their relationship in formal terms. Placing stress on the fact that God unilaterally imposed his covenant should not cause us to lose sight of the obligations on those in that relationship. Deuteronomy shows that it was a mutual relationship, and that the covenant people were expected to respond in obedience to all that their sovereign God had done for them. Redeemed people, in covenant with God, had to act in the pattern he established for them, and no aspect of their lives was exempt from his ethical demands.

5.3 The Concept of the Land

The word 'land' (Heb. *'erets*) is the fourth most frequent noun in the Old Testament, occurring 2,504 times. It occurs quite often in Genesis, Exodus and Leviticus, but it becomes even more frequent in Numbers and Deuteronomy. While Exodus and Leviticus are more concerned with the aspect of relationship between God and his people, Numbers and Deuteronomy concentrate on the aspect of the land. In Numbers the idea of movement towards Canaan appears at the outset as the census is taken. Israel at that stage was being prepared for military conquest. The real movement of the people actually begins in Numbers 10:11-12 as Israel sets off from the wilderness of Sinai to the place that the LORD had promised (10:29). In Numbers 31-35 nothing is embodied in the narrative that does not relate to the land.

In Deuteronomy everything is focussed on this theme, and therefore special attention has to be given to it. By its end the point is reached where the people are on the edge of possessing the land, but it is still not reached. It is over-stating the case to suggest that Deuteronomy only refers to 'the land' as *the* patriarchal promise, as references to the promise of a large family occur in 1:10; 10:22; and 28:62. However, it remains true that Deuteronomy is replete with references to the land, and the most characteristic phrases used of it are 'the land you are to possess' (22x) and 'the land which the LORD your God gives to you' (or, 'us') (34x).

The Land as Promise

The fact that the LORD swore an oath regarding the land is referred to in 1:8, 35; 4:31; 6:18, 23; 7:8, 12, 13; 8:1, 18; 10:11; 11:9, 21; 13:18; 19:8; 26:3, 15; 28:11; 29:12; 30:20; 31:7, 20, 21, 23. It is notable that most of these occur in the introductory section up to the end of the exposition of the First Commandment, and then in the concluding section from chapter 26 onwards. The reference is to the oaths made to the patriarchs, and some further comment on them is needed. The promise regarding a large family and a land are inter-connected. The large family needs living space, just as a land needs not only vegetation but occupants.

The story of Abraham opens with the promise of the land (Gen. 12:1ff.). He was told that he was to go out from his own land to a country which he would be shown. This promise is made more specific when it was indicated to him in 12:7 that this country was to be the land of Canaan. It was repeatedly confirmed to him that God was going to give his descendants that land (13:14-17; 15:7, 13, 16-18 [with geographical indications]; 17:8). The promise of the land is embedded in the covenant formulations in chapters 15 and 17. It is probably better to speak of the 'sworn land' rather than 'the promised land' as Hebrew has no specific word for promise. In English translations 'promise' can be a rendering of

the verbs 'to say' (Heb. *'amar*) or 'to speak' (Heb. *dibber*), but
the Old Testament's most frequent expression in this connection
is of the land which the LORD swore (*nishba'*) to give to Israel.
The stress falls on the fact that the gift of the land is a free and
sovereign one by God, but also on the connection between
obedience and the fulfilment of God's promise (cf. Gen. 22:16,
'because you have done this'; Gen. 26:5, 'because Abraham
obeyed me').

The promise was repeated to Abraham's descendants, with
specific reference back to the promise to Abraham. At a time of
famine Isaac was told not to go down to Egypt but to stay in the
land and enjoy the blessing of the LORD. The assurance was given
to him: 'For to you and your descendants I will give all these
lands and will confirm the oath I swore to your father Abraham'
(Gen. 26:3b). These words simply re-echo what was promised in
the earlier passages already cited. Later in the same chapter there
is the account of the dispute between Isaac's servants and the
herdsmen of Gerar over wells. Finally they dug a well which was
called Rehoboth, of which Isaac said: 'Now the LORD has given
us room and we will flourish in the land' (Gen. 26:22).

The promised blessings flow to Jacob, not to Esau. At Bethel
the promise of the land is repeated to him, and again it occurs
with reference back to Abraham. The LORD identified himself as
the God of Abraham and Isaac before going on to assure him: 'I
will give you and your descendants the land on which you are
lying . . . I am with you and will watch over you wherever you go,
and I will bring you back to this land. I will not leave you until I
have done what I have promised you' (Gen. 28:13-15). Later, when
Jacob returned to Bethel from Paddan Aram, God again confirmed
the same promise, saying: 'The land I gave to Abraham and Isaac
I also give to you, and I will give this land to your descendants
after you' (Gen. 35:12).

Once Moses was called to be God's agent in delivering his
people from Egypt, the LORD reaffirmed his promise regarding
the land. He spoke of delivering his people from their bondage
and bringing them into the land flowing with milk and honey
(Exod. 3:8, 17). The covenantal character of the oath regarding

the land is re-affirmed in Exodus 6:4. As the people of Israel celebrated the first Passover, they were reminded of the need for their obedience when they entered the land the LORD had sworn to them (Exod. 12:24-25). The presence of Israel in Egypt was one aspect of the testing in regard to this promise.

The Content of the Land
The geographical boundaries are specified in various ways in the Old Testament.

Genesis 15:18	From the river of Egypt to the great river, the Euphrates.
Exodus 23:31	From the Red Sea (Heb. *Yam Suf*) to the Sea of the Philistines, and from the desert to the River.
Numbers 34: 1-10	A detailed description including the southern boundary (the wilderness of Zin), the western (the Great Sea), the eastern (the slopes east of the Sea of Kinnereth = Galilee), and the northern (a line from the Great Sea eastwards to Lebo Hamath).
Deuteronomy 11:24	From the desert to Lebanon, and from the Euphrates to the western sea.
Joshua 1:4	From the desert (south) and from Lebanon (north) to the great river, the Euphrates (east) and to the Great Sea on the west.
Psalm 80:8-11	The vine out of Egypt (Israel) covered the mountains and the mighty cedars, its boughs went to the Sea (the Mediterranean), and its shoots as far as the River [Euphrates].

In Deuteronomy there are various descriptions of the land. While in Exodus 3:17 and Numbers 34:2 it is called the land of the Canaanites and Canaan respectively, in Deuteronomy 1:6 it is described as the land of the Amorites. In 7:1 it is described by reference to seven nations then dwelling within its borders. The only occasion in Deuteronomy in which the territorial boundaries are given is in 11:24 where its boundaries are described as being from the desert to Lebanon, from the Euphrates to the western sea. While the territory was never defined with geographical precision, yet its location and general borders were given with sufficient clarity.

It is referred to variously as 'the good land' (1:25, 35; 3:25; 4:21, 22; 6:18; 8:7, 10; 9:6; 11:17), and 'the land flowing with milk and honey' (6:3; 11:9; 26:9, 15; 27:3; 31:20). The summary report of Moses concerning the mission of the spies reported in 1:22-25 also includes the reference to the bringing back of produce to show how good a land it was. It is extolled as a land rich in natural products. The reference to 'milk and honey' parallels a similar expression on a tablet (written in another Semitic language, Ugaritic) found on the Mediterranean coast to the north of Israel. In one document (KTTU 1.6) Baal is said to send fertility and abundance in the form of fat/oil and honey.

13 The heavens rain fat/oil
14 the wadis flow with honey.

The use of the phrase in the biblical texts may well be a polemic against Canaanite concepts and thus a reminder to Israel that the real source of blessing is the true and living God.

Fuller descriptions are given of the possessions they will have in the land (see especially 6:10-12; 8:7-9; 11:10-15). Clearly Canaan was regarded as fertile, not just in comparison with the wilderness through which they had wandered, but also in comparison with Egypt (see especially 11:10, 11).

Another way in which the blessings of the land are described is to speak of 'rest' in the land (Heb. *menuchah* 3:20; 12:9; Heb. *heniach* 12:10; 25:19). The reference in 25:19 is important because it links together the gifts of rest and of the land. In the section dealing with covenant curses expulsion from the land is described as lack of rest (28:65). This 'rest' meant the end to life as refugees, so that Israel could look forward to enjoying a sedentary pattern of life. It also meant security from their enemies. It was to be life in the full enjoyment of God's blessings, along with the absence of war and conflict.

In Psalm 95 God encourages his people not to be like the wilderness generation, and the closing verse of the Psalm (verse 11) speaks of his oath that his people would not enter into his rest

(Heb. *menuchati*). The reference appears to be to Numbers 14:23, 30 or to Deuteronomy 1:34, 35, except that instead of 'land' the psalm uses 'rest'. Clearly rest and the promised land were equated. The epistle to the Hebrews draws upon this psalm in a unit dealing with believers entering into the eschatological rest (Heb. 3:7-4:13). Just as rest awaited the church in the wilderness, so rest yet awaits New Testament believers. In this section of Hebrews 'rest' is identical with 'the heavenly country' sought by believers, 'the lasting city which is to come' (Heb. 13:14; cf. Heb. 11:16).

Israel had no claim on the land

Eighteen times Deuteronomy mentions God's promise of the land to Israel, and in fifteen of these reference is made to God giving it. These references are important for two reasons. First, they emphasise the fact that it was not by sheer historical coincidences that Israel came into possession of Canaan. Long before Israel was constituted as a nation God had sworn an oath concerning the land. Israel's occupation of Canaan was, therefore, part of God's action in history. Secondly, the terminology used points emphatically to Canaan as God's provision. It was a gift of pure and undeserved grace. There is a clear connection between the idea of the land as a gift and the stress on God's free grace to his people. The initiative was God's, and his actions, including provision of Canaan, were an expression of his love for his people.

There was no natural right of Israel to the land. In entering the land Israel had to remember that it was not because of her righteousness that this was happening, but because of the wickedness of the nations previously in possession of it. When the sin of the Amorites reached full measure (Gen. 15:16), they would be driven out. Even before God permitted them to enter, the Israelites had to learn the Song of Moses (Deut. 32) which was to be a testimony against them. In telling Moses to write down and teach the children of Israel the song, the LORD indicated that even before he brought them into the sworn land he knew what they were disposed to do (Deut. 31:29). Israel had no claim of herself to rights over the land.

This point is underscored in another way in Deuteronomy for

there is stress on the fact that Israel can never own the land. It belongs to the LORD, not to Israel. He had proclaimed his ownership of the land in the words, 'the land is mine' (Lev. 25:23). Now in Deuteronomy the people are reminded that they can only enter into an allotment by inheritance (Heb. *nachalah*, 4:21; 19:10; 21:23; 24:4; 26:1) or by entering the land to possess it (Heb. *yarash*, 5:31; 19:2, 14; 21:1). At times these two expressions are combined when Israel is told that she is entering the land as an inheritance to possess it (Heb. *nachalah l^e rishtah*, 15:4; 25:19). The references to inheritance have to be understood in light of the fact that Israel was God's son. Since God's gift of the land is so prominent in Deuteronomy, this means that the idea of sonship is much more central to the book than might at first sight appear.

Three important consequences followed from this general concept. The first was that the Israelites were not tenants to an earthly landlord. Just as Israel protected the alien or sojourner in the land, so Israel was a sojourner under the protection of the LORD (Lev. 25:23), and to him the land belonged. Secondly, Israel was different from Canaan and other neighbouring countries in that no provision appears in the Old Testament for sale of land. That explains Naboth's refusal to sell his land to king Ahab (1 Kings 21). It could only come to others by inheritance. Pointing to a piece of land, along with the stated intention, was equivalent to a formal transfer. This was what the LORD did for Abraham (Gen. 13:14) and also for Israel through the covenant mediator Moses (Deut. 34:1-4). In one sense all the land was allotted to Israel, but God also arranged the individual allotment of territory to the specific tribes. Thirdly, because the inheritance belonged to the whole nation no one was to be denied access to the privileges bestowed by life in the land. The benefits of the good land had to be shared with the Levites (Deut. 14:27) and also with the sojourners, the widows and the orphans (Deut. 26:12-13). Provision is also made for some of the harvest to be left behind for the needy (Deut. 24:19-21) and for a tithe of the crops for them every third year (Deut. 14:28-29).

There are difficulties in knowing how far these principles were observed throughout the Old Testament period. Clearly kings did accumulate property for themselves, just as Samuel warned would happen (1 Sam. 8:14), and kings such as Uzziah had vast estates (see 2 Chron. 26:6-10). It may well be that kings altered the legal system to make such aggrandisement possible (see Isa. 10:1-4). Perhaps kings and other wealthy people obtained land by taking it as a pledge, and then retained it when the loan could not be repaid. They could not sell the land but they could use it for their own advantage. This in effect was a way of getting around the provision that the land belonged to the Lord and that it could not be sold (Lev. 25:23). Redemption of the land was possible under some conditions (Lev. 25:25-28), and the law of the jubilee provided another means of ensuring return of the property to its original owner.

Loss of land may well have had wider social consequences. For example, participation in the local assembly may well have depended upon possession of property. If deprived of property a person would be excluded from the assembly. This would explain why the widow and the orphan were in such a disadvantaged position. The widow had no right of inheritance of property, and also had no place in the assembly, and was therefore unable to plead her own cause in that legal forum.

The gift of the land threw emphasis back on the giver

Time and again expressions are used that refer back to the one making the oath, the covenant God. The focus of attention is on the God who made the oath to the patriarchs, and who was the giver of the land. The ceremony described in Deuteronomy 26:15 highlights this fact. This ceremony consisted of various facets.

a) It was to take place when Israel had come into possession of her inheritance of the land (verses 1, 2, 3, 9).

b) The individual Israelite was to take some of the produce of the land and bring them in a basket to the sanctuary (verse 2).

c) To the priest he was to make the declaration: 'I have come to the land that the Lord your God swore to our forefathers to give us' (verse 3). The priest was then to take the basket and place it in front of the altar (verse 4).

d) The Israelite was then to make a fuller declaration concerning his 'father' Jacob, and concerning the way God had fulfilled his word and redeemed his people from their bondage in Egypt.
e) Along with the Levites and aliens the Israelite was to rejoice in the bounty of God's provision.

At the time of bringing in the first-fruits Israel would recall how God had fulfilled his promise of a land, and this recollection would take place every year on this occasion.

Gift of the land meant possession and care of it

The book of Deuteronomy recognises the rights of Israel to use the land and its products, but only in the context of the Israelites being the covenant people of the LORD. When enjoying the good things of the land the people had to remember that their own power had not achieved possession of the land for them. 'But remember the Lord your God, for it is he who gives you the ability to produce wealth, and so confirms his covenant, which he swore to your forefathers, as it is today' (Deut. 8:18). This was the controlling motive to govern their use of the land, and for many aspects of social and religious behaviour. They had to share their land with those like the Levites who were not given an allotment (Deut. 14:28-29), or with the aliens who had no right to land (Deut. 24:19-22). Their experience as slaves in Egypt should have given them a sense of compassion for the strangers in their midst. The land could be desecrated by certain actions as well, and they had to take care to fulfil all their obligations lest this happen (cf. Deut. 21:22-23 in reference to not leaving the body of an executed criminal on the tree overnight).

Israel's relationship with the land was quite different from the surrounding peoples and from the Canaanites. With those other nations there was often a mythical explanation of their connection with the land. Thus Babylon was Marduk's city, while Thebes was 'the honourable hill of the Primeval beginning'. Israel did not regard the land as divine, but rather saw it as a provision of God through historical events which he controlled. The connection with the land came through history, not mythology.

Continued possession of the land depended on obedience
The land was granted to Israel on condition she remained true to
the requirements that God had placed on her. The threat of exile
from the land is first stated in Leviticus 26:27-35, and then repeated
in Deuteronomy 4:26-27. See also Deuteronomy 6:18; 8:1; 11:8,
21; 16:20; 28:11 ('if you fully obey . . . the LORD will grant');
28:58-63 ('if you do not faithfully follow all the words of this law
. . .you will be uprooted from the land you are entering to possess');
30:17-20.

This same point is made clear too by the fact that the earlier
generation did not go into the land because of unbelief and
disobedience, and that included Moses! Later, when the prophets
were threatening the disobedient people with exile, they often seem
to echo the very language of the covenant curses of Deuteronomy
(see especially a passage such as Isaiah 5:26-30 in comparison
with Deuteronomy 28:49-68).

6. The Prophetic Significance of Deuteronomy
Like all of the Old Testament revelation Deuteronomy points
beyond itself. It marks off another stage in God's dealings with
Israel and preparation for fuller disclosures of his grace. Not only
was revelation progressive in the Old Testament but it was
prospective as well. That is to say, at each stage there were
elements present pointing to revelation yet to come. In this way
expectation was quickened, and believers were encouraged to look
for God's future activity and disclosures.

In Deuteronomy two offices were designated that were to
become central for later Old Testament history. These were
kingship (17:14-20) and prophecy (18:9-22). The basic functioning
of these institutions was set out by Moses, but yet considerable
time was to elapse before they became operative. Kingship became
firmly established under David, while the prophetic role came
simultaneously to bear on every aspect of life. In addition, the
priestly office continued to be related both to the worship of Israel
and the ministry of instruction in God's law. The prophets were
to take up all three offices and speak of the coming of the Messiah
in terms of prophet, priest and king. Given the inherent

imperfection of all the Old Testament institutions and the partial nature of the revelation it contains, Deuteronomy forms part of the older covenant scriptures that point to new covenant days. Prophet after prophet reminded Israel of what God had done through Moses at the time of the Exodus and of the law he had given. That law was a schoolmaster to lead to Christ (Gal. 3:24).

Christians cannot read the book of Deuteronomy (or any other part of the Old Testament) as if they were standing in the shoes of the original recipients of its message. It has to be read from the standpoint of the fuller revelation in the New Testament. The proclamation of Jesus and his disciples drew directly on Deuteronomy. Jesus quoted it in his temptations (Matt. 4:4, 7, 10 and parallels) and reaffirmed its emphasis on an all-embracing love to God (Matt. 22:37-38 and parallels). The apostolic preaching recorded in Acts draws upon it, especially to point to the fulfilment of the word concerning the prophetic office in the person of Jesus (Deut. 18:15; Acts 3:22). In at least seven New Testament epistles there are quotations from Deuteronomy, with application made of its teaching to varied aspects of Christian doctrine and conduct. Perhaps the most significant of these is the quotation in Galatians 3:10-14. No one could perfectly keep the law, and so God's curse was universal in extent. It is only through God's redemptive work that the curse can be removed and blessing bestowed. Deuteronomy cannot be understood without an appreciation of the sequel set forth in the New Testament. By itself it is part of an overture that requires the finale provided in the fuller New Testament revelation. The institutions and general teaching set out in Deuteronomy only find their fulfilment in Christ.

7. Outline
The text of Deuteronomy can be divided in the following way:

A. Historical Review (1:1–4:49)
1. God's Word to Israel (1:1-8)
2. Horeb to Hormah (1:9-46)
3. Progress towards Canaan (2:1–3:11)
4. Division of Territory (3:12-20)
5. The Line of Succession (3:21-29)

Commentary

A. HISTORICAL REVIEW (1:1–4:49)

Deuteronomy commences with four chapters providing an historical framework against which the rest of the book should be viewed. They bring the covenant history up to date and indicate that the important renewal of the covenant took place in Moab on the eastern bank of the Jordan. The persons involved in the renewal, as well as the place and time, are clearly specified.

1. God's Word to Israel (1:1-8)

1 The book begins with a short introductory section which leads into the historical review. It opens with the expression 'these are the words' from which the Jewish title of the book has been taken (*The Words*). Deuteronomy claims to record Moses' addresses which were delivered in the desert east of the Jordan to all Israel. The expression 'east of the Jordan' is possibly a general geographical description denoting the region of Transjordania, though originally it meant 'across the Jordan' (either east or west depending upon the standpoint of the author). The 'Arabah' is the rift valley running from the Sea of Galilee down to the modern Eilat on the Gulf of Aqabah, and then down into central Africa.

The place names cannot be identified with precision. Both Paran and Hazeroth are mentioned elsewhere in the Old Testament (e.g., Paran in Gen. 21:21; Num. 10:12; 1 Kings 11:18; and Hazeroth in Num. 11:35; 12:16; 33:17) but it is difficult to know if the same places are intended here. 'Suph' means 'reed', and it occurs in the Old Testament Hebrew phrase *yam suf*, 'Sea of Reeds', which expression is used of both the Gulf of Suez and the Gulf of Aqabah (Exod. 13:18; 1 Kings 9:26). While attempts to identify the sites are interesting, the reality of the events does not depend upon our ability to identify the sites with precision today, any more than our belief in the crucifixion and ascension of Christ depends upon discovering the exact locations on which they happened. Probably all the Deuteronomic sites instanced are in the region of Moab.

2 A note is appended to indicate the time taken for travel from Horeb to Kadesh Barnea. Horeb and Sinai are synonymous terms, but in Deuteronomy Horeb is used almost exclusively with the only occurrence of Sinai appearing in 33:2. In the 19th and 20th centuries this time period of eleven days was tested and proved quite possible. The reason for this statement here is, however, not just a matter of curiosity. Rather there is a sharp contrast between 'the eleven days' here in this verse and 'the fortieth year' in the following one. Because of their disobedience Israel was to experience those long and bitter years in the wilderness and only at the end of that period are they again on the borders of Canaan.

3 The only specification of time in the whole book occurs here. Moses' proclamation took place on the first day of the eleventh month of the fortieth year. This fits with other time indicators in Numbers and Joshua. Miriam died in the first month (Num. 20:1), and Aaron died on the first day of the fifth month (Num. 33:38). The Jordan crossing took place on the tenth day of the first month in the forty-first year (Jos. 4:19). The content of Moses' proclamation did not originate with himself but was a declaration of instructions he had received; and they were intended specifically for all Israel.

4 The reference to the defeat of Sihon and Og is important. Israel had to realise that the LORD was continuing to fulfil his promises. Moses had led them to victory over these two Amorite kings. Edrei could well have been another capital that Og occupied, rather than the place where he was defeated. The following chapters spell out details of these victories.

5 It was just prior to Moses' death that he undertook to expound the law to them. Aware of his coming death, Moses gives his final instruction to the people and prepares to hand leadership to Joshua. The reference to 'this law' most probably includes the basic demands of the covenant as law. It is used elsewhere as virtually synonymous with covenant (Isa. 24:5; Hos. 8:1). 'The book of the law' is a fitting description of the entire covenant document (Deut. 28:61).

6 Moses begins by referring back to Horeb and the initiative for moving out from there. It did not come from the Israelites themselves but it was 'the LORD our God', says Moses, who gave the directions. Events at Sinai had seen the Israelites pledging themselves to their God, and now the time had come for advance into hostile territory.

7-8 The people were instructed to move forward and to enter Amorite territory in southern Canaan. They were also to attack in the Jordan Valley (the Arabah), in the low country between the Judean hills and the Mediterranean (the Shephelah), and the desert extending from around Beersheba north to the hills of Judah (the Negev). In the north they were to reach Lebanon, and the Euphrates in the north east, all this being the land promised to the patriarchs (see Gen. 12:1; 15:18-21; 17:8). Abraham had to leave his home land of Ur, but was promised much more in its place. The same promise was also given to Isaac (Gen. 26:3) and to Jacob (Gen. 28:13f.; 35:12). At the very outset of this book the theme of the land appears and it is dominant throughout. The people are reminded that God was fulfilling an oath he had made (Gen. 15). The land which was to be their possession was a sworn land, for God had in solemn covenant pledged it to Israel.

The territorial extent noted here agrees with other descriptions given elsewhere (Num. 34:1-12; Jos. 1:4). The closest Israel came to possessing it was during the reign of Solomon (1 Kings 4:21, 24) or during the reigns of Jeroboam II in the north and Uzziah in the south. After the exile the people acknowledged that the promise of the land had been realised (Neh. 9:8).

2. Horeb to Hormah (1:9-46)

(i) The Appointment of Leaders (1:9-18)
Moses now calls attention to an event prior to the giving of the law on Sinai. He recalls the record in Exodus 18:13-26 when he, acting on the advice of his father-in-law Jethro, appointed leaders and judges to assist him in the task of leading and governing Israel. This section in Deuteronomy looks back to the decentralisation of legal processes in Israel.

9 Moses recalls how he recognised the heaviness of the task committed to him. By himself he was unable to bear the burden of caring for Israel. The reminder of this fact is important as Israel prepares to go into the land under a new leader, but already it had other recognised officials who were able to assist.

10 The covenant given to the patriarchs had promised a large family (Gen. 12:2, 'a great nation'; 26:4, 'descendants as numerous as the stars in the sky'; 35:11, 'a nation and a community of nations will come from you'). Having already referred to God's covenant oath (verse 8), Moses points to the fulfilment of this promise in respect to the large family. Despite the then childlessness of Abraham and Sarah God fulfilled his promise. Abraham had been 'fully persuaded that God had power to do what he had promised' (Rom. 4:21).

11 Moses' prayer is for an even greater fulfilment of the promise than that already experienced. He specifically mentions the blessing of Israel (cf. Gen. 12:2). Probably the thought is of spiritual blessings which would accompany and proceed from the increasing size of Israel. The conjunction of the two ideas is already explicit in the promise to Isaac (Gen. 26:4).

12 The question posed by Moses relates to burdens which press down on him ('problems' and 'burdens' are practically synonymous terms) and to the legal questions ('disputes') that he had to settle. As his father-in-law rightly perceived (Exod. 18:18) some lightening of his burdens, especially in the legal sphere, was necessary.

13 The invitation was given for the people to choose men of practical wisdom and insight; and who were also men of proven ability, for appointment over them. Appointees were to be from each tribe so that those possessing authority over a particular tribe would be chosen from it.

14-15 The proposal being accepted by the people Moses proceeded with the appointments. Leading men were chosen to exercise authority over the various divisions within Israel ('thousands', 'hundreds', 'fifties', 'tens'). At this time there was little separation of general leadership responsibilities, i.e. military roles and legal functions.

16 The judges had the task of hearing disputes, whether they were between native Israelites or involving an alien. The people who had just come out of slavery, without rights as aliens in Egypt, now have to show concern for the alien in their midst. Such aliens would not have the full rights of an Israelite, but are to be accorded respect in legal disputes.

17 In giving judgment the newly appointed officials had to show impartiality, as is stressed twice in this verse ('Do not show partiality in judging; ... do not be afraid of any man'). The additional reason is given that judgment was the prerogative of God himself. God was the LORD to whom they were bound by covenant bonds, and within the theocracy of Israel God was the ultimate judge. He therefore required administration of justice in the earthly kingdom over which he ruled to be a true reflection of his own uprightness as judge over all. The most difficult cases were to be referred to Moses.

18 If God's law was to be administered rightly in the land to which they were going, the people must first show obedience to his commands. The content of their instructions extended to 'everything' that God had commanded through Moses.

(ii) The Exploration of the Land (1:19-25)
These verses summarise the exploration of the land by the twelve scouts. A fuller account appears in Numbers 13. The spies went as far north as the region around Lebo Hamath, which is probably the modern Lebweh in Syria (Num. 13:21). Both accounts focus attention on the Valley of Eshcol and the samples of its bounteous crops which were brought back.

19 At God's direction the Israelites left Horeb and journeyed through the desert until they reached Kadesh Barnea. They were then poised for advance into the hills of southern Judah, which at that time were home to the Amorites.

20-21 Moses reassures the people concerning their right to the land and that their God was in the process of giving them possession of it. There is express mention of the covenant promises concerning the land for 'the LORD, the God of your fathers', said Moses, had given it to them. This covenant faithfulness of God stands in marked contrast to the rebellion of the people that is described later in the chapter (verses 26-46).

22 The people en masse approach Moses suggesting that there should be reconnaissance of the land prior to invasion. They wanted knowledge of the actual situation ('the towns') and also the most appropriate way ('the route') to make the incursion into Canaan.

23 Here Moses accepts the proposition and chooses one spy from each of the twelve tribes. In Numbers 13:1-3 it is stated that it was at the LORD's express command that Moses sent out the spies. Clearly the proposal of the people met with divine approval.

24-25 The spies explored the valley of Eshcol in the vicinity of Hebron, an area still noted for its grapes. Taking some of the fruit (the Hebrew word used, *peri*, is the general word for fruit) the spies returned with a glowing report concerning the land that the LORD was giving to Israel.

(iii) Disobedience and Failure (1:26-46)
26 This verse provides a summary of Numbers 13:26-33. In spite of all God's promises, the spies' report on the land's bountiful nature and Caleb's urging to advance, the people baulked. The word 'rebelled' is a technical term for breach of covenant regulations.

27 That the people grumbled in their tents implies that to one another they spoke rebellious words against the LORD. They even considered that God had brought them out of Egypt because he hated them and wished to destroy them. They had already forgotten that God had brought them out because he loved them and had displayed his sovereign grace in the Exodus. The memory of this event was to remain throughout coming generations in the words of one historical psalm: 'They grumbled in their tents and did not obey the LORD' (Ps. 106:25).

28 The people now questioned where they could go as the report of the spies had made them utterly discouraged. They wanted to transfer the responsibility for their rebellion to the spies. The report was that the Canaanites were stronger and taller (some Hebrew mss. have *numerous* here in place of *taller*, conforming this verse to the expression in 2:10, 21), and living in fortified cities. 'Anakites' seems to be used as a general expression for giants, though it may well originally have been the name of a particular tribe.

29 Moses then tried to re-assure a frightened Israel that there was nothing of which to be terrified or afraid (cf. his earlier words in verse 21). The reality of the opposition awaiting them was not denied, but with God on their side why should they be afraid *of them*?

30 If the people wanted re-assurance for the future they should simply remember the past. They were eye-witnesses of what had transpired in Egypt when God brought them out 'with an out-stretched arm and a mighty hand'. This same God was going before them and would fight their battles.

31 In their desert experiences they had seen the protection which God had afforded them right up to that very moment. It was constant, fatherly protection. The imagery here is important because it relates to the unique relationship between God and Israel. Earlier when Moses was told what to say to Pharaoh in Egypt, this was the message: 'Then say to Pharaoh, "This is what the

LORD says: Israel is my firstborn son, and I told you, 'Let my son go, so that he may worship me' " (Exod. 4:22). Israel had been adopted into a position of privilege and service, and during all the experiences since the Exodus they had known God's fatherly care.

32-33 Even remembering all that God had done for them, they still did not put their abiding trust in him. The verb used here for 'trust' comes from a root which means 'sure, steadfast'. One form of the Hebrew verb (the Hiphil) came to mean 'believe, trust', and the participle here points to a constant characteristic of the people. It was not an isolated incident of unbelief, but an abiding manifestation of distrust. Their attitude was all the more reprehensible, because they had a constant manifestation of God's presence.

34-36 Though the people thought that their murmurings were known only to themselves, the LORD heard them. What they said provoked his anger and his response was in terms of another oath. Whereas the previous one (see verse 8) was an oath concerning possession of the land, this one was to ensure that those of the present generation would be excluded from it. The first oath pledged the land to Israel, as long as obedience was shown to the covenant requirements. Because this generation had proved themselves disobedient they were not to have any part in the blessings of the good land. The only exceptions were Caleb and Joshua (see verse 38). Caleb is described as having 'followed the LORD wholeheartedly'. The Hebrew text literally means 'he filled (himself) after the LORD'. Caleb's commitment was total, and this fact was reflected in his report about the land (Num. 13:30). The territory which he had traversed was promised specifically to him and to his descendants. Joshua 15:13 refers to this promise and notes the allocation to Caleb of Hebron.

37 Against Moses the LORD also displayed his anger. It is possible that on two occasions the LORD was angry with Moses. The first is mentioned here at the start of the wilderness wanderings and the other was much later when Moses struck the rock at Meribah (Num.

20:1-13). However it may well be that Moses brought in here a reference to the later incident as the consequence of his sin was that he too shared in the exclusion from Canaan. Psalm 106:32-33 refers to the same incident and makes the same connection between Moses and the people: 'By the waters of Meribah they angered the LORD, and trouble came to Moses because of them; for they rebelled against the Spirit of God, and rash words came from Moses' lips'. Such thematic linking of ideas, not necessarily in chronological order, is quite common in Old Testament narratives. The reference highlights the fact that it was on account of Israel that Moses was punished. The unique position that Moses occupied as leader of Israel is also emphasised. In the Hebrew text this is indicated both in Moses' words and the quotation of the LORD's words. A literal translation brings this out: 'With me also the LORD was angry on account of you, saying, "You also shall not enter there."'

38 The exclusion of Moses meant that another leader had to be appointed for the covenant people. This may well be a reference to another later incident which is also mentioned here because of the thought of Moses' impending death. In Numbers 27:12-23 there is the account of the designation of Joshua as Moses' successor, while later in Deuteronomy 31:1-8 the actual appointment is described.

He is called here Moses' assistant. The Hebrew text says that he stood before Moses, using a technical Hebrew description for a servant. His task would be to see that Israel truly entered into the promised inheritance.

39 The narrative now reverts to the present situation. In the reference to the children the element of hope appears. Not only are Caleb and Joshua to enter the land but a new generation as well. The rest of this book is concerned to spell out for that and succeeding generations their responsibilities before the LORD. It would seem that the Israelites had also used as an excuse for their own disobedience their fears that their children would be taken captive by their enemies. Those children were not to be punished because they had not reached years of maturity. They could discern between good and evil (cf. the use of a similar phrase in connection with the Messianic child in Isa. 7:16).

40 Moses instructed the people to turn away from Canaan and to travel into the wilderness along the road to the Yam Suf. This seems to have been a road which ran along the rift valley south of the Dead Sea down to the Gulf of Aqaba at present day Eilat. Thus Yam Suf would appear to be a description of the Gulf of Aqaba and not of the sea which the Israelites crossed as they came out of Egypt.

41 The people had a change of mind and wanted to go up and fight. Their confession of sin ('we have sinned against the LORD') was not a genuine one as they still had not grasped the significance of their rebellion. Instead of looking to their God to fight for them, they thought that they could achieve it by themselves. So they made their preparations for battle.

42 Through Moses the LORD warned the people not to venture into battle because now he was not in their midst. The outcome could only be certain defeat in battle.

43 Even when the LORD's message came to them they persisted with their disobedience and presumptuously marched into battle. It was not only a reckless act but one which involved direct covenant rebellion.

44 Defeat was inevitable. The Amorites are likened to vicious bees on the attack (for use of this simile cf. Ps. 118:12; Isa. 7:18-19). They were defeated and had to flee before their attackers from Seir to Hormah, which appears to have been north-east of Kadesh. Later Hormah was part of the territory allotted to Simeon after the conquest (Jos. 19:4).

45 The first verb in this verse (NIV 'you came back') can be used in Hebrew of a mental turning or repentance but here it is best to understand it as a literal return. They appeared before the LORD

(presumably the sanctuary is intended) and wept. Now it is the
LORD who does not listen and pays no attention to their
lamentations.

46 The last verse in the chapter records that Israel remained at
Kadesh for quite a long time. The expression seems to be a general
and indefinite one. It was not that they now remained for as long
a period as they had previously stayed there. Israel had to learn
through bitter experience that what was required was humble and
willing submission to the LORD's clear commands.

3. Progress towards Canaan (2:1–3:11)
After wandering in the hill country of Seir, Israel had to move
northwards and pass through the territory of their relatives the
Edomites (descendants of Esau). Coming into the southern part
of Transjordania they would make contact with Moab and Ammon,
both of whom were descended from Lot (see Gen. 19:36-38). Their
territory had been assigned to them by the LORD and therefore
they were not to be dispossessed (see verses 9, 19). Heshbon and
Ammon were in a completely different category and therefore
they could be completely destroyed. The historical narrative in
this section is important because it records the slow progress
towards Canaan. It also shows how Israel was being taught that
their covenant God had control of all nations.

(i) Problems with Edom (2:1-8)
1 Under divine direction (see 1:40) Israel now turned *away* from
the promised land. After an unspecified time at Kadesh (1:46),
they were starting their wilderness wanderings wherein the
unbelieving generation was to perish. The general area of their
wanderings was the hill country of Seir, south-east of Kadesh.

   At the conclusion of this period the Israelites were told to turn
to the north, thus setting themselves again on the way to Canaan.
The actual route taken is not specified, so they could have gone to
the west of Edom or round the eastern boundary. If the place names
in Numbers 33:41ff. (especially Punon) could be identified, we
might be able to fix the route with some precision. Most probably

the Israelites skirted round Edom by moving along the southern boundary then turning north along the eastern border.

Directions were then issued to the people and indications given to them of the relationship of Israel to Edom. The Edomites are called 'your brothers the descendants of Esau' who have chosen to dwell in the hill country of Seir (cf. Gen. 36:1-29). The comparative friendliness towards Edom shown here and later in this book (23:7-8) was typical of the earlier Old Testament period. Only from later times we have the invocation of curses against Edom (see Amos 1:11-12; Obad. 1-21; Jer. 49:7-22; Mal. 1:2-5). In the Song of the Sea in Exodus 15 Moses and the Israelites sang that 'the chiefs of Edom will be terrified' (verse 15). Moses now reminded them of this fact ('they will be afraid of you'), and also of the need to be on their guard as they meet them. The fear of Israel stands in marked contrast to the relationship between their forefathers Jacob and Esau. When Jacob returned from Paddam Aram it was he who feared Esau (Gen. 32:3ff.).

5 The Israelites were warned not to take any provocative actions against the Edomites as none of their land fell within the territory promised to them. Rather, it was by divine allotment that the Edomites occupied Seir. In his blessing of Esau, Isaac had said that his dwelling would be 'away from the earth's richness, away from the dew of heaven above' (Gen. 27:39). God had determined the exact places in which they should live (cf. Acts 17:26) and none of Esau's inheritance was to be transferred to Israel.

6 In this verse and verse 28 mention is made of the offer to purchase food and water from the Edomites. In neither verse is it said that they did so, for the reference in verse 29 to the descendants of Esau may just be to the permission to pass through their territory mentioned in verse 28b, rather than the note in verse 28a to food and water. Thus the account in Numbers 20:14-21 and Deuteronomy 2 do not conflict.

7 In their wanderings Israel had to think back on all the provision the LORD had made for them. Past benevolences should be the encouragement to look for future provision from the same source. Forty years experience should have taught them that those who truly seek the LORD would lack no good thing (Ps. 34:10). Since their God had provided for them over the past forty years, he would not fail them now.

8 The summary statement in this verse does not mention Edom's refusal of Israel's formal request to pass through their territory. Numbers 20:14-21 tells that because of their fears, the Edomites forcefully prevented the movement of the Israelites through their country. The full narrative was unnecessary here for Moses was concentrating mainly on Canaan as the promised inheritance of Israel. By Edom's action the people were forced to turn off the Arabah road that ran northwards from Elath. Moses' intention may well have been to point out that Elath and Ezion Geber were identical, for sometimes the conjunction in Hebrew can indicate that the second name is simply another for the same person or place (cf. the use of the conjunction to link the synonyms Tiglath-Pileser and Pul in 1 Chron. 5:26). Instead of pursuing their original route they now had to take the desert road of Moab.

(ii) Journey through Moab (2:9-15)
9 The Moabites also were a people related to Israel. Both Moab and Ammon were descendants of Abraham's nephew Lot (Gen. 19:36-38). The LORD warned Israel through Moses not to trouble Moab, nor provoke warfare with them, for the territory they possessed was theirs by his allocation. Ar may well have been a synonym for Moab, or else one of its major settlements. The LXX identifies it with Aroer, but this is uncertain.

10-12 Here some particulars are inserted to explain who were the original inhabitants of the territory now occupied by the Moabites. A similar insertion comes in the next section when Ammon is the subject (verses 20-23). If these historical notes are by Moses, the reference to 'the land the LORD gave them as their possession' (verse 12b) must be the territory which Israel acquired by conquest on the east bank of the Jordan. More probably they are from the hand of the unknown editor who completed the whole book after Moses' death (see the comment at the commencement of chapter 34).

The immediate predecessors of the Moabites were the Emites. Along with the Anakites (see note on 1:28), they were also known as Rephaites, who are mentioned in Genesis 15:20 as being the occupiers of some of the promised land. It is not known whether these are ethnic or descriptive terms. The Horites were the Hurrians, and the Edomites had dispossessed them of the territory around Seir. In a similar way Israel had dispossessed those within the borders of the land promised by the Lord.

13 The narrative concerning the Lord's instructions now resumes. The words 'And the Lord said' are inserted in the NIV to make the connection clear. The other possibility is that they were Moses' words of command to Israel. They crossed the brook Zered which marked the southern boundary of Moab.

14-15 This decisive event is marked by a time reference – 38 years since the Israelites had set out from Kadesh Barnea till this moment. God's judgment against the fighting men of the wilderness generation was now complete. The Lord's oath had been fulfilled (see commentary on 1:34-35) and the wilderness provided the graves for the rebellious men. Their deaths were not just due to natural causes but the direct result of divine judgment. As so often in biblical history, judgment began with the house of God.

(iii) Journey Through Ammon (2:16-23)
16-19 When judgment on the men of the wilderness generation had been completed, new instructions were given to Moses. Territory belonging to the Moabites was passed. As in verse 9 Ar could be either the territory as a whole (and thus used in apposition to Moab) or the name of a major settlement or even the capital. Israel was to approach another nation descended from Lot and again the same instruction is given as that regarding Moab (cf. verse 19 with verse 9). They were not to be oppressed, nor was

their land to be taken from them, because to the sons of Lot, the LORD had allocated territory as their possession.

20-23 As in verses 10-12 another historical note is appended. Previously the Ammonite territory was considered as belonging to the Rephaites (see verse 10), whom the Ammonites called Zamzummites. These may have been the same people who are called Zuzites in Genesis 14:5. Like the Anakites they were a strong and powerful people. However, the LORD's hand was behind their destruction so that a dwelling place for the Ammonites could be provided. That allocation of territory was to remain and Israel obeyed the instructions of the LORD in this respect (see verse 37). The note in verse 22 gives the same information as contained in verse 12. Another reference is appended in verse 23 concerning a similar dispossession of territory. At one time Avvites lived in the south-west of Palestine as far as Gaza but the coming of the Caphtorites from Crete had resulted in their destruction. The Caphtorites then occupied that area. It is generally held that the Caphtorites are the Philistines, who later occupied much more territory. The role that the Philistines played in Canaan is commemorated in the name Palestine, which is a corruption of Philistia. The name 'Palestine' was imposed by the Romans in the second century AD after the Bar Cochba rebellion.

(iv) Conquest of Heshbon (2:24-37)
24 Instructions were given to advance into Amorite territory, whose southern border was Arnon Gorge. Long before (Gen. 15:16) the LORD had spoken of the Amorites when he referred to the sojourn of Israel in a foreign land (Egypt) followed by re-entry into Canaan. The sin of the Amorites would finally reach full measure. Canaanite territory fell within the borders promised to Israel (Gen. 15:18-19), hence Israel could be assured that God had put the Amorites into their power. Whereas Moab and Ammon were not attacked, the Amorites were to lose their territory through military action.

25 Encouragement was given to Israel to attack because reports about them would cause fear and anguish. In the Song of the Sea (Exod. 15) Moses and the Israelites had sung:

> *The nations will hear and tremble;*
> *anguish will grip the people of Philistia.*
> *The chiefs of Edom will be terrified,*
> *the leaders of Moab will be seized with trembling,*
> *the people of Canaan will melt away;*
> *terror and dread will fall upon them.*
>
> (verses 14-16a)

From Balaam's second and third oracles we know that the reports of the Exodus were well known to the peoples of the area (Num. 23:22; 24:8). Rahab later confirmed that the people of Jericho were well aware of what God had done for Israel and were terrified (Jos. 2:11). That 'very day' God would begin to cause terror before Israel. Whenever the report came there would be distress and anguish on account of the nearby presence of Israel.

26 Though he knew of God's promises Moses sent messengers to Sihon king of Heshbon seeking a peaceful passage through his territory. Sihon ruled over the area east of the Jordan and the Dead Sea from the Arnon in the south to the Jabbok in the north. Heshbon could have been the name of the whole kingdom or else the name of his capital situated about 15 miles east of the northern end of the Dead Sea. The desert of Kedemoth was north of the eastern part of the Arnon and later fell within the territory allotted to Reuben (Jos. 13:15-18).

27 In his message Moses expressed the desire to go through Sihon's lands without deviating from the main highway. The second clause in this verse, 'we will stay on the main road', is the translation of the Hebrew which literally means, 'I will go on the road, on the road'. The last clause clearly explains this phrase to mean direct travel by staying on the major highway.

28-29 Moses reminds Sihon of how the Israelites had traversed the country belonging to the Edomites and Moabites. He desired to act in the same way with Heshbon, purchasing, not seizing, the necessary food and water. The only thing he wished was freedom to travel on foot through Heshbon. Moses encouraged Sihon to grant this permission because the ultimate goal of Israel was really to cross the Jordan 'into the land the LORD our God is giving us'. The land promised to Israel was west of the Jordan, but possession of the territory to the east was to be an additional gift.

30 Sihon was unwilling to grant the request for God had hardened his heart. Just as Pharaoh had hardened his own heart (Exod. 9:34-35) and had then known God's hardening of it (Exod. 10:20), so Sihon, having set himself against Israel, experiences God's hardening. The same terminology used here in Deuteronomy 2 is used later of Zedekiah, the last king of Israel. He did evil in God's eyes and failed to humble himself before the prophet Jeremiah ('He became stiff-necked and hardened his heart and would not turn to the LORD, the God of Israel', 2 Chron. 36:13). As is customary in the Bible, divine sovereignty ('For the LORD your God had made his spirit stubborn') and human responsibility ('but Sihon king of Heshbon refused') are held in apparent tension.

31 With the hardening of Sihon's heart the handing over Heshbon into Israel's hands had commenced. The main task lay ahead of them and so the people were directed to commence with the conquest of Heshbon.

32-33 A longer account than given in Numbers 21:23-26 is presented here. Sihon with his entire army came out to meet Israel at Jahaz. The location of Jahaz is unknown, though the name occurs in Isaiah 15:4 and in Jeremiah 48:34 and also in the Mesha inscription (lines 18ff.). This inscription on black basalt was left by Mesha king of Moab to commemorate his revolt against Israel when Ahab died (see 2 Kings 3:4-5). Because God gave Sihon over to them, the Israelites struck him down together with his son (the Jewish Massoretes' marginal reading is the plural 'sons') and his whole army.

34 As a result of Sihon's actions he and his people were the first to suffer the judgment of total destruction. They came under God's curse or ban, as did the Canaanites shortly afterwards. Complete destruction of the towns and their inhabitants took place.

The first of six occurrences in Deuteronomy of the Hebrew verb meaning 'devoted' or 'dedicated to destruction' (2:34; 3:6[x2]; 7:2; 13:16; 20:17) occurs in this verse. The related noun (*cherem*) also occurs three times in Deuteronomy (7:26[x2]; 13:17). Comment is needed on this idea for the concept is almost exclusively a biblical one. The main occurrence outside the Bible is in the Moabite inscription commemorating Mesha's victory over Israel (see note on the previous verse). Mesha tells how he took Nebo from Israel and devoted to destruction all within the tower to his god.

The basic idea concerned the dedication of something to God. Anything devoted to the LORD was to be regarded as most holy (Lev. 27:28). It may well have been placed in the treasury of the LORD's house, as were the precious metals and vessels of iron and bronze taken from Jericho (Jos. 6:24). Any person devoted to the LORD was to be put to death (Lev. 27:29). From this latter application the idea came to be linked with God's judgment, and so the expression occurs most often in the case of God's judgment upon the Canaanites. In reference to what happened at the time of the conquest the idea has to be linked to the curse on Canaan (Gen. 9:25-26; see also Gen. 15:16-21). The principle behind this ban is not the ordinary biblical ethic, but rather the principle which will ultimately apply in the kingdom of God. This is when Christ will have subdued and destroyed all kingdoms, authorities and powers and handed them over to his father (1 Cor. 15:24-25). The application of this curse on the original inhabitants of Canaan was an anticipation of the final destruction of all evil. The last Old Testament prophet ends his message with the warning that even Israel could find herself under the same divine curse which she administered to others (Mal. 4:6).

35 When the ban was applied everything was to be destroyed. Here an exception is made without explanation, for the Israelites carried away the livestock and plunder. When an exception occurred in the case of Jericho (Jos. 6:24; 7:1ff.) God's judgment followed, first on Israel as a whole, and then particularly on the transgressor Achan.

36 The boundaries of the conquered territory are noted. Aroer was in a strategic position on 'the rim of the Arnon Gorge' (Jos. 12:2) and it marked out the southern limit of Heshbon territory. In the north, Gilead, the land across the Jabbok river, formed the northern boundary. Throughout all this region there was no town too strong for Israel because the LORD had put them into Israel's hand. In conquest the people learned how to overcome their fears of fortified cities (1:28) by trusting in their God.

37 The first great conquest was achieved by implicit obedience to the LORD's commands. As instructed (see 2:19) the Israelites did not take any of the land of the Ammonites.

(v) The Conquest of Bashan (3:1-11)

The narrative of Moses also told how the LORD gave Bashan into the hand of Israel. This attack took them far to the north of where they would cross the Jordan, but secured for them that whole area on the east bank to their rear as they moved into Canaan. The same strategy was later attempted by Pompey and also successfully used in the first Muslim invasion in the seventh century AD.

1 The Israelites next took the road leading to Bashan, which was north of the Jarmuk and east of the sea of Galilee. The name Bashan indicates the nature of the soil in the area – clearly it was a plateau well-known for its lush pastures and fat cattle (Amos 4:1; Mic. 7:14). Og led out his army and the battle was fought at Edrei, the present day Deraa.

2 Encouragement was given to Israel by the LORD. Og's kingdom was clearly quite extensive (see verse 4), but the Israelites were not to fear him. Their God had put this giant (see verse 11) and his kingdom into their hands. The same treatment already given to Sihon was to be given to him.

3 The summary statement that 'the LORD our God also gave into our hands Og king of Bashan and all his army' gives no hint of the problems the Israelites faced, nor of their feelings as they tackled a kingdom far greater than that of Sihon. But with the LORD's promise to strengthen them they went into battle and devastated their opponent.

4-5 All the territory or confederacy (the Hebrew word *hevel* can mean either a territory or a band of men) of Bashan was conquered, including all its cities. While cities here do not mean anything like our modern cities, the reference makes it plain that there were many settlements in this area. The Hebrew word *qiriat* is used when referring to the sixty cities, and this word would be better rendered by 'hamlet' or 'town'. Argob may either have been part of Bashan or another name for the whole region (see verse 14 below).

5-7 The towns were well fortified, and in addition many unprotected agricultural settlements were captured. All these details accentuate the triumph which the LORD gave to Israel over Og and his people. As was the case with Heshbon (see 2:34), Bashan was put under the curse. The inhabitants were killed and the cattle and spoil were carried off.

8-9 This section of the history is rounded off with summary statements and some further particulars about Og. First there is reference to the territory captured, which extended from the Arnon Gorge as far north as Mount Hermon. In the joy of victory Israel gave a new name to that peak on the Anti-Lebanon range which was called Sirion by the Sidonians and Senir by the Amorites. In Psalm 29:6 Hermon is also referred to as Sirion, while 1 Chronicles 5:23, Song of Solomon 4:8, and Ezekiel 27:5 use the word Senir.

10 All the territory of Og was captured including the plateau, all of Gilead (thus including the two parts north and south of the Jabbok held previously by Og and Sihon respectively) and Bashan as far as the south-eastern border, which was marked out by Edrei and Salecah.

11 A historical note is appended which indicates that Og was the last of the Rephaites (see 2:11, 20). While the Hebrew word *'eres* can mean 'bed' or 'couch', it is better to take this as a reference to a sarcophagus or monument in honour of Og, and not necessarily his last resting place. Made out of basalt (which contains iron and is extremely hard) this monument was of considerable size (4m x 1.8m.). This size may be a reflection on Og's physical stature or may just denote the large proportions of the monument. It may well have been erected in Rabbah (present day Amman) to celebrate a victory by Og. If so its capture by the Israelites was further evidence of the triumphal conquest which God had given them.

4. The Division of Territory (3:12-20)
While Moses was not spared to see the main territorial allotment in Canaan, he was responsible for distributing the land captured in Transjordan (verses 1-2). The reference to 'at that time' (which occurs several times in these chapters, 3:18, 21, 23; 4:14) is important. It is not so much a date, as an emphasis on the dramatic moment in Israel's history when the promised land was about to be entered.

Reuben and Gad were allocated the territory from 'Aroer by the Arnon Gorge to the hill country of Gilead' in the north, where half of it, with its settlements, was given to Gad. Probably this territory was what Sihon had previously possessed (see 2:36). The other part of Gilead and all of Bashan, which had previously been Og's territory, was given to half the tribe of Manasseh. The other half of Manasseh had to wait till later when they received their allotment (Jos. 17:7-11). A historical note is added to indicate that the region of Argob was previously known as the land of the Rephaites. As with the previous mention of the Rephaites (see 2:11, 20) the intention is to stress the fact that the conquest had not been achieved by the might of the Israelites themselves. Their possession of the land was a gift of God's grace.

14 After giving the general description of the east bank territory in verses 12-13, Moses now records additional details regarding them. One of Manasseh's descendants, Jair, 'took' (i.e. as his possession) the whole of the Argob up to the borders of the two small states of Maacah and Geshur. The latter was situated east of the sea of Galilee, while Maacah occupied territory around the Jordan just south of Mount Hermon. The Geshurites and Maacathites were not dispossessed of their lands (Jos. 13:13) and both seem to have survived as small (semi-) independent states for some centuries (Geshur, 2 Sam. 3:3; 13:37; 15:8; Maacah, 1 Chron. 19:6; 2 Sam. 10:6).

The territory taken by Jair was renamed after him, Havvoth Jair (see also Num. 32:41). Havvoth is of uncertain derivation. It could be from a Hebrew word which means 'settlements', or from the plural of the Hebrew word for life. In that case it would be a similar usage to the way in which the German *leben*, 'life' is used in place names, e.g., Eisleben. In Judges 10:4 it is connected with a later Jair, one of the judges. Either the later figure bore the same name as his famous ancestor, or a second recovery of this territory was named in the judge's honour.

The expression 'to this day' has often been taken to indicate that a later hand has added this note. However, the same expression occurs in Moses' reference to the victory over Egypt in the Hebrew text in Deuteronomy 11:4 and in Joshua 9:27 with reference to the fate of the Gibeonites (NIV omits it in its translation of Deut. 11:4). Rather than being a later reference the expression may well mean something like 'and so it remained' or 'irrevocably'.

15 The particular triumphs of another descendant of Manasseh, Machir, were also recognised in the allocation of Gilead (see Num. 32:39-40).

16-17 Further particulars are given of the territory allotted to Reuben and Gad, even specifying that the southern limit was to come 'in the middle of the gorge' of the Arnon. The reference to the eastern border is probably to an upper tributary of the Jabbok which flows from south to north. Thus it formed the western boundary of Ammonite territory. The western border for the two and a half tribes was the Jordan River and the two seas, Kinnereth (the sea of Galilee) in the north, and the Salt Sea (the Dead Sea) in the south. Thus Reuben and Gad had the eastern part of the Jordan in their territory, including the area east of the Sea of Galilee, called here Kinnereth (probably the name for the district as in 1 Kings 15:20) down to the slopes of Pisgah to the east of the northern end of the Dead Sea. Nebo was one of the peaks of Pisgah.

18 Those tribes which were given their allotment on the eastern bank could not disclaim responsibility for helping their kinsmen of the other tribes to conquer Canaan. They had to be prepared to cross over and help secure rest for their brethren. The way into Canaan was not going to be easy and therefore due preparations for battle were to be made. Armed men were to be in the vanguard as the Jordan was crossed. The original instructions are given in Numbers 32:20-24.

19 The wives and little children were to be left behind, along with the large numbers of cattle. In the ancient world possession of livestock was a much more obvious sign of wealth than land. They were to stay in the towns already occupied.

20 The military responsibilities of those crossing the Jordan would not cease until 'rest' was achieved in the land the LORD their God was giving them. Only then could they return to their territory in the east. This concept of entering into 'rest' in the promised land is an important one in Deuteronomy and elsewhere (see also 12:9,10; 25:19; 28:65).

Israel's unity was important. It was *one* nation under *one* God and going in to possess *one* land. When Joshua later encouraged the two and half tribes to assist in the occupation of the land west of Jordan he reminded them of this command (Jos. 1:12-18). Their obedience was commended when the task was completed (Jos. 22:1-2). The basic concept of unity was sometimes later forgotten and the eastern tribes were criticised for their failure to help fight against the Canaanites' confederacy in the time of Deborah (Judg. 5:15-17).

5. The Line of Succession (3:21-29)

This section contains the recollection by Moses of two important events, the transfer of leadership to Joshua, and his own prayer that he be allowed to enter the land of Canaan. The context, with the people poised ready to cross the Jordan, suggested both subjects. The impending death of Moses becomes the reason for the transfer of leadership to Joshua. Moses had sinned and judgment had been passed on him (Num. 20:9-13) and Joshua had been designated as his successor (Num. 27:18-23). The actual transmission of leadership is recorded in Deuteronomy 31:1-8. With the land in sight Moses pleaded for permission to cross the Jordan, and to see there the continuation of the mighty deeds already witnessed. The prayer may not have been wrong in itself but it suggested that Moses' eye had shifted from the LORD of the promise to the promise itself.

21 Again there occurs in this verse the phrase which points to the critical nature of that moment in Israel's history, 'at that time'. The events in recent history were made to serve as promises or pledges of what God would to do in the immediate future. As Joshua had seen what had happened to Sihon and Og, so would he see similar happenings as the people move into Canaan. The cause of their future victories would still be the LORD.

22 Accordingly, the people need not fear. The form of the Hebrew verb is second person plural, indicating that the new leader, Joshua, and all of Israel, could put their full trust in their God. He was the one who would go before them and fight their battles. The warfare in which they were engaged was indeed a holy war in which God himself was active. Israel had the guarantee that God himself would fight against the kingdoms in Canaan.

23 The second incident concerned Moses' request that he be allowed to go across Jordan. This request is not mentioned in Numbers 27:12, where reference is made to the Lord's instruction to him to go up and look at Canaan. Moses' prayer is based on the words already spoken to him by the LORD (1:37). The word 'pleaded' translates the Hebrew verb that conveys the idea of pleading for mercy.

24 Moses began his prayer by addressing God as Sovereign LORD, using a combination of 'adonai' (Heb. *'adonay*), Sovereign, and the covenant name 'LORD'. The reference to the things which God had begun to show probably refers to the recent events, not the more remote events of the Exodus. God's greatness and mighty hand (an anthropomorphic reference to his deeds) were apparent to Moses, his servant, who now approached his master with a request. The question, which forms the latter part of the verse, does not suggest that there are other gods in existence. It is very similar to the question in the Song of the Sea in Exodus 15:11: 'Who among the gods is like you, O LORD? Who is like you – majestic in holiness, awesome in glory, working wonders?' The same expression as here occurs in almost identical form in Psalm 86:8: 'Among the gods there is none like you, O Lord; no deeds can compare with yours'.

25 The plea he makes is pressed home as an entreaty. The Hebrew uses a particle (*na*) after the imperative 'let me'. It softens it somewhat to 'please, let me', and indicates the intense longing of Moses to go over into 'the good land beyond the Jordan'. From his vantage point on Pisgah the promised land does appear to be a range of mountains, and so Moses referred to it as 'that fine hill country and Lebanon'. Already in 1:7 Lebanon had been included in the territory promised to Israel.

26 The response of God was decisive and grim for Moses. God was angry at him on account of the people's sin (see the comments on 1:37), and he is told that it is enough, and to desist from further speech about the matter. According to the New Testament Moses was one of those who was 'commended for their faith, yet none of them received what had been promised' (Heb. 11:39). Though God's anger may have abated, yet he carried the guilt of Israel to his grave. There was need for a mediator of the new covenant to come and suffer and die outside the camp (Heb. 13:12-13) so that the sins of his people (under both Old and New Covenants) would be blotted out (Rom. 3:25).

27 The only consolation afforded to Moses was to look from the top of Pisgah over the promised land. As he was told before (1:37), so now he is emphatically told again that he was not to cross over the Jordan.

28 Under the New Covenant the one and the same person is he who begins and ends (Heb. 12:2). Under the old covenant Moses began the task, but it fell, by divine appointment, to Joshua to continue it, and others after his death to complete the conquest. The land Moses could see was the territory which Israel was to inherit. Moses' encouragement to Joshua was later echoed when God himself encouraged him: 'Be strong and courageous' (Jos. 1:9).

29 This final verse of the chapter notes that the people stayed in the valley opposite Beth Peor. The mention of that location would have recalled the Balaam episodes which happened there, as recorded in Numbers 22-25. To some of these events Moses returns in 4:3ff.

6. The Covenant in Miniature (4:1-40)
The major part of chapter 4 is a speech by Moses. He encourages the people both by recalling the past blessings and by stimulating them to obedient service in the future. Interspersed are warnings, including the threat of exile (vv. 25-31), if God's ordinances are forsaken.

This speech is really a covenant document in miniature with all the features of the extra-biblical covenants, though not in the precise order in which they occur in those documents. The identification of the covenant-maker is stressed on several occasions, and his basic demands on Israel are re-affirmed. The blessings and cursings are set out, with appeal to heaven and earth as witnesses (verse 26). Succeeding generations had to be taught the knowledge of this covenant (verses 9-10).

This chapter assumes that the people were familiar with treaty documents. God's use of this form was a condescension to their weakness and frailty. In order to let them grasp something more of the significance of the treaty which the Great King was renewing with them, he set it in a familiar pattern. While strict legal form is not followed, the basic elements stand out clearly in Moses' speech.

(i) The Appeal for Obedience (4:1-14)

1 The transition from historical review to application is marked by the opening word in the Hebrew text (*vᵉ'attah*, 'and now'), as so often in biblical passages (cf. Exod. 19:3-5; Deut. 10:12; Jos. 24:1). The same usage occurs in the extra-biblical treaties. Israel was called upon to listen and obey 'the decrees and laws' that he was teaching them. For the Israelites there should be no unthinking acceptance of their Sovereign's demands. They had to apply those demands to their lives and so use their minds in the service of their God. The New Testament application of this principle is seen in Paul's words in Romans 12:1: 'Present your bodies as living sacrifices, holy and pleasing to God, which is the service of your mind' (Gk. *ten logiken latreian humon*).

The distinction between decrees (Heb. *chuqqim*) and laws (Heb. *mishpatim*) is not very fixed, and both expressions are used with a certain degree of flexibility in Deuteronomy. Both seem to be used of the directions which make concrete the general principle contained in 'the command' (or the plural *commandments*, Heb. *mitsvah*, pl. *mitsvot*; see following verse). This expression often occurs along with 'decrees and laws', and it is clearly the more comprehensive idea (see for example 6:1; 7:11 for the singular; and 5:29; 8:11; 11:1 and 30:16 for the plural). Like 'testimonies' (Heb. *'edoth*), it expresses the fundamental ideas of relationship to the covenant God, while 'decrees and laws' spell out the application of this basic principle. Moses was the appointed teacher of the people and they had to obey these directions if they wanted to *live*. This word means not simply 'be alive' but enjoying to the full God's blessing and favour. The immediate task was 'to go in and take possession of the land that the LORD, the God of your fathers, is giving you'. The present covenant renewal was in direct continuity with the earlier covenants with the patriarchs in which the land has been promised to them. The present tense 'giving' (in Heb. the active participle) stresses that the promise was then in the process of fulfilment.

2 No additions could be made to 'the word' which Moses was commanding them (NIV 'what I command you'). Here it may refer to the whole law which was given to them. Neither was any subtraction to be made from it. This instruction is parallel to the curse against the alteration which occurs in some of the tablets recording the extra-biblical treaties and also on boundary marker stones. The New Testament expresses the same principle in Revelation 22:18-19, though there as here the reference is not to the whole biblical canon but a restricted portion of it (here, 'the word which I am commanding you'; in Rev. 22:18, 'this book').

3-4 In order to reinforce the instruction in verse 1 Moses appealed to the incident at Beth Peor given in Numbers 25:1-18. Probably Baal Peor is just another name for Beth Peor (3:29). Israel had joined in the worship of the Baal of Peor. Canaanite worship of Baal often involved sexual immorality, and in this case Israelite men were involved in sexual relationships with Moabite women. The resulting plague and also the execution of the leaders was God's judgment. However, those who remained faithful to the LORD were living proof of the truth of his word. Clearly Moses wanted his listeners to emulate those who remained faithful to him during that time of trial.

5 Two major reasons were adduced by Moses to encourage obedience. The first, given in verses 5-8, is that the obedience of the people in taking possession of the land will be a testimony to the surrounding nations. Moses had given Israel the LORD's decrees and laws in order that they would obey them and become the type of nation depicted in verses 6ff.

6 In obeying these decrees and laws Israel would show that greatness did not depend upon size of population or military might.

Rather it depended on showing wisdom and understanding to the nations. The biblical concept of 'wisdom' (Heb. *chokmah*) and 'understanding' (Heb. *binah*) is not of abstract understanding but practical wisdom displayed in daily life. When the others looked at Israel they would say, 'Surely this great nation is a wise and understanding people'. Israel was to fulfil a missionary task, and the principle indicated here comes to fuller expression later in the Old Testament, especially in the prophets and psalms.

7 When other nations learned of Israel's belief and practice, they would be logically compelled to acknowledge that God was near his people. This belief was later expressed in Psalm 145:18: 'The LORD is near to all who call on him, to all who call on him in truth.' Israel's continued existence would be a testimony to the reality of Israel's God who heard and answered prayer.

8 The other important aspect was that Israel also possessed what no other nation had – 'righteous decrees and laws'. Moses praised the law which he was about to give anew to Israel (see 5:6ff.), which, having its origin with God, was also to be characterised as righteous. What he did for Israel he did for no other nation; they did not know his laws (Ps. 147:20).

This section is important for the later Wisdom literature of the Old Testament. It looks back to the covenant statutes and applies them to the practical affairs of life. It is never theoretical wisdom, but spiritual knowledge and insight applied to the full scope of human life.

9 The second reason encouraging obedience is given in verses 9-14. Appeal was made by Moses to the manner in which God appeared to them at Sinai. The people had to be consciously on their guard ('Only be careful, and watch yourselves closely') lest they forgot the momentous events which occurred there at that time. They had seen with their own eyes what had happened and these things had to be held in their hearts. This was not just a temporary matter, but one with permanent validity ('as long as you live'). Moreover they were required to pass on their knowledge to successive generations. This is the first of several references in Deuteronomy to the important principle of parental instruction (see on 6:7; 6:20; 11:19; 31:13; 32:46). The knowledge of God's covenant was to be transmitted from generation to generation. Later Israel was to sing that 'the things ... we have heard and known, things our fathers have told us. We will not hide them from their children; we will tell the next generation the praiseworthy deeds of the LORD, his power, and the wonders he has done' (Ps. 78:3-4).

10 In the Hebrew text the verse begins abruptly with 'the day you stood before the LORD'. This connects on from 'watch yourselves closely so that you do not forget' in the previous verse. In English we need to insert some words such as 'do not forget' or 'remember'. The people came before the LORD because he had so directed. The instruction given to Moses was to assemble the people before the LORD. From the Hebrew word rendered 'assemble' we have the Old Testament concept of the congregation which was taken over into the New Testament as the *ekklesia*, the church. The purpose of the gathering was to hear words from God which were to give direction to the people right throughout their lives. They and their children were to fear the LORD. This important concept of the fear of the LORD is mentioned several times in this book (see especially on 6:2). It was to provide an abiding principle which would guide from childhood to old age. Again the emphasis is placed on the need for parents to instruct their children.

11 The account here is a summary of what is described more fully in Exodus 19:16-19. God descended in fire upon the mountain, so that it seemed to be burning to the very heavens (Heb. *to the heart of the heavens*). There was darkness, and clouds are described using two terms – heavy rain clouds and heavy mist (Heb. has simply three words after 'heavens', *choshek* ['darkness'], *'anan* ['clouds'], and *'arafel* ['darkness, gloom']).

12-13 The purpose of the meeting was for the communication of God's words to the people. The people were able to hear the voice,

but they 'saw no form'. This is emphasised by the addition in
Hebrew of two words, 'only a voice' (Heb. *zulati qol*). What was
communicated by God to the people is called 'his covenant, the
ten words'. Moses was reminding them that that meeting was in
connection with God's covenant of which the Ten Words (as the
Hebrew text consistently calls the Ten Commandments) formed
a vital core.

The communication was not just in oral form but written down
on stone tablets by the LORD. The two stone tablets were duplicate
copies, as was normal in treaty situations in the extra-biblical
world. Normally in a secular setting one tablet would be placed in
the shrine of the king who had conquered, while the other would
be placed in the shrine of subject king, over whom he now ruled.
In the case of the tablets written at Sinai by God, they were both
placed in the tabernacle (Exod. 25:16, 21; 40:20; Deut. 10:2).

14 In the Hebrew text emphasis falls on Moses' role ('And *me* the
LORD commanded') as the teacher of Israel. What he has instructed
the parents to do, he exemplified in his own ministry to them. He
was already looking ahead to the time when having crossed the
Jordan they would be living in the land of Canaan. This explains
why on so many occasions the laws are directed to a new situation.
With that in mind minor modifications occur even in the Ten
Commandments (see especially the comments on 5:15 and 5:21).

(ii) Warnings against Idolatry (4:15-31)
Idolatry would be a snare to the Israelites in Canaan, just as it had
been in Egypt. The people must remember that great care was
needed to keep themselves from corruption (verses 15-20). If they
did succumb to idolatry that would be tantamount to rejecting
God's covenant (verses 21-24). Punishment, including exile to a
foreign land, would come upon them because of their rejection of
the LORD (verses 25-31).

15 The Israelites had to be on their guard lest they compromised
themselves by being attracted to, and engaging in the worship of
gods of other nations, particularly those of Canaan and Egypt. In

the majestic appearance of God at Horeb, when he spoke to them out of the fire, no visible form was seen. There was no doubt about the reality of the experience, but there was no form of God seen.

16 Moses now detailed snares which Israel was to shun. Moral and religious corruption were dangers to be strenuously avoided. There was to be no place in their experience for the male and female deities of the Canaanites, nor was their physical representation to be depicted in image or statue form. This presumption would apply as much to male and female animals as to humans. God must not be limited by the images made by men.

17-19 These verses spell out the dangers with clear allusions to practices in the heathen nations, particularly Egypt, where there were many animal deities. All animals, birds and reptiles were themselves part of God's creation and images of them could in no way represent their creator. These verses not only forbid the representation of Israel's God by images, but more widely prohibit idolatry in general.

It was not only the false gods of past experience that were in view, but also new expressions of idolatrous worship which they were to meet in Canaan. These included worship of the sun, moon and stars (verse 19). That the Canaanites worshipped the sun is evident from the name Beth Shemesh (= house of the sun), while Jericho may come from the Hebrew word for moon (*yareach*). Through Jeremiah (Jer. 8:2) the LORD later expressed the future judgment on Israel. The day would come when the bones of kings, priests, prophets and people would be 'exposed to the sun and the moon and all the stars of the heavens, which they have loved and served and which they have followed and consulted and worshipped'. The prohibition does not deal with physical manifestations of idolatry in the form of idols or images, but with the very worship in itself of the heavenly bodies. Like the living creatures in verses 17-18 these heavenly bodies were created by God and served a function for all nations which he had allotted to them.

20 The distinctiveness of Israel is emphatically emphasised in the opening phrase in Hebrew, which the NIV catches well with the translation 'But as for you'. Their previous condition in Egypt is described as being in 'an iron-smelting furnace', which description emphasises both the affliction they experienced and also the purifying especially at the time of the Exodus. Later Isaiah spoke the LORD's words to Israel and said: 'See, I have refined you, though not as silver; I have tested you in the furnace of affliction' (Isa. 48:10). Jeremiah also contains a reference to the deliverance from the iron-smelting in Egypt (Jer. 11:4). The exclusiveness of Israel's position is further emphasised by the words 'the people of his inheritance'. This phrase is practically synonymous with the expression 'treasured possession' (7:6; 14:2). Both phrases emphasise the fact that Israel was the possession of the LORD, not in a temporary way but as an enduring object of love and affection.

21 The thought in verses 21-24 now turns to the way in which apostasy from the true worship would in fact be tantamount to a breach of covenant commitment. The emphasis is decidedly on the LORD's action against Moses. This is the third time this has been mentioned in Deuteronomy. On the first occasion (1:37) it is to emphasise the terrible nature of God's judgment. On the second occasion (3:23-26) it points to the glorious nature of the inheritance in the land, while here it was to teach the Israelites the lesson of thankfulness. Moses, by reason of a divine oath (this is not mentioned previously) is only able to gaze at the inheritance, but the rest of the people will enter in and enjoy it.

22 The contrast in this verse between 'this land' (i.e. the east bank of the Jordan) and 'that good land' (i.e. Canaan) highlights the poignancy of Moses' words. It is accentuated also by the contrast between 'I' and 'but you'. The good land was something which by divine grant the people would soon enjoy. The seriousness of Moses' position was that he was excluded from it.

23 In this verse two themes from previous verses are repeated. The opening words 'Be careful' resume from verse 15, while the thought of not forgetting the covenant goes back to verse 9. The warning here is, 'Don't forget the LORD's covenant by making an idol!' If they did forget the covenant demands of God and deviate into idolatrous ways, such would be tantamount to rejecting the covenant. The themes of 'not forgetting', or the positive aspect of 'remembering', are repeatedly brought before the people in Deuteronomy ('not forgetting' in 6:12; 8:11, 14, 19; 9:7; 25:19; and 'remembering' in 5:15; 15:15; 16:12: 24:18, 22).

24 God who appeared at Sinai as a devouring fire was the God to whom Israel must be accountable. To those within the covenant bond love was the expression of his attitude to those 'married' to him. To those outside, including those who put themselves in that position by their own sinful actions, he was a jealous God who would come in judgment as a devouring fire (cf. the words of the Second Commandment, Exod. 20:5; Deut. 5:9). In contrast to this, New Testament believers are reminded that we 'have not come to a mountain that can be touched and that is burning with fire' (Heb. 12:18) but rather 'to Mount Zion, to the heavenly Jerusalem, the city of the living God' (verse 22).

25 This verse introduces the statement of curses to be expected if the people disobey. Such curses were a standard feature of the extra-biblical treaties and here in summary fashion they are described. For even fuller examples we may look at Leviticus 26:14-46 and Deuteronomy 27:15-26 and 28:15-68. In effect this section works out in greater detail what is implicit in verse 24. If the God of Israel was 'a consuming fire' and 'a jealous God', then the people could expect judgment if they disobeyed his commands. One danger which Israel would meet in the future was not external but internal, because the dramatic events of Mt Sinai and the wilderness experiences would recede from living memory. Second and third generations would not have the same personal appreciation of God's covenant, and could turn aside and make some form of idol. Such an action would provoke the jealous God to anger against his people.

26 In the vassal treaties the gods of the suzerain and the vassal are involved as witnesses. This was because it was thought they had the power to carry out the curses of the treaty. Within the biblical framework of covenant the heavens and the earth are called upon, as part of God's creation, to be witnesses to his covenant with his people. This is the first of three occasions in this book that this appeal is made (Deut. 30:19; 32:1). The prophets often reflect this covenant form as they appeal to people who have transgressed its demands (cf. e.g. Isa. 1:2; Jer. 2:12; Mic. 6:1-2). The threat of exile was here set before the people even before they entered the land. Spiritual and moral corruption would lead to a comparatively brief sojourn in the land ('you will not live there long'). The thought of the coming judgment is emphatically stated twice in this verse ('you will quickly perish, you ... will certainly be destroyed').

27 The judgment would be in the form of scattering the people among the nations. The Hebrew expression used here (*hêfîs ba 'ammim*) is used in the prophetical books when describing the Exile in Babylon (Jer. 9:16; Ezek. 22:15; 36:19). However here in Deuteronomy it is used in a general way, so that there is no need to restrict it to the Exile of 587 BC. The same threat had earlier been given by Moses to Israel (Lev. 26:33), and is spelled out in greater detail later (Deut. 28:64-68). The surviving remnant would be very small. This fact stands in marked contrast to the promise of increase in numbers if Israel remained faithful to the LORD (Deut. 1:10,11; 6:3; 7:13).

28 In exile Israel would not only be attracted to false gods, but actually come into the service of 'man-made gods of wood and stone'. These idols could not speak, hear, smell, feel or walk. They were lifeless and all who trusted in them would be like them (Ps. 115:8). Isaiah (Isa. 44:12-20) later ridiculed those who worshipped idols. From one piece of wood they fashioned an idol and also got their firewood (Isa. 44:14-17). A sense of futility in such worship might well bring them to fresh experience of the only living God.

29 The final verses of the section contain the promises or blessings which were attached to the covenant. If there was whole-hearted seeking of the LORD, Israel would find that their covenant God ('the LORD your God', says Moses) would be near to them again. 'Heart' means the centre of one's life, while 'soul' describes the inner, spiritual life of men (for later use of these words in Deut. see especially 6:5 and 10:12).

30 Distress and affliction would have the effect of drawing the people back to their God. The verb 'return' is used both of literal turning or returning to someone or something, and also metaphorically of a change of heart, especially in relation to God (cf. Isa. 10:21). Moses describes this happening as occurring 'in later days'. The Hebrew phrase (*beacharit hayyâmîm*) is used in the prophets with the note of eschatological finality, of the events in connection with the coming of the great day of the LORD. Here it may well carry something of that meaning, especially as it occurs in the Balaam narratives with this force (Num. 24:14). The end result would be a renewed obedience to the voice of the LORD.

31 The character of God remained the foundation of all the covenant promises. In wrath God would remember mercy (Heb. 3:2), for he was a compassionate God, one who would remember the covenant made to the fathers. As in 4:1 'the fathers' were Abraham, Isaac and Jacob. The same sort of reference to the confirmation in covenant form given to the patriarchs occurs in the promise section of Leviticus 26 (verse 42). A gracious God, who had made his oath by two unchangeable things 'in which it is impossible for God to lie' (Heb. 6:18), would not abandon his people.

(iii) A Chosen People (4:32-40)
32 The section is tied closely to the preceding one by the opening word (Heb. *kî*). It moves to a climax in verses 39-40, with the renewed assertion of the exclusiveness of Israel's God. First, however, there was the evidence supporting that conclusion. It was grounded in the revelation that God gave in word and action. The practical proof of God's compassion was manifest in the

Exodus events. The whole passage is elevated prose, thoroughly in keeping with the subject matter.

All Israel were encouraged to enquire about their early national history ('the former days'), going as far back as creation itself. They could enquire anywhere for evidence that events like the ones they had witnessed have occurred elsewhere. The expected answer is, of course, that these events were without parallel.

33 Another rhetorical question gives the answer. No other nation had heard God speaking out of the fire and yet survived. That theophany had revealed God to them, and yet they still lived! Such theophanic manifestations of God were pointing to the full manifestation when the Word became flesh and dwelt among men (Jn. 1:14).

34 Preceding that experience at Horeb had been the miraculous happenings in Egypt. Some of the plagues like the hail (Exod. 9:13-35) were things which were part of natural occurrences, but most others were abnormal. These events were judgments on the Egyptians and their gods (Exod. 12:12). The ineffectiveness of the Egyptian gods was in view here, along with the exaltation of Israel's God. The thought of God taking Israel for himself looks back to the description in verse 20 of Israel as 'the people of his inheritance'. The manner in which God did this was a very practical expression of his electing love (taking 'one nation for himself out of another nation').

35 The momentous events which took place before the very eyes of the Israelites demonstrated the reality of their God, the one living and true God. To 'know' God in the biblical sense is not just to have an intellectual appreciation of his existence and character, but to know by personal experience the reality of his presence. The confession of monotheism followed the exhibition of his power over all the gods of Egypt. It was by revelation ('you were shown these things') that Israel came to a monotheistic faith.

36 That this revelation was divine in origin is stressed by the

description of the manner in which it came. 'From heaven' the
LORD spoke (cf. Exod. 19:20, 'the LORD descended to the top of
Mount Sinai') in order to discipline Israel. The word 'discipline'
reflects on the father-son relationship between Israel and the LORD.
The same Hebrew verb (*yasar* Piel) occurs in Deuteronomy 8:5:
'Know then in your heart that as a man disciplines his son, so the
LORD your God disciplines you'. The manner of this disciplining
is indicated by the last part of the verse. Out of the fire God spoke
to the people, and the content of that revelation (the Ten
Commandments) is given in the following chapter.

37 Again Moses draws the attention of Israel back to the ultimate
source of their blessings. God had both 'loved' the patriarchs and
'chosen' Abraham's seed after him as the means of fulfilling his
purposes. The conjunction of the verbs 'to love' and 'to choose'
is important because they stress the sovereign nature of God's
relationship with Israel. The NIV version (as with many other
English versions) translates the object of the verb 'choose' as 'their
descendants after them'. The Hebrew text has the singular 'his
descendants after him'. Clearly Abraham is in view as the one to
whom the original promise, repeated to Isaac and Jacob, was given.
The God who brought his people out of Egypt did so 'by his
Presence'. This is echoing the language of Exodus 33:14 where
the LORD promised: 'My Presence (Heb. *panîm*) will go with you,
and I will give you rest'. In the Exodus context it is clear that
God's presence or face going with the people was identical with
his own going (cf. Exod. 33:15). Isaiah says that the angel of God's
presence (Heb. *mal'ak panav*, 'the angel of his presence') saved
the people (Isa. 63:9). God's presence was manifested by what he
did for his people when he showed 'his great strength'.

38 God's intended purpose was to bring the people into possession
of land which at that time was held by much greater and more
powerful nations. In moving into the land they had to recognise
the hand of God in dispossessing other nations and giving them
their inheritance.

39-40 Here is the climax of Moses' address to the people. On the basis of the facts which have been set out, Moses asks for the only fitting response from the people. They should acknowledge from their own experience that 'the LORD is God in heaven above and on the earth below'. He is the universal LORD; no other God exists. This is the expression of the monotheistic faith of Israel. The consequence of this fact was that Israel should render obedience to all the decrees and commands that the LORD was giving them through Moses. Only by so doing would they ensure the continuity of covenant blessing ('that it may go well with you'), and continued occupation of Canaan. Neither original possession of the land nor continuity in it was due to Israel's own might or power. The land was a gift to a covenant people, and disobedience could lead to expulsion from it. The conditional element of the gift had at all times to be in the people's consciousness. Only in that way would they be saved from presumption and disobedience.

7. The Cities of Refuge (4:41-43)

These verses are appended to the historical prologue to show that in the territory already occupied on the east bank of Jordan Moses had carried out faithfully the LORD's instructions (see Num. 35:6-34). As with other parts in the book which speak of Moses in the third person (31:1-34:12) they were probably written by the writer(s) who carried on the covenant history in the Former Prophets (Joshua, Judges, 1 and 2 Samuel, 1 and 2 Kings). Those writers may well have been the priests and elders who had responsibility for reading the law to the people every seventh year (Deut. 31:11). This passage indicates that Moses, who had instructed Israel to keep all God's commands (verse 40), was himself obedient. Even before his death he allotted the three asylum cities in Transjordania.

The report is also significant in the light of the extra-biblical treaty patterns. In those treaties the historical prologue included a reminder to vassals of the territorial allocations the suzerain had made to them. Before going on to consider more fully the LORD's stipulations to Israel in the following chapter, acknowledgment of his grace already was highly significant. In the Transjordanian territories and the allocated cities of refuge there Israel had a pledge of what was yet to come.

No explanation is given here of the fuller meaning of these asylum cities. The principle was stated in Exodus 21:12-14 that a manslayer could find refuge at the altar. This is broadened in scope in Numbers 35, and Deuteronomy 19:1-13 notes the provision of the other three cities later allocated on the west bank (see for fuller comment the section on Deut. 19:1-13, and cf. also the names of the cities in Jos. 20:7-8). The actual practice of asylum is only referred to in the Old Testament in 1 Kings 1:50-53 and 2:28-34.

These verses make it plain that the provision was for unintentional manslayers. There had to be no prior record of hatred towards the victim. Of the cities mentioned nothing is known regarding the exact location of Bezer and Golan. Bezer is known from extra-biblical sources, especially the Moabite inscription of Mesha (see comment on 2:32-33). We only know that it was situated in the Reubenite territory, just as Golan was in the territory allocated to Manasseh in Bashan. Ramoth in Gilead may well be the modern town of Tell-Ramîth.

8. Introduction to the Law (4:44-49)
These verses give the location of the law-giving, along with historical and geographical notes. Such notes are important because biblical revelation is rooted in history. The renewal of the covenant took place on the eastern bank of the Jordan, and readers are reminded that significant victories had already been achieved over two Amorite kings.

44 The use of the word 'law' (Heb. *torah*) is equivalent to 'covenant' in contexts such as this. Whereas 'law' can elsewhere be used to refer to the whole of the Pentateuch, here it clearly denotes the collection of principles that Moses was about to enunciate.

45-47 This understanding of 'law' is confirmed by the use of the expressions ' stipulations, decrees, and laws'. Of these 'stipulations' is the more general term, and then 'decrees and laws' specify more closely the nature of the stipulations. There is no apparent difference between 'decrees' and 'laws', both being used to indicate covenant requirements. The reminder is given that these were not new demands on the people, but ones already given between the exodus from Egypt and the encampment at Beth Peor. The reference to Sihon and Og is part of historical recapitulation that is typical of Deuteronomy (see 1:1-5; 3:1-11).

48-49 This is a summary description of what has already been given in 3:8-22. The land extended from Aroer in the south to Mount Hermon in the north. Hermon is called 'Siyon', which is probably a variant of 'Sirion' (see on 3:9). The final detail notes in conformity with 3:17b the geographical area taken in the central part of the country.

B. THE FOUNDATION OF
THE COVENANT RELATIONSHIP (5:1-33)

1. The Ten Words (5:1-21)

The opening verses of chapter 5 refer to the covenant made forty years before on Sinai. Moses was the mediator on that occasion (verse 5, and see later verses 24-27) to declare God's words to the people. The historical prologue in chapters 1-4 has dealt with the period following the inauguration of the covenant at Sinai and leading up to the covenant renewal ceremony in the plains of Moab. This present section deals with the stipulations given by God for life in the covenant. As was common when extra-biblical treaties were renewed, there are some modifications to the stipulations. What is presented is a general rehearsal, with some slight reformulation of requirements made upon Israel at Sinai. Fittingly Moses begins with the Decalogue and then goes on to show its significance for the life of God's redeemed community.

In the non-biblical covenants it was common for some alteration to the stipulations to occur in renewal ceremonies. Similarly here in Deuteronomy 5. Comparison with Exodus 20 clearly shows that (apart from some minor verbal changes) there are three basic alterations:

1. In Exodus 20 the reason for keeping the Sabbath is God's pattern of creating and then resting. Here it is God's redemption of his people from Egypt. These two ideas of creation and redemption are important. God's pattern of work and rest was to be imitated, but entry into God's ultimate rest would only be by redemption (see Heb. 3:12–4:11).

2. The Fifth Commandment is expanded by the addition of 'as the LORD your God has commanded you' after the opening instruction, and then the addition also of the words 'and that it may go well with you'.

3. In the final commandment there is a reversal of the order of 'wife' and 'house', and the word 'land' is added. Now that Israel was about to enter the sworn land and become a sedentary people the addition of 'field' was necessary.

The common English term, 'the ten commandments', never actually occurs in Scripture. In Hebrew they are called simply 'the ten words' as in Exodus 34:28, Deuteronomy 4:13 and 10:4, or 'the words of the covenant' (Exod. 34:28; Deut. 29:1). From the former expression we have borrowed the word *Decalogue* (via Greek and Latin) into English. Though the expressions 'the ten words' or 'Decalogue' are more accurate as translations, yet as the expression 'the Ten Commandments' is more common in English there is no reason to avoid its use. Nowhere are we told how the ten words are to be divided, and three different ways are still current.

1. Protestants and Greek Catholics follow Josephus (*Antiquities* iii.5.5) in having a preface and followed by the Ten Commandments, separating exclusive worship of God from the prohibition to idolatry.

2. Roman Catholics and Lutherans also have a preface, but combine the first two commandments together, and then separate the tenth into two commandments, one dealing with coveting a neighbour's house and the other with coveting a neighbour's wife and property.

3. Jewish scholars from the early Christian centuries have taken the preface as the First Commandment, then combined the exclusive worship of God and the prohibition of idolatry as the Second Word. The remaining commandments are the same as in the Protestant enumeration.

Clearly Deuteronomy 5:6 is not the prologue to the covenant, as this is really Deuteronomy 1:1-5. It makes far better sense to take that verse (5:6) and combine it with the exclusive worship of God in 5:7. The sin of having any other god then becomes all the more pointed, as the opening words of the Decalogue relate to the redeemer God who saved his people from their bondage in Egypt.

Law and grace go together in the biblical setting. Even granting the covenant and giving the law was purely of grace. This fact is highlighted by the close proximity of the mercy seat and the testimony within the Tabernacle. The mercy seat and the testimony in close proximity in the Tabernacle (Lev. 16:13) draw attention to this fact. The law is a reflection of God's own character and it sets the pattern for imitation. Israel was obliged to be holy, because God was holy. The negative character of so many of the ten words reminds us of the inherent sinfulness of those to whom they came, while the recurring 'you' strikes a very personal note.

1 Words preceding the restatement of the Decalogue serve to emphasise the importance and significance of the exposition that follows. Instead of the simple 'And Moses summoned' we have 'And Moses summoned all Israel, and said'. Not only were the people of Israel to listen to the stipulations of the covenant, but they were to order their lives in obedience to them. To be loyal to the covenant the people had to respond to these demands of God. The call by Moses for them to hear, learn, and follow (verse 1) is repeated in essence at the end of the chapter (verses 32-33). They had bound themselves by a solemn oath to keep these obligations of the King. Significantly, then, the solemn command to follow carefully all requirements of the covenant both precedes and follows the actual Decalogue.

2-3 The present ceremony was but a renewal of the existing covenant relationship with the LORD. That theocracy had been established at Sinai forty years earlier, and although many of those present then had since died, clearly Moses considers the covenant as being made with the nation as an organic whole. He traces the covenant back even further – to the fathers. Calvin thinks that 'the fathers' are those who died in Egypt, but it is better to take it as a reference to the patriarchal fathers (cf. 4:31, 37; 7:8, 12; 8:18). They had died without receiving the promises, but the present generation was privileged to approach the promised land and enter it. The negative 'not' is to be taken in a relative sense of 'not only'. This means that Moses is asserting the continuity of God's covenantal dealings with his people, just as he had done at the outset of his exposition of the law (1:8). The meaning is therefore 'not only with our fathers but also with us'. The emphasis falls on the responsibility of the present generation to observe the covenant made not only with their forefathers, but with them also. The word 'us' is inserted to emphasise the suffix on the Hebrew word 'with us', which is still further strengthened by adding, 'all these of us who are here alive this day'.

4 At Sinai the LORD spoke with them 'face to face'. This must refer to their hearing the voice speaking, for it is expressly said that they saw no likeness or appearance (Deut. 4:15-19). It emphasises the directness with which the LORD gave his revelation, and the solemn and impressive way in which the covenant was inaugurated. To avoid any doubt as to the identity of the speaker there was a visible manifestation of God's glory in the fire (cf. both the voice and the visible descent of the Spirit at Jesus' baptism, Luke 3:22). It could only be God's voice that spoke from the fire.

5 This forms a parenthetical remark on the position of Moses, who was the mediator between God and Israel. This office of mediator was all the more necessary because Israel feared face to face confrontation with the fiery theophany. If this remark refers to the giving of the Decalogue, it would mean that God's voice was audible but indiscernible to Israel, for it is expressly said that Israel heard God declare the Decalogue (e.g., 4:12). However, it is possible that this is a proleptic comment and refers to revelations after the giving of the Decalogue, and verses 22-31 seem to support this interpretation. Moses acted as mediator to declare to the people the word of the LORD. The word 'saying', or 'he said', at the end of verse 5 refers back to the word 'spoke' in verse 4.

6 The opening of the Decalogue identifies the God of the covenant, and presents the prime motives for obedience at the very outset. God asserts his authority over Israel by reminding them that he is the self-existent LORD, but also the one who had entered into a covenant with Israel. Hence he can make the claim to them that he is 'your God'. Then there follows a reminder of what God did in sovereign grace and omnipotent power in delivering them from the bondage of Egypt. They were brought out in order to serve the LORD, and the recollection of God's grace and mercy in past history should encourage them to yield living obedience to covenant requirements.

7 The teaching of the Pentateuch as a whole is clearly monotheistic. Israel's God, the creator of heaven and earth, was the only God. All other so-called gods were 'worthless idols' (Deut. 32:21). They appealed to men because worship given to them was really given to demons (Deut. 32:17; Ps. 106:37). The obligation stated here was a demand that they know God as their God, the God who had revealed himself in salvation. Seeing that there was only one true God, they were not to have any other gods either 'beyond me' (Heb. *'al* as in Ps. 16:2) or 'in addition to me' (as in Gen. 31:50; Deut. 19:9). The latter translation would make it the equivalent of the LXX rendering 'by the side of me'.

8 The prohibition in this Second Commandment is closely linked with the preceding one and it defines an important aspect of worship. It is not a question of all painting and sculpture being forbidden, but the construction of figures of God (see especially the words used in the preceding chapter, 4:15-23). There could be no representation of God by means of an image.

9 If such images did exist in other cultures, Israel was not to prostrate herself before them in worship nor was she to enter into bond-service to them (cf. the use of the same Hebrew verb in verse 6 when describing their condition in Egypt). The reasons given to enforce this prohibition are basically the character of their God and the threats and promises which he gives to encourage obedience. The assertion 'I am the LORD your God' repeats the opening statement of the Decalogue, and then places in apposition to it the words 'a jealous God'. This jealousy expresses itself in the way in which the LORD deals with transgression from his law. Where there is rebellion against him and a hatred towards him, he will punish that iniquity for several generations.

10 On the other hand, the constancy of God's covenant love is promised to those who love him and keep his commandments.

The concept of love to God is a frequent one in Deuteronomy (with God as the object 6:5; 7:9; 10:12; 11:1, 13, 22; 13:4; 19:9; 30:6, 16, 20; of God's love to his people 4:37; 7:8, 13; 10:15; 10:18; 23:5). This expression of covenant love is promised 'to the thousandth generation'. Neither in verse 9 nor in verse 10 does the word 'generation' occur in the Hebrew text, but clearly if it is inserted in the translation of verse 9 then it also has to appear in this verse. That this verse is speaking of a thousand generations is made all the more likely because of the express use of the phrase a thousand generations in 7:9 in a very similar context.

11 The Third Commandment forbids bearing God's name in vain. The Hebrew verb used (*nasa'*), when standing alone, never refers to speech. It means to bear or to carry. The object expressed is 'the name of the LORD'. The name of something in Hebrew meant far more than just the vocable by which it was known. It was rather the character or reputation of the person. To bear God's name was to bear his character by living as the people of God. The Israelites were commanded to demonstrate by their actions that they were the LORD's chosen people. The phrase occurs in this Word as a prohibition, and it has attached to it the adverbial phrase 'in vain', or 'hypocritically' (NIV 'misuse'). There could be no hypocrisy concerning his service, which is made plain by the application of the covenant curse. Anyone in Israel who did live hypocritically was in grave danger, 'for the LORD will not hold anyone guiltless who misuses his name'. He would stand as guilty before God and his transgression would be punished.

12 The Fourth Commandment points to the structuring of time which God required from his people. The Sabbath was set apart by God from creation, bestowing his blessing on it (Gen. 2:3). There is no further mention of the Sabbath until the narrative concerning the provision of the manna in the wilderness (Exod. 16). When the covenant was instituted on Sinai the principle of Sabbath rest was engraven in its provisions. Here in Deuteronomy 5 there is mention of that occasion with the words 'as the LORD your God has commanded you'.

This Commandment involves the most significant of the variations in the form of the Decalogue as set forth in Deuteronomy as compared with that of Exodus 20:2-17. Here 'keep' (Heb. *shamar*) replaces 'remember' (Heb. *zakar*) but there seems to be no real difference in meaning between these two verbs in this context. 'Remember' is not so much 'recall to mind' but 'remember to do'. The reference to keeping the Sabbath holy is an echo of Genesis 2:3. The pattern of God's actions becomes the exemplar which man is to follow.

13 Before prohibiting work on the Sabbath, the Fourth Commandment speaks in positive terms of the nature of activities on six days of the week. In following God's own actions, his people are called to a life of activity in which work has its rightful and necessary place. The day of rest only has meaning in relation to the preceding labour.

14 The distinctive character of the seventh day was that it belonged to the LORD as a Sabbath. It was his Sabbath, not Israel's. As the owner of the Sabbath the LORD had exclusive claims to it, and therefore could require abstinence from work by men and animals. The purpose clause at the end of the verse gives the ultimate goal, 'that your manservant and your maidservant may rest, as you do'. The use of the verb 'rest' here may well echo another statement in the Exodus form of the Decalogue, for God is said to have *rested* on the seventh day (Exod. 20:11).

15 In Exodus the reason for keeping the Sabbath is the pattern set by God during creation. He worked and then rested, and so man must follow his example. The entire work of God comes to its consummation, and the Sabbath was an exhibition of that consummation principle. Here the reason is the redemption from Egypt, for the same consummation principle in God's salvation results in God bringing his people into their rest. The writer to the Hebrews spells out the concept most fully when he points to the ultimate Sabbath rest which awaits the people of God (Heb. 3:16–4:11). The manner of speaking of the deliverance from Egypt, 'with a mighty hand and an outstretched arm', is a standard way used in Deuteronomy to draw attention to the greatness of God's power shown in the redemption of Israel from Egypt (the combined phrase occurs elsewhere in the Old Testament in 4:34; 7:19; 11:2; 26:8; 'mighty hand' alone in 3:24; 6:21; 7:8; 9:26; 34:12; 'stretched out arm' alone in 9:29).

16 'The first commandment with a promise' (Eph. 6:2) is a positive direction to honour father and mother. The verb 'honour' has a wide range of meaning. It is used of honouring and esteeming other human beings, but it is also used of the response of worship given to God (1 Sam. 2:30; Ps. 86:9; Prov. 3:9; Isa. 24:15). Fellow men and neighbours are to be loved (Lev. 19:18), but parents are to be honoured or 'feared' (Lev. 19:3, using a term normally reserved for God).

The fact that this command is addressed to adults points to the fact that something more than just one's parents was in view. The latter part of the verse confirms this. Long life in the sworn land would depend upon obedience to God's commands and recognition of his duly appointed representatives who would exercise his rule in the various facets of human life. In these words there is yet another warning to Israel. Lack of respect for parents would amount to rebellion against God, and it might result in abrupt cessation of possession of Canaan. Later on one of the sins mentioned as a reason for the Exile was disrespect for parents (Ezek. 22:7, 10-11). The reference in 'as the Lord your God has commanded you' is either to the original giving of this instruction (Exod. 20:12) or else to passages such as Exodus 21:15, 17, Leviticus 19:3 and Leviticus 20:9.

17 The Sixth Commandment, which occurs like the Seventh and Eight Commandments in the shortest formulation in the Decalogue, deals with the security of life against attack. The root used here (Heb. *ratsach*) denotes in the Old Testament both killing in general and more specifically murder, manslaughter. It is not the most common verb for taking life in the Old Testament, occurring 46 times in comparison with 'kill' (Heb. *harag*, 165x) and 'put to death' (Heb. *hêmît*, 201x). Underlying the command was the basic concept of the sanctity of human life, for man was the image-bearer of God (Gen. 9:6). No one was to take the law into their own hands out of feelings of personal vindictiveness. The lack of an object for the verb leaves it very open and general, including both murder and even suicide in its scope. When describing the abuses of the covenant community both Hosea (4:2) and Jeremiah (7:9) include this verb in their lists. There were various exceptions to this prohibition. It relates only to humans, not to animals. It does not apply to the defence of one's home (Exod. 22:2) or to accidental killings (Deut. 19:5) or to the loss of life in war (Deut. 20:13).

18 Both the Old Testament and the extra-biblical texts from the Near East call adultery 'the great sin' (Gen. 20:9). This Seventh Commandment prohibits the breach of the sanctity of marriage. The verb here (*na'af*) is used in the Old Testament of both men and women, though far more commonly of men. That this word was understood literally is shown by its use for sexual intercourse of a man with another man's wife (Lev. 18:20; 20:10; Deut. 22:22), of sexual intercourse of a man with the fiancee of another man (Deut. 22:23-27), and of intercourse of a wife with a man, presumably a married man (Hos. 4:13; Ezek. 16:32).

The seriousness with which this sin was viewed is shown by the way in which Jeremiah (5:7) links it with the worship of 'no-gods', and by Hosea's linking it with deceitful swearing and killing (4:2). Breach of the prohibition was primarily sin against God (cf. Joseph's words, 'How then could I do such a wicked thing and sin against God?' Gen. 39:9), and this explains the directness of the references to it and the severity of the penalty for its breach. There is also interconnection of the concepts of human marriage and the idea of the marriage relationship between God and Israel. He was zealous for the sanctity of human marriage bonds, as he was for his own marriage bond with Israel. The prophets, echoing references to Israel's own 'great sin' (Exod. 32:21-34), use the same verb (*na'af*) to describe Israel's breach of the covenant bond by indulging in idolatry (Isa. 57:1-13; Jer. 3:6-9; Ezek. 23:36-49).

19 Theft always results in a disruption of relationships, as well as being a disrespect for the rights of individuals and groups to hold property. Thus the Eighth Commandment is a comprehensive prohibition of all forms of stealing, with the verb used here (Heb. *nagav*) lacking an object (cf. the Sixth Commandment). In the Old Testament God was the one who possessed all things (Ps. 24:1), and he entrusted them to others. Rightful ownership of property had to be respected. Hence even when those in debt were forced to sell either their property (or themselves as slaves), the sabbatical or jubilee years brought a reversion to the original ownership (Exod. 21:1-2; Lev. 25; Deut. 15:1-18).

20 The Ninth Commandment is directed towards preserving the sanctity of truth. The thought of bearing false witness points to a law-court situation in which a fellow member of the covenant community was on trial. This is because the terms 'false witness' and 'answer' reflect a legal background, just as 'neighbour' is a term describing a full citizen. However, the expression seems to go beyond this, as truthfulness is presented here as a requirement of the LORD, not just something which was embodied in a legal code. The alteration here in Deuteronomy to 'nothingness, emptiness' in place of 'false, fraudulent' which occurs in Exodus 20:16, serves to strengthen the breadth of the prohibition. This is also borne out by other passages containing prohibitions against lying (e.g., Exod. 23:1-2, 7; Deut. 17:6; 19:15-21; 22:13-21), as well as the way in which Hosea lists lying as one element in his catalogue of the sins of the people (Hos. 4:2). Not only is lying forbidden by this Word, but any false or unfounded statements in general, wherever in life they might occur.

21 The final Commandment relates not so much to outward actions as to inward motives. In Exodus 20:17 the Hebrew verb *chamad* occurs twice, while in Deuteronomy the second verb is changed to *hit'avveh*. Both verbs are very similar in meaning, but the introduction of a new verb here may well emphasise further the aspect of emotion rather than emotion plus associated action. This prohibition comes at the end of the Decalogue in a summarising fashion. Illicit desire was the root from which all the other sins would spring. Both Testaments indicate that coveting comes from the heart (Prov. 6:25) and ultimately brings forth sin, which expresses itself in the act (Jas. 1:14, 15). The list given in this verse is very typical of the ancient Near East, and it is aimed at spelling out the extent of a man's property. Sinful desire for the possessions of another extended to everything he had.

2. Historical Review 5:22-31

The basic stipulations having been given in the Decalogue, Moses proceeds to explain and expound them (for fuller discussion on the order of chapters 5-26 see the Introduction). This section of historical review marks the transition from setting out the basic law to its exposition. It follows on from the section of the previous chapter that recalled to the people's minds the events at Horeb (4:9ff.). Here we have a fuller description of the events than that given in Exodus 20:18-21. Later on Moses returns to this topic in 9:7ff., though with special reference to the events which followed the giving of the law.

22 The proclamation on Sinai was made in circumstances which stressed the solemnity of the event. The 'loud voice' of the LORD was heard 'on the mountain from out of the fire, the cloud and the deep darkness'. The majestic way in which the words came to Israel was in keeping with the whole setting of the covenant ceremony (cf. Gen. 15:17-18). What has just preceded is described as 'these words' (NIV 'these are the commandments'). They formed the very core of the covenant commitment and in the Shema it is 'these words' (6:6) that are to be upon their hearts.

The uniqueness of what had happened is stressed in two ways. First, Moses said that God had not added anything further to this basic covenant proclamation, and secondly, that he had committed them to writing on two stone tablets (see comment on 4:13 in reference to the duplicate tablets). These tablets were delivered into the hands of Moses. Exodus 34:28b makes it explicit that the text on the stone tablets and the Ten Words were identical. Those words were complete and God added nothing to them. The exposition of the Ten Words which follows was not given directly by God but through the covenant mediator, Moses (4:14; 5:31).

23 The appearance of the presence of God in such an awe-inspiring way provoked a response from the people. Both testaments bear witness to the fact that God, 'who alone is immortal and who lives in unapproachable light', is the one 'whom no one has seen or can see' (1 Tim. 6:16). The people wanted Moses to act as their mediator, and so their representatives approach him with their request.

24-27 The people acknowledged that what had taken place was a self-revelation of God himself. He had shown them 'his glory and his majesty'. The addition of the latter word draws attention to the greatness of God, and to the character of the covenant God before whom they came at that time. While they saw no figure, yet they distinctly heard a voice from the midst of the fire. They then knew that it was possible for a man to speak with God and still live. That was an experience which no other nation had had (cf. 4:33).

Their mortality was brought home to them by that revelation. Hence they said that a prolongation of their experience at Sinai could lead to their death. If they stayed any longer there the fire might well consume them. They recognised (verse 26) that there was no mortal man (Heb. *basar*, 'flesh') who could continue to have this experience of the living God and still survive. The fear expressed by the people was not sinful in itself. In fact, it was the very opposite, for the people recognised that what had happened was a revelation of their God (cf. the threefold usage of the 'LORD our God' in this section verses 24, 25, 27).

The request that the leaders of the people make to Moses (verse 27) recognised the uniqueness of his position, as well as their own need of a mediator. Though he too was flesh (NIV 'mortal man') yet they considered him able to hear safely God's words and transmit them to the people. They pledged themselves to both listen and obey. That reminder of their promise at Horeb was apt in the circumstances as the covenant was being renewed. As they had done at Horeb (Exod. 24:1-11), so would they shortly be called upon to do again (cf. 30:11-20).

28 Moses received his mandate as mediator from God himself. His role as such raised a basic problem for Israel in the future. What would happen to the people when their mediator died? The role of Moses in Deuteronomy pointed ahead to another greater mediator whom God would raise up *like Moses* (18:15; cf. Acts 3:21-23). Mention is made here of the LORD's response (cf. Exod. 20 where this is omitted). Moses had no need to carry the people's request to the LORD as it was heard already. Approval was given to it because the request stemmed from a sense of their own unworthiness before him.

29 The LORD then expressed a wish! In Hebrew the sentence starts with words which are regularly used to express a desire or wish (*mi yitên*, lit. 'who would give?' cf. Exod. 16:3; 2 Sam. 19:1; Job 6:8, 13:5, 14:13; *mi* is also used with other verbs as in 2 Sam. 23:15 and Mal. 1:10 to express a wish, but the usage with *natan* is the most common). The people had often failed to show a heart in line with God's commands. Now the LORD longed to see constant obedience to his words and the consequent enjoyment by them of covenant blessings ('that it might go well with them').

30-31 The division between Moses and all the others in Israel is made plain. He is instructed to remain before God while the people as a whole are dismissed to their tents. He would be taught 'the commands (Heb. has the singular *mitsvah*, 'commandment'), the statutes and the judgments' for transmission to the people. These instructions were to be practised by the people as they entered into possession of the land of Canaan.

32 The account of the giving of the law having been completed, Moses commenced his summons to Israel to hear and to obey. The way of the LORD was plain, and there could be no deviation from it. He was concerned, therefore, to remind Israel that all God's commands had to be practised and his pathway followed.

The expression to 'turn aside to the right or the left' is common in the Old Testament when faithful obedience to God's will is being described (cf. Deut. 2:27; Jos. 1:7; 1 Sam. 6:12; 2 Sam. 2:19; 2 Kings 22:2; 2 Chron. 34:2).

33 The instructions given by the LORD constituted a way of life for Israel, being intended for the nation and also for all the individuals that made up Israel. This imagery is taken up in various places in the Old Testament (see e.g., Ps. 119:105; Prov. 4:18) and in the New Testament (see especially Jesus' words in the Sermon on the Mount, Matt 7:13-14). Moses reminded the people that obedience was necessary so that they might live. The wilderness generation had perished because of unbelief and disobedience (cf. Ps. 95:7-11; Heb. 3:7-19). Warning had already been given (4:26) that if the people were disobedient they would quickly perish from the land. This summarised the covenant curses of Leviticus 26:27ff. concerning expulsion from the land.

The expression 'that you may live and prosper' (Heb. $v^e tov$ *lachem*) involves a covenant concept. The Hebrew word *tov*, 'good', is often used in covenant contexts (e.g., Deut. 23:6; 2 Sam. 2:6; 7:28; Ps. 23:6; Hos. 8:3) to show the bounty promised to faithful covenant servants. As with the extra-biblical texts, the Old Testament often uses etymologically related words to indicate 'friendly relations established by treaty.' The Psalmist can pray that goodness and steadfast love (Heb. *tov vachesed*) will follow him as long as he lives (Ps. 23:6). Continuity of living in the land they were to possess was dependent upon their obedience. God's promises concerning it would not apply automatically. The same idea is present in the Fifth Commandment with the thought of prolonging their days in the land.

C. EXPOSITION OF
THE TEN COMMANDMENTS (6:1–26:15)

1. The First Commandment (6:1–11:32)

(i) Introduction (6:1-3)

1 Then Moses began to spell out the implications of what he had received from the LORD. The commands, decrees and laws that God required were to be taught to the people by him. These instructions were to be their guide as they moved into the land to possess it.

2 This teaching was to motivate the present generation and those to come, to 'fear the LORD your God'. There is no Old Testament expression more all-embracing in describing religious life than this one. This fear is not the abject fear of a cowering slave, but heartfelt devotion of a redeemed sinner. This aspect of redemption was mentioned earlier (cf. 4:20, 34, 37; 5:6, 15) and in the next few verses comes the expected response to God's sovereign care for them. In the Old Testament the fear of the LORD was the beginning of wisdom (Ps. 111:10) and without that fear there was no spiritual life. This requirement of fear towards the LORD was valid all the days of their lives. The presence of that fear would be demonstrated in obedience to God's covenant conditions. The same principle carries over into the New Testament, where our Lord reminded his disciples: 'You are my friends if you do what I command you' (Jn. 15:14). To remain in Christ's love is to keep his words (Jn. 15:7, 10).

3 Moses reminded Israel of the need to hear and carefully observe all that the LORD commanded. Covenantal blessings were contingent upon their obedience. If they obeyed, then all would 'go well' with them. The Hebrew expression comes from the root *tov* (see above on 5:33 for the noun), and the verbal form occurs here. Significantly this phrase occurs in a covenant context, for mention is made later in the verse of the promise given to the patriarchs. A large increase in the national population was a covenant promise (see Gen. 12:2; 15:2-6; 17:2). If Israel wanted

full enjoyment of the good things promised by the LORD, then
wholehearted obedience was essential. The land they were going
to enter was a land flowing with milk and honey. Such description
of Canaan first appears in the words of the LORD to Moses at the
burning bush. God said: 'I have indeed seen the misery of my
people in Egypt. I have heard them crying out because of their
slave drivers, and I am concerned about their suffering. So I have
come down to rescue them from the hand of the Egyptians and to
bring them up out of that land into a good and spacious land, a
land flowing with milk and honey' (Exod. 3:7-8). When the spies
brought back their report they confirmed that it was a land flowing
with milk and honey (Num. 13:27). To us today, Israel may seem
dry and barren in spite of modern irrigation, but in ancient times
its produce was far more abundant than that of Egypt or its
immediate neighbours.

(ii) The Shema (6:4-9)

The words in verses 4-6 play an important role in both Jewish and
Christian thought. Orthodox Jews recite these words morning and
evening, and wish to die with them on their lips. In addition to
these words, the Jews often add Deuteronomy 11:13-21 and
Numbers 15:37-41. It may well be that this Jewish practice
suggested to the early Christians that they too should confess their
faith in summary statements. Examples in the New Testament
include passages such as Romans 10:9, 10; 1 Corinthians 15:3-8;
Philippians 2:6-11; 1 Timothy 3:16, 6:12-16; and 1 John 4:2.

Deuteronomy 6:3 commences with the Hebrew word *shema*',
and thus the passage as a whole gets its name from this word
which means 'listen' or 'hear'. It carries the implication that
hearing will be followed by obedience. Hebrew has no word for
obey (cf. in Greek *akouo* is 'to listen', and *hupakouo* 'to obey').
In the New Testament, verses 4-5 appear in our Lord's answer to
a Pharisee's question about which was the greatest commandment.
Jesus said (Matt. 22:36) that the most important one was that which
is embedded here in Deuteronomy 6:4-5. To this Jesus appended
as the second most important commandment the words from
Leviticus 19:18: 'Love your neighbour as yourself' (Mark 12:28-
31; cf. also Matt. 22:37-39 and Luke 10:27).

4 Twice in this verse the covenant name of God occurs. It comes into English in the hybrid form of 'Jehovah'. The name was so sacred to the Jews that to avoid an unworthy use of it they refrained from using it at all, and substituted the word *Adonai*, 'Lord'. In writing they placed the vowels of Adonai with the consonants of the sacred name, YHWH. This name, because of its four consonants, is often called the Tetragrammaton (Gk., 'four letters'). It has become customary to print the English word LORD in capital format to mark the occurrences of this divine name, reserving Lord (with only an initial capital) for Adonai.

While *El Shaddai* ('the Almighty') was the common title for God in the patriarchal period, clearly LORD was also known. This is evident from the name of Moses' mother, Jochebed, for the first part of her name is a shortened form of the Tetragrammaton. That the people already knew their God by this name is evident from the way in which God instructed Moses prior to the Exodus. Moses was instructed to say to the people: 'The LORD, the God of your fathers – the God of Abraham, the God of Isaac and the God of Jacob – has sent me to you. This is my name for ever, the name by which I am to be remembered from generation to generation' (Exod. 3:15). Similarly the elders and Moses, when they went to Pharaoh, were to say: 'The LORD God of the Hebrews has met with us; and now, please, let us go three-days journey into the wilderness, that we may sacrifice to the LORD our God' (Exod. 3:18). Both instructions presuppose a prior knowledge of who the LORD was. The later references to audiences with Pharaoh do not mention the presence of the elders.

Some reference is also necessary to Exodus 6:2-3, especially to the way in which God declared that he was the LORD and that he had made himself known to the patriarchs by the term *El Shaddai*. By his name the LORD did not make himself known to them (Exod. 6:3). It is possible that the second part of this verse is a question: 'And by my name the LORD did I not make myself known to them?' The absence of an interrogatory particle, which is the more usual way of asking a question in Hebrew, is not absolutely decisive, as Hebrew sometimes depended on voice inflection to indicate a question. However, the better explanation

would seem to be that the Israelites knew the name *the* LORD but
did not understand the true significance of it until the events of
the Exodus. They then came to know him as redeemer and saviour,
the covenant God of Israel. This same conclusion can be reached
by taking the negative in a relative sense and so translate, 'and by
my name the LORD I was not only known to them'.

The second part of Deuteronomy 6:4, in which the name *the*
LORD occurs twice, is difficult to translate. This is because in simple
Hebrew sentences in which two nouns (or a noun and an adjective)
are equated with one another, no verb is necessary. Here we have
four words (*the* LORD, *our God, the* LORD, *one*), and several
translations are possible. They include:

a. The LORD our God is one LORD.
b. The LORD our God, the LORD is one.
c. The LORD is our God; the LORD is one.
d. The LORD is our God, the LORD alone!

Of these translations the last is probably to be given the preference.
Grammatically such verses as Genesis 42:19, 1 Chronicles 19:1
and Zechariah 14:9 show that this translation is quite acceptable.
Later references in this chapter (verses 5 and 14) indicate that the
stress is on both the unity and the uniqueness of Israel's God.
This was not just a theoretical confession on the part of Israel.
Rather it was a confession based on the fact that God had redeemed
his people and had now brought them to the edge of Canaan. The
monotheistic confession was based on God's redemptive actions
(cf. also 4:35 and 5:6, 7).

5 As a consequence of the uniqueness of Israel's God, the
command is given, 'love the LORD your God'. He had set his love
on Israel (4:37; 7:7-8) and that exclusive love demanded a response
by Israel. The idea of love to God may be grounded on the son/
father relationship of Israel to God and also on the marriage
relationship that bound them in covenant bonds. The language of
the marriage relationship is used of religious attachment in Exodus
34:15 where the Canaanites are described as those who 'play the

prostitute with their gods.' The marriage covenant was later used by several of the prophets to describe both the love of God and the binding nature of the relationship between God and Israel (see Hos. 1-3; Jer. 2:2; Mal. 2:10-16). If all marriages were covenants, then the use of this imagery would have been particularly fitting (cf. Prov. 2:17; Mal. 2:14).

The loving response of Israel to God had to be with all their 'heart' and all 'their soul'. These terms seem to be used here as synonyms. God is represented as being jealous for the total response of their lives to rest on himself. 'Your strength' (Heb. *me'odeka*) is a rare word in the Old Testament, appearing only here and in 2 Kings 23:25, where Josiah's strong commitment is described. All the personality had to be directed to responding to God's love, by loving in return and by displaying this love in obedience.

When questioned about the greatest commandment and also about inheriting eternal life Jesus responded by citing these words. He freed his followers from the legalistic obedience to this command which had evolved among the rabbis. Jesus taught that this love must find expression in practical ways. This point comes out clearly in the Lucan account of the question about inheriting eternal life. In response to the further question 'Who is my neighbour?' Jesus told the story of the Good Samaritan (Luke 10:25-37). Having come to fulfil the law and the prophets (Matt. 5:17), Jesus fulfilled both commands (love to God and love to one's neighbour) in his life and death.

6 One way in which God expressed his love was in the revelation to Israel of himself and his will. Moses was the covenant mediator who taught these words to the people. The expression 'these commandments' seems to imply more than what is contained in verses 4 and 5. It is probably a comprehensive term for all the teaching given in chapter 5 and what he was at this point giving to them. The LORD's words were to be so impressed upon them that they could be said to be upon their hearts. This meant treasuring God's words in their minds and remembering what he had done (cf. the use of Heb. verb *zakar*, 'remember' in Deut. 5:15; 7:18;

8:2; 9:7; 16:3, 12). God's revelation had to be a vital and living reality in their daily lives.

7 The words of the LORD had to be passed down from generation to generation. The word translated 'impress' (Heb. *shanan* Pi.) literally means 'to repeat'. This parental role of educating the children in the covenant words is emphasised again in Deuteronomy 11:19. The basic principle is reiterated in Psalm 78 where appeal is made to what the LORD had commanded the people to teach their children. The whole aim was that succeeding generations would know of the LORD's deeds and his instructions and that they would put their trust in him (Ps. 78:1-8). The LORD's words, in addition to being the driving force in the life of the individual, had also to be a living reality in family life. Whether at home or outside, in whatever activities were taking place, God required his words to be discussed. Clearly in such situations the discussion would be provoked by children's questions, such as Moses envisaged them asking at the time of the Passover (Exod. 12:26ff. 'When your children ask you ...').

8-9 The instructions in these verses were taken literally by the Jews in later time and many orthodox Jews continue to do so down to the present. That this was so in New Testament times is clear from our Lord's reference in Matthew 23:5 to phylacteries. These were small wooden boxes containing miniature scrolls with some verses inscribed on them, and which were worn on the forehead and left wrist. From the Hebrew word for doorposts used in this verse comes the term 'mezuzot' to refer to the boxes attached to the doorposts. One such 'mezuza', found in one of the caves at Qumran at the northern end of the Dead Sea, contained the text of Deuteronomy 10:12-11:21. Orthodox Jews still place a small container with scrolls on the right doorpost of their house. Often they touch it with their fingers when entering or leaving the house and then kiss their fingers.

The context suggests, however, that the words should be interpreted metaphorically. The reasons for this are as follows:

1. This passage re-echoes words found in Exodus 13 in connection
   with the consecration of the firstborn. That observance was to
   be like a sign on their hand and a reminder on their forehead
   (Exod. 13:9, 16). Clearly the Exodus passage is drawing a
   comparison, not describing a literal occurrence.

2. The teaching in question is expressed by 'these commandments'
   in verse 6. That meant much more than just the words of verses
   4-9. It embodied all the teaching that Moses was giving, and
   this amount would be far beyond a literal fulfilment of these
   verses.

3. In this context Moses has spoken of God's word in their hearts
   (verse 6) and on their lips (verse 7). It fits in well with the
   context if verses 8-9 are understood as expressing the reality
   of God's words demonstrated by their actions.

(iii) Warnings (6:10-18)

This section deals with two problems facing the people after they
have come into possession of the land. The first is that when they
have everything – houses, vineyards, wells, abundant food – they
are to beware lest they forget it was God who redeemed them and
gave them all these things. Without him they would still be slaves
in Egypt rather than proprietors in the Promised Land. The second
danger was that of contamination by the Canaanites. With
Canaanitish worship all around them, there would be the
temptation to worship and serve the gods of the Canaanites instead
of the living God. The two ideas are linked together because the
Canaanites believed that their gods gave fertility and abundant
crops.

10-11 Moses then spoke in prophetic style to the people (Heb.
$v^e hayah\ ki$, 'And it shall be when ...') regarding the situation they
would find in Canaan. They were being brought there by their
God, who was fulfilling the oath he had made to the patriarchs.
The Israelites would come into possession of the culture of the
land, including 'large and flourishing cities' which they themselves
had not built. They are reminded that their possession of the land

and its contents was all of grace, and the adjectives used ('large', 'flourishing') emphasise the bounty of God to his people. Similarly they would live in houses stocked with provisions, and they would not need to dig cisterns or plant vineyards. They could eat their fill from the good things they were to find there.

12 Such experiences could easily bring a false sense of security to Israel. Hence the call to them: 'Be careful that you do not forget the LORD' (cf. 4:9). The danger would be that they would forget their deliverer who brought them 'out of the land of Egypt, from the house of bondage' (NKJV). Constantly Israel needed reminding of their abject condition of slavery in Egypt. Their God had delivered them so that they themselves could be masters and lords. In their new situation they had to look always to the source of their deliverance from bondage.

13 In the Hebrew text emphasis falls on the words 'the LORD your God', 'him', and 'his name': *'The LORD your God* you shall fear and *him* you shall serve and *by his name* you shall swear.' Love (see verse 5) and fear do not exclude one another. 'Fear' is an expression of religious life and devotion (see comments on verse 2). In speaking of the Israelites' service of God, Moses uses a word which is connected in Hebrew with the word for *bondage* in the previous verse. They were now slaves to a new sovereign. To swear by the name of the LORD seems to indicate something broader than simply taking an oath. While its origins may well have been in the formal covenant oath, it denotes public confession of the very character of God. The *name* of God is not just the vocable by which God was known but his character, his self-manifestation (cf. Jesus' use of name in this way in his high-priestly prayer, 'I have revealed your name ... I have made you known to them', Jn. 17:6, 26). Their lives had to witness to the one God (verse 4) who had redeemed them and on whom they were totally dependent.

14 The expression 'to follow other gods' may well be derived from the ritual of processions after an idol. In the extra-biblical treaties 'to go after' has the idea of serving as a vassal. If Israel

forgot God, then the temptation would be to show allegiance to
Canaanite gods. To swear by God's name would mean renouncing
allegiance to them.

15 Reference to God as a jealous God has already occurred in
4:24 (see commentary) and in the Second Commandment (5:9).
The words here, 'for the LORD your God, who is among you, is a
jealous God', form a parenthesis between the end of verse 14 and
the second half of this verse. They emphasise that God is both
jealous and zealous for his own honour. The danger for the people
was that God would reveal his wrath and that they would be blotted
out from the earth (cf. the covenant curse in 4:26 and more fully
in chap. 28, especially verses 36ff.). Here the expression seems to
denote utter destruction, not just removal from their own land.

16 Israel must not put God to the test as they did previously at
Massah. There they grumbled when they had no water and said to
Moses, 'Why did you bring us up out of Egypt to make us and our
children and our livestock die of thirst?' (Exod. 17:3). They put
the LORD to the test by saying, 'Is the LORD among us or not?'
(Exod. 17:7). Moses cited the past experience of Massah as a
warning against future temptations to react in this same manner.
These words of verse 16 are cited later in the Bible in two very
different ways. When requested by Isaiah to ask for a sign from
the LORD, Ahaz hypocritically replied using these words (Isa. 7:12).
Even though he would not ask, a sign was given by the LORD, that
of Immanuel (Isa. 7:14). The words are also cited in a far different
way by Jesus during his temptation by the devil. When asked to
throw himself down from the temple he replied: 'Do not put the
Lord your God to the test' (Matt. 4:7).

17 The task before Israel was to obey the commands, stipulations
and decrees that God had given them at Horeb. The corollary of
not going after other gods (verse 14) was that they were to keep
diligently what their covenant God demanded of them.

18-19 This verse explains further what is meant by 'be sure to keep the commands' in the previous verse. What was good and upright to the LORD was to be the standard for them. Possession of the good land (cf. verses 10-11) was not to be automatic, but dependent upon obedience. The last part of verse 18 is explained here in other words. What the LORD had promised was that he would drive out other nations before Israel so they could settle in Canaan. The motive for obedience is underscored once again.

(iv) Instruction for the Future (6:20-25)

20 Parental instruction was to be so important for the future life of Israel. The people had already been told to learn the ordinances of the LORD (5:1). Now they are told of their responsibility to teach these things to their children. The pattern of question and answer had already been set in connection with the Passover (Exod. 12:26ff.). Now Moses explained further what imprinting the words of the LORD on the children's hearts meant (verse 7). In time to come children would ask about the significance of what they were being taught.

21 Once again the emphasis is placed on the terrible reality of bondage in Egypt. From that God had redeemed them and had shown his sovereign power. This was the first answer which the children were to be given. Their God had acted in history when he displayed his redeeming power. The Song of the Sea (Exod. 15:1-18) stressed the nature of the victory which the LORD had achieved.

22 God had not acted in secret but openly before his people when he took action against Egypt, Pharaoh and all his house. He had done so with plagues which displayed his power and which had shown his superiority over all the gods of Egypt (Exod. 12:12, and cf. the use of these terms 'signs' and 'wonders' in 4:34).

23 The Hebrew text accentuates the object of God's favour. '*Us* the LORD brought out,' says Moses, in order to give the land about which he had sworn an oath. As in verse 18 the emphasis is placed on the faithfulness of God in fulfilling his oath.

24-25 Here is the second thing which the children were to be told. God had revealed his instructions to guide them in his service. The people, on the point of entering Canaan, were at that moment conscious of God's blessing, and continuation in that blessing meant the required pathway of obedience. It would be their 'righteousness'. The term is used here in a way very similar to that in the epistle of James (see Jas. 1:20; 2:22-24; 3:18). The reality of a relationship with God is expressed in commitment to his commands. Continuity of blessing in the future and even for all the days of their lives depended on faithful obedience to what God had commanded.

(v) Privilege and Responsibility (7:1–26)

(a) The Wars of the Lord (7:1-5)
Israel's special position before the LORD meant that it had to deal with the other nations, especially those in Canaan, in an extraordinary way. Following the proclamation of *one* God in the previous chapter (see comments on 6:4), the position of *one* people of God is now emphasised. These verses set out the policy of destruction of the Canaanites and the placing of the 'curse' or 'ban' on them (see comments on 2:34). They were to implement a policy of 'holy war' or to use a term employed later in the biblical history (1 Sam. 18:17; 25:28), they were to engage in 'the battles of the LORD'.

1 Moses then fixed the attention of the people on the task immediately in front of them. However, explicit in Moses' words was the further reminder that it was really the LORD who was going to perform these actions. He would bring them into the land and drive out the nations already there. The verb 'drive them out' (Heb. *nashal*) is significant. It is used in Hebrew for loosening a sandal (Exod. 3:5; Jos. 5:15), while another form of the verb describes how Rezin drove out the Israelites from Elath (2 Kings 16:6). Here it is used to convey graphically how the LORD would free the Israelites from the heathen nations just as a sandal is freed from the foot. Seven nations are mentioned as being in the land and as being greater and more powerful than Israel. In other passages different listings of the nations appear. The table of the nations in Genesis 10:15-18 lists eleven, while in Genesis 15:19-21 ten names appear. Exodus 3:8 and 33:2 have six, and Exodus 23:28 three. Why then seven here? Probably because seven was a number used to denote completeness.

2 God was going to put the nations into Israel's hands. They would then have to apply the curse upon them. It is clear from what follows that Moses did not have in view the destruction of every single person in these nations. Nor did he envisage complete occupation of all the territory immediately (see comment on 7:22). The dangers for Israel included intermarriage (see below) and entering into treaties with them, which would mean renunciation of the sole lordship of God over them. In the Book of the Covenant (Exod. 20–23) the warning was given of making treaties with the nations in Canaan or 'with their gods' (Exod. 23:32). In Joshua 9:1-27 we have the account of how the Israelites were later tricked into making such a treaty with the Gibeonites. They would also be faced with the temptation to show pity. Later in this book (chap. 20:1-20) further details regarding warfare are given.

3 Intermarriage was to pose a continuing problem for the Israelites. In itself it was not impermissible, as is seen from the fact that Moses' two marriages were with foreign women (with Zipporah from Midian, Exod. 2:21, and with a Cushite, Num. 12:1). The dangers became very real in the cases of Solomon (see 1 Kings 11:1-13) and Ahab (1 Kings 16:31-33). Here the proscription of mixed marriages comes in close proximity to the instruction regarding treaties. Hence most probably the thought is that of marriages intended to cement the external policy of entering into alliances with the surrounding nations.

4 The danger of intermarriage was that coming generations would be induced to follow other gods. Moses said that they would turn away 'from following me'. Either he repeats the words given to him by the Lord, or else he speaks as the mouthpiece of the Lord and thus identifies himself with the LORD. In Exodus 34:15-16 the warning about this had already been given, immediately after the assertion that the LORD was a jealous God. Here in Deuteronomy 7 it follows the same assertion given in 6:15. Such betrayal of the LORD by following other gods would not go unpunished, but would bring about sudden punishment (cf. 6:15 for the same warning). Instead of the heathen nations being destroyed, Israel herself would be.

5 When Israel came into Canaan the people would immediately be confronted with the whole apparatus of cult worship. The Canaanites had their places of sacrifice and sacred stones (Heb. *matstsevot*), standing stone pillars that somehow represented a deity. They also had wooden poles which symbolised the fertility goddess Asherah. Out of wood and stone they cut idols of their gods. All these were the outward expression of Canaanite religious belief. Israel had one God, the LORD, who was not to be depicted in any way by idols (cf. 4:15-24; 5:8). In accordance with the instruction in the Book of the Covenant (Exod. 23:24) these cult objects were to be broken down, smashed, cut down and burnt respectively. To leave them where they were would provide constant temptation to the Israelites.

A Further Note on the Cherem Principle
The Hebrew verb *charam* (Hif.) means 'to devote to the ban', or 'to dedicate to destruction', while the noun *cherem* refers to what is 'dedicated to destruction', or 'placed under a curse'. The application of the principle in these verses requires further comment. Clearly Israel did not carry out the instructions fully, and from later in Deuteronomy we see that humanitarian considerations had to have play as well. Thus citizens in a besieged city could be offered terms – either submit to Israel and become slaves, or else suffer death (Deut. 20:10-15). While Israel had to be separate from the other nations, yet she had a missionary task (Deut. 4:6-8), which was a concept which would become a dominant factor in the life of the New Testament church as a result of the death and resurrection of Jesus.

The application of the principle of the *cherem* has to be seen as foreshadowing the ultimate judgement of God. The banning or cursing was not just a verbal action, but it involved the handing over of someone or something so that they were at the exclusive disposal of God. What was banned belonged henceforth to God alone. Achan was to find out how serious his sin was in keeping back what was *cherem* for his own use (Jos. 7:1-26) and Israel never forgot his sin, as mention in the post-exilic genealogies shows (1 Chron. 2:7 where *Achan* is called *Achar*. The reference is clear however as he is called 'The son of Carmi ... the troubler of Israel, who transgressed in the accursed thing' [NIV 'who brought disaster on Israel by violating the ban on taking devoted things']). The destruction of the Canaanites was an intrusion of God's judgement into Israel's history and it shows the same pattern of separation that will take place when God irrevocably separates believers and unbelievers. The judgements of hell are really the principle of the curse come to full and final manifestation. God had appointed his rule over Israel (the theocracy) as a divinely appointed symbol of the ultimate kingdom of God. Hence in the period of the theocracy there is an intrusion of the ethical pattern that will prevail at the final judgement.

Two further points should be noted. First, in commanding the Israelites to apply the *cherem* principle, Moses was also speaking about actions which they had already committed themselves to perform. After the defeat of Israel by the king of Arad, Israel made this vow to the LORD, 'If you will deliver these people into our hands, we will totally destroy their cities' (Num. 21:2). Secondly, the task which Israel was to carry out was also a surgical operation to prevent their own destruction through rampant venereal disease (Num. 25 and 31). Israel had had the experience of contamination through the Midianites, and the danger from the Canaanites was just as real.

(b) A Special Treasure (7:6-11)
This section forms the very heart of this chapter. Preceding verses have dealt with the position of Israel in relation to other nations. Now the fuller explanation is given of the privileged position which

Israel enjoyed before God. The origin of Israel's status was solely dependent on free and sovereign love.

6 For the first time in the Old Testament Israel is called a *holy people* (Heb. *'am qadosh*). In Leviticus 19:2 God had said: 'Be holy, because I, the LORD your God, am holy'. The holiness of the people was more a promise than a demand. The basic idea of holiness in the Old Testament is that of separation. By God's choice of them, the people of Israel had been set apart for the LORD himself.

Out of all the nations he had made choice of Israel to be his 'treasured possession' (Heb. *segullah*). The Akkadian cognate of this word is *sikiltu,* which occurs on a treaty seal from Alalah in reference to the king as a 'treasured possession' of his god. Alalah was a city-state on the Orontes River in northern Syria, where many tablets were found dating from 1900-1400 BC. This expression is not common in the Old Testament as it only occurs eight times. The first occurrence is in Exodus 19:5, a passage which is echoed here in Deuteronomy 7:6, and also in the two other occurrences in this book (Deut. 14:2; 26:18). In 1 Chronicles 29:3 it is used of special treasure belonging to David, which he was giving towards the temple of his God, and in Ecclesiastes 2:8 it similarly means 'treasure'. The expression also appears in Malachi 3:17 of those whom the LORD will gather to himself at his coming. The AV uses 'jewels' in that passage and this has been taken over into English hymnology ('When He cometh, when He cometh, to make up His jewels'). The final occurrence is in Psalm 135:4, and it is significant because, as here in Deuteronomy 7, the word is used along with the verb to choose (Heb. *bachar*). Because of God's choice in love of Israel, she was elevated to a special position of privilege and service in his sight.

7 The reason for Israel's special position is now further explained. Other nations were far greater in number, and in comparison the Israelites were 'the fewest of all peoples'. The explanation could only be that God had set his sovereign love upon them. God's firstborn son was chosen in love, a truth which also applies to New Testament believers. Paul reminded the Ephesians that God had chosen us in Christ 'before the creation of the world to be holy and blameless in his sight. In love he predestined us to be adopted as his sons through Jesus Christ, in accordance with his pleasure and will' (Eph. 1:4-5).

The same theme is taken up later in Deuteronomy 9:4ff. There was nothing intrinsic in Israel which moved God to separate her from the other more powerful nations. The thought is carried over into the New Testament and the language from this passage is applied to the church. In Titus 2:14 it is said that our Saviour gave himself to redeem us and to 'purify for himself a people that are his own'. Peter takes the words over even more graphically when he tells his readers 'you are a chosen people, a royal priesthood, a holy nation, a people belonging to God, that you may declare the praises of him who called you out of darkness into his wonderful light' (1 Pet. 2:9).

8 The opening phrase of the verse continues the theme of God's unmerited love for Israel, as it re-echoes the language already used in 4:37. With the words 'and because he would keep the oath he swore to your forefathers' Moses gives the second reason why God redeemed his people from Egypt. God had bound himself by an oath to their forefathers that he would bring their descendants out of the land of Egypt (Gen. 15:13-16; Exod. 2:24, 25). He had delivered and redeemed his people according to his pledged word. The action of God is described as redeeming his people. The Hebrew verb 'redeem' (Heb. *padah*) comes from the business world, as compared with the other common word of similar meaning (Heb. *ga'al*) which comes from the realm of the family (for the participial use of *ga'al* later in Deuteronomy see 19:6, 12). In its use in Deuteronomy (Deut. 7:8; 9:26; 21:8; 24:18) the word used here for 'redeem' stresses the ransom price rather than the restoration of a relationship. God in his love had taken the initiative to redeem his people from oppressive slavery under Pharaoh.

9 The term 'know' is also a technical covenantal expression. From God's side it is used in a way almost the same as 'choose' (cf.

Amos 3:2 'you only have I chosen', Heb. 'known'). Of humans in
the Old Testament (as in the New Testament) it describes a
relationship with God based on personal experience of him. The
outcome for Israel of the prior actions of God was that there should
be the acknowledgment of Jehovah. Their God had kept his sworn
word and shown covenant love (Heb. *chesed*) to those who loved
him and were obedient to his commandments. Later in the Old
Testament Abraham is called God's lover (Isa. 41:8; 2 Chron.
20:7), as he set the pattern for his descendants of a true response
to God's love. The phrase 'to a thousand generations' comes at
the end of the Hebrew sentence. However it is rightly to be
construed along with 'keeping his covenant' as it alludes to the
words in the Second Commandment, 'showing love to thousands
of generations of those who love me and keep my commandments'
(Deut. 5:10, and Exod. 20:6). Covenant love would continue to
be shown by a faithful God to countless generations to come.

10 In contrast with the covenant love to thousands, swift judgement
was promised to those who showed open hatred to the LORD. Such
basic antagonism to him and disrespect for his sovereign rights
could only result in appropriate judgement. Clearly 'hate' here is
the opposite of 'love' in the previous verse. Just as the antagonism
was shown openly so would there be open punishment upon those
who set themselves against the LORD. The LORD would not delay
the execution of his judgment.

11 The conclusion is drawn by Moses that the people have to
follow carefully everything which he as covenant mediator was
commanding them. A chosen people, possessing great privileges,
had also to demonstrate by obedience their commitment to the
LORD.

(c) Abounding Blessings (7:12-26)
This section can be divided into two parts. The first (verses 12-
16) consists of a reminder of the blessings promised to an obedient
people, and then the reminder concerning the command to destroy
their enemies (verse 16). That instruction placed additional

emphasis on the need for complete obedience. The second part
(verses 17-26) follows the same pattern. There is a recital of
promised blessings, especially that relating to God's presence and
assistance, and then the command to set aside truly the things that
were covered by God's ban (verse 26).

12 The blessings of the covenant were contingent upon obedience
by the people ('if you ...'). Their experiences in the future were to
depend so much upon their response to the demands of the
covenant. The Hebrew text conveys the idea that the blessings are
the reward of obedience, as a particle ('*eqev*) is used which implies
recompense. This particle seems to be equivalent to a fuller
expression used in Genesis 22:18 (Heb. '*eqev 'asher*) and it is
often used with the thought of reward and punishment (Num.
14:24, NIV 'so'; Deut. 8:20, NIV 'because'). Mention is made of a
double-sided obligation. The people have to keep God's
ordinances, while he keeps his covenant of steadfast love in
accordance with his oath. On God's side there is the continuation
of his promises, for he does not go back on his word. He fulfils all
the obligations he has so freely taken on himself.

13 Now the promised blessings in regard to material prosperity
(verses 13-14), health (verse 15) and military success (verse 16)
are set out. Further expansion of Israel is mentioned ('increase
your numbers') in this verse, along with various material blessings.
The stress on such material blessings is not surprising as they are
viewed as the guarantee of blessings that come to an earth, cursed
since the Fall. Thus heaven and earth feature in eschatological
scenes in both Old and New Testaments (a new heaven and a new
earth). We need also to remember that the patriarchs were
conscious that they were strangers and pilgrims in the promised
land and looked for the coming heavenly reality (Heb. 11:13-16).
As Christians we should also realise this. We have the present
experience of the kingdom of God within but we know that the
fuller reality of it is still to come. The material blessings include
the basic foods of Palestine – corn, grape juice and olive oil. The
expression 'the offspring of your flock' (NIV, 'fruit of your womb')

is interesting for it is literally 'the *ashterot* of your flock'. This Hebrew word is the plural of the name for Astarte, the goddess of the Sidonians (see 1 Kings 5:5. 33). Perhaps it was used for polemical reasons to show that all these blessings were to come from the LORD and not from a Canaanite fertility goddess. On the other hand, any link with the goddess may have been lost. Israel had to constantly be reminded that these blessings were inseparably linked to the land which God was giving to them.

14 Not only animals, but humans also were to know abundant fruitfulness. In treating the people in this way the LORD was fulfilling his oath of multiplying them (see previous verse). In both verses the contrast between Israelites and Canaanites is obvious. The latter offered up wives and daughters to try and secure fruitfulness. Israel had no need of such forbidden practices because their God was the source of all blessings.

15 Israel was also to be distinguished among the nations by the absence of 'the horrible diseases you knew in Egypt'. Just after the experience at Marah, Moses promised the people: 'If you listen carefully to the voice of the LORD your God and do what is right in his eyes, if you pay attention to his commandments and keep all his decrees, I will not bring on you any of the diseases I have brought on the Egyptians, for I am the LORD, who heals you' (Exod. 15:26). It is well-known that in Egypt diseases such as elephantiasis, dysentery and ophthalmia were rampant. But in this Exodus context here it is better to understand the sickness mentioned as being the plagues which the LORD had brought on the Egyptians. As long as the people were faithful, they need not fear similar punishment.

16 The first part of the section concludes with the command to destroy the nations whom the LORD would put into their hands. They were not to pity them (cf. verse 2) nor be attracted by the gods of the Canaanites. A purely human feeling of sympathy could so easily lead finally to idolatry. We cannot draw the conclusion from a passage such as this that as Christians we have a right to conduct a military crusade against the heathen. Crusaders, Conquistadors and others in recent times have falsely adopted such an approach. This command was a unique one in relation to the occupation of Canaan. No such command was given them in regard to the Egyptians. On the contrary, special mention is made later in this book of the permissibility of Egyptians being incorporated into the congregation of Israel (Deut. 23:7-8). People are brought into God's kingdom not at the point of a sword, but by the work of the sword of the Spirit in their hearts (Heb. 4:12-13).

17 This second section deals with the fear which would arise in Israelites' hearts as they viewed the powerful nations they would soon confront. If they looked at the impending conquest in human terms alone, they would ask, 'How can we drive them out?'

18 Fear could be dispelled by remembering what the LORD had done to Pharaoh and to Egypt. Appeal had already been made in 4:34ff. to what God had done there. 'Remember well' translates a Hebrew expression (*zakor tizkor*) which emphasises the action of remembering. It is almost equivalent to saying, 'You must remember'. That mindset of remembering was a continuous requirement for Israel, not just a temporary injunction for that time.

19 Most of the people of the Exodus generation had perished. Those who remained alive could declare that they had been eye-witnesses of God's actions in Egypt when he displayed 'great trials, the miraculous signs and wonders', and by his arm of power he had led Israel out. That action was the pledge of God's continuous provision for his people.

20 The promise for the future consisted of two elements, of which the first is mentioned here. The 'hornet' has been often interpreted metaphorically. For example, older Jewish exegetes explained it as leprosy, while other modern scholars have thought of it as a reference to the Pharaoh of Egypt or as the spirit of despondency in the people. In view of the fact that the great confusion of verse

23 seems to indicate a literal happening, it is best to take hornet here as literal also. A general plague of stinging insects may well have been intended.

21 Moses reassured the people that the LORD their God was among them. In apposition to 'the LORD your God' he says: 'a great and awesome God'. The presence of such a great God should inspire awe in Israel and among the other nations. A similar contrast is drawn by Isaiah when he told the people of Judah not to fear the alliance of Israel and Syria but rather he says: 'The LORD Almighty is the one you are to regard as holy. He is the one you are to fear, he is the one you are to dread' (Isa. 8:13).

22 This verse takes up the thought of verse 1 and the same Hebrew verb (Heb. *nashal*) is used of God's action in expelling the Canaanites. However, now the people are told that possession of the land in its entirety was not to be given at once as a matter of practicality. It was to be done 'little by little', an echo from Exodus 23:30. If the conquest was completed too quickly much of the land would have reverted to wilderness. The book of Joshua describes how in principle the land was occupied (Jos. 11:23; 21:43-45) but yet much remained to be done to complete the conquest. Because of the apostasy of the people after Joshua's death this gradual dispossession of the Canaanites was set aside by God as a punishment on the people (see Judges 2:20-23; 3:1, 2). It was not until the period of David that full possession was taken of the promised territory.

23 The second element of promise is now given. God would throw the other nations surrounding Israel into great confusion. Later this is called a panic sent by God when Saul's army attacked the Philistines (1 Sam. 14:15). Here the expression is used to describe God's activity in bringing confusion to Israel's enemies.

24 The kings would not be able to stand against Israel and their obliteration would mean the disintegration of their armies and the social life of their countries. An illustration of this is later given in Joshua 10.

25 Again the command is given to destroy the Canaanite images lest they become a snare to them (cf. verses 5 and 16). Their continued existence would be a temptation to sin. Not every transgression is called 'detestable' (Heb. *to 'avah*), for the term is reserved particularly for things which were connected with the foreign gods and their worship. Thus the Canaanite practices of divination were later to be called 'detestable practices' to the LORD (Deut. 18:9-12).

26 Nothing which was an abomination could be taken to their dwellings because all such things came under the ban. Infringement of this prohibition would cause the offending party himself to suffer God's judgement. The section concludes with the command to 'utterly abhor and detest' what was set apart in this heathen way. This whole chapter, which has been devoted to the exclusive worship of Jehovah, concludes with this note of warning.

(vi) A Call to Remember (8:1-20)

The whole of this chapter is taken up with impressing on the people the danger of letting slip from their memories what God had done for them. The call to remember comes both at the beginning (verse 2) and at the end (verse 18). The intervening verses consist of recollections of God's abundant provisions for them in the wilderness experience, together with warnings not to forget him when they enter into the bounty he has pledged himself on oath to provide for them. Themes that have already been mentioned in chapter 7 are taken up again and developed more fully including the danger of feeling self-sufficient (7:7-11; cf. 8:2-3, 11-14, 17-18; see also 9:1-6) and the remembrance of the great deeds of the LORD (7:8b, 18b-19; cf. 8:15-16).

In proclaiming to the people the demands of the LORD in reference to the promised land and their obedience to his claims, Moses' address takes on a format which emphasises the message. It is as follows:

1. Admonition: Remember (Heb. *zakar*)
   A. (verses 2-5) The Desert
     B. (verses 7-10) The Promised Land
2. Admonition: Don't Forget (Heb. *'al shachak*)
     B^1 (verses 11-14a, 17) The Promised Land
   A^1 (verses 14b-16) The Desert
3. Closing Admonitions
   Remember (verse 18)
   Don't Forget (verse 19)
4. Prediction of Rebellion, verse 20

(a) Admonition (8:1)

1 In a manner similar to 4:1, Moses begins anew to reinforce the lessons that Israel needed to know as they considered entry into the promised land. The immediacy of the instruction is reinforced by use of the present tense and addition of the word 'today' (see its use again later in verse 11, 'this day').

(b) The Desert Experience (8:2-6)

2 The theme of remembering the great deeds of the LORD is taken up (cf. 4:10), especially the experiences that he had brought upon them when leading them in the desert for forty years. Those years were intended both as a humbling experience and a test for Israel. No further specification is given about the testing, but undoubtedly all the experiences of that time are intended. Their purpose was that the LORD could gauge the attitude of the people (lit. 'to know what was in your heart') and then to make them know something very important (verse 3). Obedience was the mark of covenant loyalty.

3 The humbling experiences included the wilderness period and the absence of the normal means of food supply. The people were fed miraculously by God, in a manner unknown either to them or their forefathers. Exodus 16:4 calls the manna 'bread from heaven' (see also Pss. 78:24 and 105:40; the description of the manna is given Num. 11:6-9), for the provision of food in this way was intended to teach Israel the lesson of continuing and daily dependence upon God. They had to learn that something more than material blessings (including all the promised good things in Canaan) were needed, if there was to be real life. They would need to listen attentively and obey explicitly all that came from the LORD's mouth, just as verse 1 had already made plain. The Lord Jesus quoted these words from Deuteronomy in his own temptation (Matt. 4:4) in order to show that the humble servant of the LORD was also living in complete obedience to the will of his father. It is noteworthy that Jesus also used other quotations from Deuteronomy in his temptation experience (Deut. 6:13 in Matt. 4:10; Deut. 6:16 in Matt. 4:7).

4 It was not just food that was miraculously provided in the desert, but God also gave their clothes greater durability and prevented their feet from swelling in the harsh terrain by seeing to it that their footwear was not destroyed. The Hebrew word translated 'swell' (*batseqah*) only occurs here and in Nehemiah 9:21. The Greek translation rendered it in both passages by a word which means hard or callused. This verse is quoted in the thanksgiving prayer of the Levites on their return from Exile (Neh. 9:21), though no previous mention is made of it in the accounts of the wilderness wanderings.

5 The hard experiences they had known were reminiscent of the way in which a man disciplined his son. Added point to the comment comes from the recollection that from the time of the exodus God called Israel his son (Exod. 4:22-23). All their experiences were intended as disciplining procedures.

6 Once again Moses reminds the people that they must observe the LORD's commands and walk in his ways. The latter phrase has already been used of following after other gods (4:3; 6:14), but now the emphasis is on commitment to the ways of the LORD. There may also be an echo from verse 2 here ('led you all the way'). The underlying motive was the fear of the LORD (see the commentary 4:10).

(c) A Description of Canaan (8:7-10)

These verses form a unit and comprise a statement to which verses 11-14 form the response: 'For the LORD your God ... be careful that you do not forget'. The language used of Canaan is reminiscent of similar descriptions in the extra-biblical treaties. Contemporary Hittite, Ugaritic and Assyrian kings included resource lists of the land they were giving as gifts to their vassals.

7 The Israelites are reminded of the nature of the land into which the LORD was bringing them. Canaan is described in three ways. First, its climate was such that it could be called 'a good land'. The word 'good[ness]' has a wide connotation and can be translated as 'nice,' 'pleasant' or 'beautiful.' The LXX and the Samaritan Pentateuch both add the word 'broad' but this seems to be a recollection of the description in Exodus 3:8. It was a land in which there were good water supplies, both from rain and also from subterranean sources. Hence, it was a suitable land for agriculture and for raising of animals.

8 Secondly, the land was intrinsically fruitful and seven products are mentioned (cf. the descriptions also in 11:14-15 and 33:13-16b). Wheat was certainly produced in abundance (see Solomon's provision for Hiram, 1 Kings 5:11), and the other products are all native to Palestine though some, especially the vines, figs, pomegranates and olives, were cultivated. The reference to honey recalls the oft-repeated phrase that Canaan was a land flowing with milk and honey. On the one hand, this phrase may have been used to contrast the LORD's provision in Canaan with the relative barrenness of both Egypt and Sinai. On the other hand, it may have been used deliberately in a polemical way as the Canaanites seem to have used the phrases 'the heavens rain fat; the wadis flow with honey' to refer to Baal's provision for them. Israel had to know that the covenant God, not Baal, was the provider of such bounty.

9 There would be no lack of bread and other products because of the natural abundance of the land. The word translated 'scarce' only occurs here in the Old Testament, though the related adjective 'poor' occurs fairly frequently.

Thirdly, there was also abundant provision of metals in the land. Some have objected to this expression on the ground that neither copper nor iron are found west of the Jordan. However, the east bank of the Jordan was also included in the promised land (see Num. 34:1-12 and Deut. 1:7) and there was certainly natural mineral wealth there (cf. Deut. 3:11 regarding Og's sarcophagus). Later during Solomon's reign copper was mined and smelted in the Arabah Valley between the Dead Sea and the Gulf of Aqaba. This has been confirmed by archaeological discovery, while the biblical text refers to the production of bronze pillars for the temple (1 Kings 7:15-16). Southern Lebanon could also have been the place intended, especially as Hiram, who did the bronze work, was the son of a man from Tyre (1 Kings 7:13-14).

10 Satisfaction with the abundance that God provided should move the people to praise him. Thankful recognition of the gifts and acknowledgment of the giver should not be lacking.

(d) Don't Forget the LORD (8:11-20)

The warning passage that now follows has certain similarities to what has already been said in 6:10-15, but it is an extension of the idea in two directions. It contains fuller recollections of the past history of Israel (verses 15-16) with the explicit warning of the threat of ultimate destruction of the nation (verses 19-20).

11 The need for immediate action in regard to this command is stressed by the final word in the verse, 'today' (NIV 'this day'). Personal attention (the imperative is second person masculine singular, 'you') had to be given in case forgetfulness became characteristic of their way of life. That very day they were being instructed to keep the commandments, judgments and statutes of the LORD. These had to be guarded carefully. In the Hebrew text there is a play on words between 'beware' and 'keeping' that can be brought out by translating: 'guard yourself lest you forget to guard the commandments ....'

12-13 After their experiences in the wilderness (excluding the provision of the manna) many in Israel would soon have an abundance – not just plenty to eat but beautiful homes, large flocks and herds, and great wealth. However, this was not to be true of everyone in Israel, for provision is made later for the poor in the land (see Deut. 15:1-11; 24:12-15).

14 The ever-present danger was going to be that material prosperity would bring with it the danger of pride. A heart lifted up with feelings of immense satisfaction and self-sufficiency would inevitably lead to forgetfulness of the LORD. This forgetfulness would be aggravated because it involved the God who had redeemed them from their slavery in Egypt. This is the first of four wonderful acts of God's grace that are cited in verses 14-16: he redeemed them from Egypt (verse 14); he led them through the wilderness (verse 15a); he provided water out of the rock (verse 15b); he gave them manna to eat (verse 16).

15-16 The wilderness experience was not a pleasant interlude in Israel's history (cf. Num. 14:26-35; Deut. 8:2-5). God sent fiery serpents among the grumbling people who were only saved by looking to the bronze serpent that Moses made (Num. 21:4-9; cf. 2 Kings 18:4 for the account of how Hezekiah broke the bronze serpent because people were burning incense to it; see also the illustrative use made of the incident in Jn. 3:14). There were also scorpions. There is a pass through the hills south-west of the Dead Sea which probably got its name from the Hebrew word used here for scorpion, the ascent of Akrabbim (Num. 34:4). The land was also thirsty. The word 'thirsty' only occurs in this form here and in Psalm 107:33 and Isaiah 35:7, and both of these passages use it of desert experiences. Miraculous provision was made of both water (Exod. 17:1-7; Num. 20:13) and food (already referred to in verse 3), and identical language to that of verse 2 is used in reference to it being a humbling and testing experience for Israel. The ultimate aim, however, was for blessing to come to them, probably referring to God's provision for them in Canaan.

17 Never would Israel be able to say boastfully: 'My power and the strength of my hands have produced this wealth for me.' Though tempted to proclaim their independence from God they should always recognise the source of their wealth. He won the battles and gifted the land to them. The closing verses of the chapter reinforce the related ideas of remembering and not forgetting. Israel had to have continuing trust in the God who was fulfilling his pledged word.

18 Praise was due to the LORD, the covenant God, who was giving them the land in fulfilment of his oath to the patriarchs (to Abraham – Gen. 12:7; 15:18; to Isaac – Gen. 26:3; to Jacob – Gen. 28:13). This was the foundation on which their prosperity was based because as a consequence of the covenant bond he gave them the ability to achieve wealth. Israel had to learn that without the LORD their building would be in vain (Ps. 127:1). The terminology used here regarding the covenant bond is significant. It is not the normal expression for making a new covenant that occurs, but the one for re-affirming an existing one. The usual Hebrew terminology for making a covenant is *karat berit*, 'cut a covenant,' whereas the one here is *heqim berit*, 'confirm a covenant.' This form also occurs in Genesis 6:18 of the re-affirmation of the covenant of creation. Just as the Sinai covenant was regarded as in direct continuity with the Abrahamic covenant (Exod. 3:15-17; Deut. 4:31, 37-38), so also the renewal of it in the plain of Moab was also a re-affirmation of the Abrahamic covenant. The words 'as it is today' emphasise the immediacy of God's dealings with his people.

19-20 These verses spell out the reward for pride and self-sufficiency. If forgetfulness of the LORD led them into the service of Canaanite gods and they prostrated themselves before them, then they would perish from the land (see 4:25-31 and commentary of that passage). In effect a circle would be completed. Having been brought out of slavery by the LORD, Israel would, because of her pride and forgetfulness, be brought back into slavery. The judgment soon to be shown to the Canaanites would be applied to them because of their failure to heed the LORD's commands. This was the reward in store for disobedience. The Hebrew particle *'eqéb* used in verse 20 quite often has the connotation of a reward for something. It occurs in a similar context in 7:12. The threat of destruction by application of the curse or ban was eventually to end the Old Testament prophetic message (Mal. 4:6). However, the thought that God would even apply the curse on Canaan to his own people was so unpalatable that the Jewish scribes (the Massoretes, about 500-700 AD) would not let the book of Malachi end on that note. They inserted a second time the words of Malachi 4:5: 'See, I send you the prophet Elijah before that great and dreadful day of the Lord comes', and this is still in the modern editions of the Hebrew Bible.

(vii) God's Grace and Israel's Response (9:1–10:22)

(a) Assurance of God's Presence (9:1-6)
The opening part of this chapter is reminiscent of chapter 7, and Moses makes two main points. First, he directs attention to the fact that the victory that they were going to achieve in Canaan would be the LORD's, and not theirs. Secondly, he notes that victory was going to be granted by God as an expression of his grace towards Israel and not because of their righteousness.

1 Just as Israel had previously been summoned to listen in 6:4-9, so again Moses calls for attention to important principles that are going to affect them in both the immediate and long term future. The usage is perhaps more closely parallel to that in 5:1, 20:3 and 27:9 than to that in 6:4. 'To cross the Jordan' is one of the expressions that occurs repeatedly throughout the book for entry into Canaan (15x). The word 'today' should not be pressed to mean precisely 'this very day'. Its usage is much closer to 'now', 'at this time', or 'about to' in English. The prospect ahead of the people was daunting, because they were on the point of facing powerful foes who lived in fortified cities which seemed impregnable.

2 In particular they were to face again the Anakim before whom they had been terrified on their earlier encounter (see 1:28). Reports were prevalent concerning the fighting capacity of the Anakim. Moses is here deliberately quoting the words of the spies (Num. 13:28; Deut. 1:28). However, the people should have remembered that God had promised that none would be able to withstand them (7:24). The point of recalling the previous experience is to re-emphasise that with the LORD in their midst they should not fear.

3 The sentence structure in this verse highlights the emphasis on the opening clause. It can be set out thus:

> Know now
> > that the LORD is your God
> > > – he is going over before you as a consuming fire
> > > – he will destroy them
> > > – he will bring them down before you.

The emphasis is again on the initial words of the Decalogue: 'I am the LORD your God', but the following clauses, each beginning with an emphatic 'he' in Hebrew, emphasise the way in which God's actions were to be shown. He was going to cross over before them as a consuming fire (see on 4:24) and destroy the occupants of the land. 'Cross over' (Heb.) is a shortened form of 'cross over the Jordan'. He was also going to humble the nations before Israel. There may be an intentional play on words here as the Hebrew word translated bring them down (*yakni'em*) has three of the same consonants as the word Canaan (*kena'an*). The word is more commonly used in the Old Testament of people humbling themselves, but it is used repeatedly of the subduing of the oppressing nations in the time of the judges (Judg. 3:30; 8:28; 11:33; 1 Sam. 7:13). Speedy success was to be attributed to the LORD, just as he had promised. The reference could be back to Exodus 23:31, but more probably, because it is in immediate context, to 7:17-24.

4 The warning now follows that Israel could never claim success in the conquest because of their own righteousness. The form of the expression recalls 8:17 where the subject was 'my power and the strength of my hands' as over against 'my righteousness' here. 'Righteousness' and 'wickedness' are set in opposition to one another. There could be no pride on Israel's part but only a recognition that the sin of the Amorites was now full (Gen 15:16) and consequently the time for divine judgment had arrived.

5-6 These verses press home to Israel the reality of the situation, first in a negative way and then in a positive way. First, in addition to the word 'righteousness' of verse 4 is added 'integrity' in verse 5, (for them in parallel cf. Ps. 7:8-10) while in verse 6 further emphasis falls on the lack of righteousness on Israel's part. In addition, Israel is called a stiff-necked people, which is a closer description of what is meant by unrighteousness or wickedness. The imagery is probably borrowed from that relating to a rebellious farm animal. It is used again in 10:16 (along with the command to circumcise their hearts) and in 31:27. Later the prophetic historian uses it in describing the reasons for the fall of the northern kingdom (2 Kings 17:14), while Jeremiah employs the phrase several times (Jer. 7:26; 17:23; 19:15). The indigenous peoples of the land (notice it is called 'their land' in verse 5) are to lose this good land on account of their unrighteousness. The positive aspect once more draws attention to the gift of the land as one of pure grace. This is done by recalling that God made an oath concerning the land to the patriarchs and so the gift of it now was a confirmation of that oath (see on 8:18). Possession of the sworn land was to be by divine judgment and divine grace.

(b) Israel's Disobedience and Stubbornness (9:7-29)

This new section concentrates on the disobedience and rebelliousness of Israel. The accusation is stated in general terms (verses 7 and 24) but illustrated by reference to specific incidents. These include Massah (Exod. 17:1-7), Taberah (Num. 11:1-3), Kibroth Hattaavah (Num. 11:31-34), and Kadesh Barnea (Num. 13-14), and especially the incident concerning the making of the golden calf. The account follows very closely the record in Exodus 32 and 34. There is some telescoping of the events, and though in general this passage condenses the Exodus account yet at other points it supplements it, as for example by referring to Moses' intercession for Aaron. It does not follow strict chronological order and deals with some of the incidents with brevity (see verses 22-24), concentrating on the breaking of the covenant at Sinai. It is not new history but a recital of well-known past events.

7-8 Individual covenant members are commanded to remember (and not to forget) how they had rebelled against the LORD from the very beginning of their covenant relationship. The imperatives are second person singular, even though plural language is used from the second part of the verse onwards. The singular form was probably used in order to press home to the people individually the LORD's demands. Their behaviour had been consistently rebellious from the time they left Egypt to the present. The technical term for rebelling against the covenant is used here in a participial form that emphasises the continuous nature of their rebellion. The identical words occur later in verse 24. At Horeb, while Moses was on the mount of God, the people expressed their rebellion by sinning in making the golden calf. This was so provoking to the LORD that he told Moses he was going to let his hot wrath burn against the people and consume them (Exod. 32:10; see also Zech. 8:14). Even those who had been born in the interval between the exodus and the present covenant renewal are regarded as part of the community who rebelled.

9-10 These verses summarise Exodus 24:12-18. Moses was summoned by the LORD to the mountaintop to receive the two stone tablets that constituted the core of the covenant. Hence here in the Massoretic Text the word 'covenant' (Heb. *berit*) is put in apposition to the words 'the tablets of stone'. As in 4:13 'covenant' and 'the ten words' are equated. God had initiated that covenant and the written tablets were an inscripturated form in which Israel received the basic requirements. The forty days and nights Moses was on the mount (Exod. 24:18) appear to be linked deliberately with the forty years of the wilderness experiences (cf. 8:2-3). This connection is made plainer still by reference to Moses not eating bread or drinking water. He, like Israel in the wilderness, was sustained by the LORD's life-giving word. In both cases the point was that complete dependence upon the LORD had to be demonstrated (cf. Jesus' experience in the wilderness temptation, Matt. 4:1-11 = Luke 4:1-13). To Moses was given two tablets written with 'the finger of God'. Most probably they were duplicate copies of the covenant as in the extra-biblical treaties. This is one of the distinctive features of the decalogue which marks it off from the rest of the Mosaic law. Unlike the covenant code (Exod. 21:1; Deut. 5:31; 6:1), it was given directly to Israel and not through the covenant mediator (Exod. 24:12; 32:16). The second part of verse 10 emphasises the precise equivalence between what was written on the tablets and the verbal declaration of the LORD as he spoke out of the midst of the fire.

11-12 At the conclusion of forty days and forty nights, God committed to Moses the two tablets, called again 'the tablets of stone, the tablets of the covenant', and no further information is added to what is in verse 10. Then he was commanded to go down from the mountain because the people had acted corruptly. Several things are significant. The repetition of the action of handing over the tablets simply reinforces the concept of them being divinely given. The LORD's speech, also exactly following Exodus 32:7-8, prepares for the actions yet to be recounted. The contrast is clear. While Moses was receiving the tablets of the covenant the people were already breaking the covenant, especially in relation to the first commandment. They had created another god in place of the LORD, and this was tantamount to rejection of the covenant. This fact is emphasised by the way in which the people are addressed – 'your people' – since they could no longer be considered as the LORD's people. God had not broken the covenant, but they had. They had quickly turned from what the Hebrew calls 'the LORD's way' (an abbreviated expression for the core of the covenant, the decalogue) and especially the inclusive claims God made for himself and constructed for themselves a moulded image (*masseka*). The word calf (*'egel*) occurs in Exodus 32:4, 8 and later in the narrative in verse 16. The fact that this is a new speech is marked in the following verse by the word 'furthermore' (Heb. *lêmôr*).

13-14 The LORD spoke to Moses expressing surprise (the word 'indeed' in the NIV represents the Hebrew *vehinnêh*) that the people are stiff-necked (cf. verse 6). No mention is made of Moses' intercession (see Exod. 32:11-13) though it is implicit in the expression 'let me alone'. The LORD did not wish to listen for he was going to blot them out so that they ceased to be a people. 'Blot out their name' means that they would no longer be called a people, in striking contrast to what is said in Deuteronomy 2:25. The threat which they were intended to carry out against the nations in Canaan was applied to them (Deut. 7:24). In place of Israel God expresses the intention to fulfil the promise of the patriarchs through one person, Moses. The idea is that even though a judgment as radical as the flood came on Israel, when few were saved, from one person God could fulfil his word.

15-16 Moses now obeys the LORD's command and proceeds from the mount where the theophany continued ('the mountain burned with fire'). In his hands were the two tablets and this is the sixth mention of them. In Exodus 32:15, the singular 'hand' (Heb. *yad* is used), but that could be in a collective sense. It is possible here that the meaning is that he had one in each hand (see NIV margin). There were two duplicate tablets, written on both sides. The way in which the statement is made may also suggest that this was all he carried, for the Decalogue was the all-sufficient revelation of God's will for his people. Immediately Moses saw the state of Israel's apostasy. The Hebrew *vehinnêh* draws attention to their sin in a very pointed way – 'and I looked and there, ...' – Moses spells out the three things which the people had done. First, they had sinned against their sovereign God (the LORD your God), and the word he uses (*chattah*) is the most general Hebrew word for sinning. Secondly, they had made for themselves a moulded calf, probably in the likeness of the contemporary bull-calf idol of Goshen in Egypt. The word 'yourselves' stresses the selfish and self-centred action of the people. Thirdly, they had quickly turned aside from the divinely appointed path of obedience. Their action was an explicit denial of the uniqueness of their God, for they had put something else alongside him.

17 Now Moses relates three actions with the two tablets. He grasped them (the word is stronger than the normal 'take' and often signifies 'to take violent hold of') and threw them out of his hands. This action was not one of rashness or sheer disappointment on the part of Moses. It was clearly a symbolic reaction to the breaking of the covenant by the people. This was consistent with ancient suzerainty covenants, where the relationship was only valid while the covenant document remained in existence. If it was destroyed then a new document had to be prepared. Seemingly the action had the LORD's approval, because it was evident to the Israelites, who were spectators but not participants, in order to demonstrate to them that judicial action had been taken to signify the broken nature of the covenant bond.

18 This speech telescopes the events of Exodus 32-33 and makes no mention of Moses' return to the mountain. He does, however, refer to two prayers (verse 18, 'Then once again I fell prostrate before the LORD'; verse 19, 'But again the LORD listened to me'). There was a repetition of his behaviour of the previous occasion, with Moses fasting on behalf of his people. As the covenant mediator he interceded for his people, even offering his own life as an atonement for their sin (Exod. 32:31-33). The expression used here ('I ate no bread and drank no water, because of all the sin you had committed') has close parallels to repeated references in Leviticus 4 and 5. Intercession is made for all the sin of Israel throughout the wilderness experiences which culminated in the sin of the golden calf.

19 The danger which Moses foresaw was the destruction of Israel. He does not use the usual word for 'fear' but one which denotes more fear that something was going to happen, a fear of consequences. Moses feared the blotting out of Israel (see verse 14). The intercession was successful and Israel was spared. The word 'also' (NKJV; Heb. *gam*) may have here the connotation more of 'indeed', 'assuredly' rather than its more common meaning of 'also'.

20 One new fact is mentioned that is not included in the account in Exodus. This is the reference to Moses' intercession for Aaron. He was guilty, and judgment could have been expected to fall on him because he had actually made the idol. It was not only the people who deserved destruction (verse 14) but even their high priest whose responsibility is spelt out in the Exodus account (Exod. 32:2-4, 21-24, 35). But Moses interceded on his behalf, praying for mercy to be shown to him. That Israel's high priest had personally to experience God's mercy was a further expression of God's grace to the people as a whole. The intercession of Moses on behalf of Aaron and the whole nation came at a crucial time in Israel's history, just as did Samuel's intercession (1 Sam. 7:5, 8-9). Much later in Israel's history, near the final collapse of Judah, the Lord referred to these intercessions in his message to the prophet Jeremiah (Jer. 15:1).

21 The opening words of the verse in the Hebrew text emphasise the guilt of the people. Moses calls the calf which they made 'your sin' and then describes its ritual destruction. It was pulverised and then the dust was thrown into the stream which flowed from the mountain. The action of Moses was a symbolic one, for the people were forced to drink that water (Exod. 32:20). It carried in effect the covenant curse (cf. Num. 5:16-28 where a broken vow is also the reason for the ritual) and judgment in the form of sickness was brought on Israel (Exod. 32:35). The idol was swept away by the living water from the mountain of God. Later kings such as Asa (1 Kings 15:13), Hezekiah (2 Kings 18:4), and Josiah (2 Kings 23:4-15) followed the action that Moses initiated here. He set the pattern for radical action of this kind.

22-24 These verses are clearly intended to be a further proof of Israel's long-standing rebelliousness. The fact that Moses does not mention the places in chronological order could indicate a decision to emphasise the increasing gravity of the people's sin. Furthermore, at Taberah fire from the LORD consumed some of the people, and hence that fact would connect the Taberah incident with verse 21, and also to the earlier references to the fire on Mt.

Sinai in verses 10 and 15. The chronological order was Massah (Exod. 17:1-7), Taberah (Num. 11:1-3), Kibroth Hattaavah (Num. 11:4-34) and Kadesh Barnea (Num. 13-14). The last incident has already been dealt with in Moses' historical preamble in this book (Deut. 1:19-46 and see commentary). At Taberah complaining Israel had only been saved because Moses interceded for them. At Massah they accused Moses of bringing them out into the wilderness in order to kill them, and Moses had to seek direction from the Lord. Judgment had fallen on the people at Kibroth Hattaavah when the people expressed their longing for the pleasures of Egypt. When commanded to go up to Kadesh Barnea and possess the land Israel refused. Again the technical term for 'rebel' is used of the reaction of Israel (verse 23), but to it is added the words 'you did not believe him' and 'you did not listen to his voice'. The occurrence of the verb 'believe' (Heb. Hif. of *'aman*) may have covenantal overtones. The root means 'to be sure' and from it 'Amen' is derived. 'Amen' was often used in covenantal situations to declare acceptance of the various stipulations or demands of the LORD (see e.g., Deut. 27:11-26). Contrary to Abraham's declaration of his 'Amen' to God (Gen. 15:6), the Israelites failed to make their affirmative declaration. The words of verse 24 repeat those of verse 7. 'You have been rebellious against the LORD ' with the addition 'from the day that I knew you'. Rebellion was not a new phenomenon with Israel but an old one, and even Moses and Aaron were themselves guilty of it (Num. 27:14).

25 Intercession was made by Moses for the people as a whole. Thus he says he prostrated himself before the LORD. The same verbal form occurs in verse 18 and the reference is to the same prayer. This is made clear in the Hebrew by two changes to the language of verse 18. The first of these is the addition of the particle *'et*, that appears in rare use denoting the subject, not, as usually, the object. The second is the presence of the article with the words 'day' and 'night' (Hebrew uses the singular form in this type of construction). These changes make the reference back to verse 18 more explicit. From a position of abject humility Moses made his request for a change in the announced intention of the LORD.

26-27 In his prayer Moses makes three requests, and in doing so addresses God as LORD God (Heb. *'adonai yhwh*). The use of this title occurs only in introduction to prayer and emphasises the fact that God was the ruler or master (*'adonai*) along with him being the gracious redeemer of the people from their bondage in Egypt (*yhwh*). The first request is that God will not destroy his inheritance. The verb used (Hebrew *shachat* Hif.) is the same as is used in verse 12 to describe the action of Israel (Heb. *'al shachat* Pi.) What Israel had done to themselves in part (destroying themselves), God intended to complete by making it total destruction. Moses pleads before the Lord calling them 'your people' and 'your inheritance'. This is a compound expression pointing to the special and intimate relationship that Israel had with the LORD (see comment on 4:20). He had redeemed them from their slavery. The verb used here (Heb. *padah*) occurs six times in Deuteronomy (7:8; 9:26; 13:5 (Heb. 6); 15:15; 21:8; 24:18). The term 'greatness' seems to be a summary of what is said later in verse 29, 'Your mighty power and by your outstretched arm'. The second request (verse 27a) is to remember 'Your servants, Abraham, Isaac and Jacob'. Appeal is made to the covenant promises given to the patriarchs and by naming them the implication is that the oath of the LORD was in view (see verse 6). He specifically calls them the LORD's servants, and thus brings into consideration their service to their covenant Lord. Thirdly, he pleads (verse 27b) that God will not turn his face to the stubbornness of the people, nor to their wickedness or sin. The latter expressions seem to define more closely what was meant by stubbornness. Wickedness draws attention to their lack of righteousness, while sin reminds of what has already been described in verse 18. The present generation ('this people') needed divine grace to forgive their rebellion.

28 At stake was the LORD's reputation in the eyes of the Egyptians (cf. Exod. 32:12). The great object before Moses' mind was God's glory. The redemptive history of Israel was meant to be seen by Egypt and other nations as a demonstration of the power of the living and true God. The destruction of Israel in the wilderness would have caused the Egyptians and perhaps others to mock God by doubting his ability to save and by claiming that God had killed them because of his hatred for them.

29 The final section of the prayer reiterates the theme of verse 26. Moses again links together 'your people' and 'your inheritance' with the thought of the manifestation of God's great power in the redemption from Egypt. Election and God's might were brought together in the same action. Whereas in Exodus 32:14 the answer to the prayer is expressly stated, here in Deuteronomy it is implied in the sequence of events that immediately follow. The prayer is important in this context because it reminds the people at a crucial point in their history that the past mercy of the LORD had spared Israel from extinction.

(c) The New Tablets (10:1-11)

The provision of the new tablets was at the direction of the LORD and importantly indicated the restoration of the covenant relationship. The events symbolically announce the restoration of fellowship. Moses' prayer had been answered, though as Exodus 33:7-11 shows, a temporary tabernacle of meeting had to be erected outside the camp. After the renewal of the covenant the true tabernacle was made and erected within the camp, and the ark, with the tablets of testimony, was brought into it (Exod. 40:21).

1 The opening words, 'at that time', link the narrative directly with what has preceded. The term has already been encountered in several passages (1:16,18; 2:34; 3:4 etc.). It never refers to a precise date but always to a general period and especially the connection between other events and the period under review. The LORD commanded Moses to prepare again two replacement stone tablets and also an ark of wood. The Hebrew word translated ark ('aron) is first used of Joseph's coffin (Gen. 50:26) and later it is used of a money box (2 Kings 12:9). The word 'ark' as a translation comes from 16th century English when it was the common word for a box or chest. It is doubtful if this was the permanent receptacle for the tablets (commanded in Exod. 25:10) and which was made by Bezaleel (Exod. 37:1). More likely the item here was a temporary case to hold the tablets for the period needed before the construction of the tabernacle.

2 The restoration of the covenant relationship did not require alteration of the basic conditions. The same words that were on the first tablets would be written again by the LORD. The manner in which the Decalogue was given sets it apart from the teaching that follows it, both in the Exodus account and here in Deuteronomy. Unlike the other commands that came through the mediation of Moses, the Decalogue was a direct divine command. It was the writing of God (Exod. 32:16), and Moses was instructed to deposit the tablets in the ark.

3-4 The making of the ark is recorded, with the additional note that it was constructed from acacia wood. Numbers 33:49 records that Israel camped near the Abel Acacia Grove in the plains of Moab. Acacia was also a well-known wood in Egypt from which furniture was constructed. Moses went back up the mountain and the Ten Words were again inscribed by the *Lord*. That fact is emphasised (Heb. *hamiktab harishon*), as is the entrusting of them to Moses (see Deut. 5:22 and 9:11 also). The majesty of the LORD's appearance on Sinai is also recalled (cf. 5:23-26 and 9:15).

5 What is recorded here stands in marked contrast to what happened to the first tablets (see 9:17). On the second occasion the tablets remain intact, for no new breach of the covenant occurred. The account appears to condense the time frame, for Moses picks out specific details of events which took place over a considerable period. The reference to Moses making the ark need not be brought into conflict with the reference to Bezaleel as its maker (Exod. 37:1). Bezaleel and others had been designated by Moses to carry out the work on the sanctuary (Exod. 35:30–36:1). A similar case is that of Solomon who built the temple (1 Kings 6:1) but did so by utilising many skilled craftsmen. The final sentence of this verse reminds the people that 'the ark of the covenant' (as it is called in 10:8; 31:9, 25; Jos. 3:6, 8; 4:7, 18 etc.) contained those covenant documents till that very day. The emphasis appears to be on the ark, rather than on the tablets, and this helps to explain the introduction of the reference to the Levites in verses 6-9.

6-9 These verses form a slight break in the speech and at first sight it is difficult to see the connection between them and what goes before and after. There is some difference in style, including the absence of the first person singular forms of verses 5 and 10 ('I turned', 'I stayed'). However, if the suggestion made above in the final comment on verse 5 is correct, the link between the two sections is the ark of the covenant. In verses 6-7 the thought is of the journeying of the people (and the ark), with Aaron and his sons responsible for the continuing ministry at the tabernacle. Then in verses 8-9 mention is made of the provision that the LORD made for the Levites to minister to him and to bless in his name. The reference to 'at that time' (verse 10) connects with the same expression in 9:1. The text in verses 6-7 and that in Numbers 33:31-33 are not directly related. It is quite possible that here the reference is to later movements of Israel, who returned to Kadesh before setting out on the final journey around Edom and to the plains of Moab. This explanation would also cover the fact that the place names occur here in a different order to that in the Numbers passage. None of the places have been identified with certainty, but most probably all are located in the Arabah region.

The reference to Aaron is the key. Moses had interceded for him and he was spared. Not only was he spared, but God also made further provision for the continuing worship of Israel in that his son Eleazar ministered as priest in his stead. The point is that Aaron's death was not shortly after leaving Horeb, but in fact, he was spared until near the end of the wilderness wanderings. Moserah may well have been the name of a wide area, or even more specifically a designation of Moses rather than a commonly used name. It must have been in the region of Mount Hor (Num. 20:27; Deut. 32:50).

The second major idea is presented in verses 8-9. At Horeb (at that time, verse 8) God made provision for the appointment of the tribe of Levi to perform specific functions. Previously the head of each house performed priestly functions, but this practice was ultimately to be superseded by the Levitical priesthood. The tribe of Levi had heeded the call of Moses to consecrate themselves to the LORD (Exod. 32:26-29). They were later marked out after the revolt of Korah, Dathan and Abiram (Num. 16-18) and again after the sin in connection with Moab (Num. 25:6-13; Ps. 106:30). The task of the Levites was a threefold one. First, they were responsible for carrying the ark of the LORD's covenant, and also for instructing the people in the law (Deut. 33:10; Mal. 2:4-5). Thus their role was much wider than simply being in charge of sacrificial arrangements. Secondly, they were to stand and minister before the LORD, i.e. they were the sanctuary attendants. Just as Joshua was the minister or servant of Moses (Exod. 24:13; 33:11; Num. 11:28; Jos. 1:1), so the Levites were the LORD's ministers. The LORD himself was the great and active worker in the sacrificial system, but the Levites were his assistants. Thirdly, a further mediatorial work was to bless in the name of the Lord. Several concepts are involved in this idea. God's name is his self-revelation (see Exod. 6:2-5) and he promised to record his name in certain places and there bless the people (Exod. 20:24; cf. Deut. 12:5). The role of the priests was to be far wider than simply using the LORD's name in prayer. They had to proclaim the salvation of the LORD and in bringing the people into a relationship with him, they brought blessing to them.

A consequence ('that is why', verse 9) of the Levites' special relationship with the LORD was that particular provision had to be made for their maintenance. In place of a territorial allocation of land, the Levites were to have the LORD as their inheritance. The term which is used of Israel as the LORD's possession (see 4:20) is here applied to the special privilege that the Levites would have. The absence of land would be more than compensated for by them having the LORD himself. He made special provision for their earthly needs by allocating certain sacrifices as their inheritance (12:19; 14:27-29; 16:11; see 18:1-8 and commentary for the detailed instruction). This statement was in accordance with what the LORD said to Aaron (Num. 18:20).

10-11 The concluding verses of this section summarise the events concerning the prayer by noting the period ('forty days and forty nights') and the LORD's answer ('the LORD also heard me at that time, and the LORD chose not to destroy you'). Mercy was shown to an erring people. The term 'at that time' (in Heb. *bapa'am hahi'*), is a different expression from that used in verses 1 and 8). It can be translated 'on that occasion', so emphasising the abundant mercy of the LORD that had been shown repeatedly, including on that occasion. Moses' intercession had prevailed and Israel was spared. The opening of verse 11 ('The LORD said to me') connects best with the last part of verse 10: 'The LORD chose not to destroy you, for the LORD said to me...'. This makes the connection clear. Israel's continuing covenant relationship with the LORD and her entry into Canaan were both dependent on the outcome of Moses' intercession. Israel could now move out from Horeb and begin the journey to Canaan, the land that God had committed by oath to their forefathers.

(d) The Fear of the Lord (10:12-22)

12-13 The style of the comments now changes as Moses challenges the people in regard to their obedience to divine commands. This change is marked by the words 'and now' (in Heb. a single word *ve'attah*). The interrogative style is one which Micah later echoes (cf. Mic. 6:8, 'And what does the LORD require of you?'). Five demands are made of the people, all of which have already been mentioned. They have to show reverence for the LORD (5:29; 6:24), to follow his paths (5:33; 8:6), to love him (6:5; 7:9) to be obedient servants (6:13), and finally to keep the commandments and statutes which Moses was delivering to them (4:2; 6:2,17). He was coming to the conclusion of his explanation of the first commandment and the warnings concerning deviation from it. Covenantal terminology permeates these words for expressions such as 'to love', 'to serve' and 'for your good' all occur in both the biblical and extra-biblical treaties. The vassals were obliged to love their masters, and to recognise that they were servants, while the promises of the covenant are sometimes called 'the good' with which the recipients were blessed. Further attention is going to be given to these themes in the immediately following context (see 10:20; 11:1,13, 22).

14-15 To press home these demands Moses returns to the theme of the electing love of the LORD. The use of a particle at the start of verse 14, 'indeed' (Heb. *hen*) serves to turn attention expressly to the character of Israel's God and his choice of the patriarchs. The greatness of God is emphasised by the assertion that everything belongs to him both in the heavens and on earth (cf. Solomon's similar language at the dedication of the temple, 1 Kings 8:27; also cf. Pss. 24:1; 115:16). He had bound himself to the patriarchs in order to continue a love relationship with them. That love was reciprocated for Abraham is called God's friend (Isa. 41:8 lit. 'God's lover'). The verbs 'delighted' and 'chose' have already come together in 7:7. The seed of the patriarchs is identified as being those to whom Moses is now speaking ('you above all peoples, as it is this day').

16 No formalism was to characterise their obedience to the Lord. Rather their relationship was to be a spiritual one as they are called to circumcise the foreskin of their hearts. Circumcision was instituted as a sign of the covenant with Abraham (Gen 17:9-14), and it was a sign of God's impending judgment if the command was not kept. A disobedient servant could expect to be cut off entirely, as Moses himself discovered (Exod. 4:24-26). Now the idea is transferred to a spiritual plane as Moses indicates that something more than mere outward observance of the covenant requirements was necessary. Obedience must be from the heart. A true Jew, as Paul later expressed it (Rom. 2:28-29), is one who possesses circumcision of the heart by the Spirit. The idea of circumcision of the heart is taken up further in the Old Testament in Deuteronomy 30:6; Jeremiah 4:4; 9:26; and Ezekiel 44:7, 9. Linked with the idea of inward circumcision is that of not being stiff-necked (see the comment on 9:6). Stephen in his speech before the council, used both of these ideas as he accused his hearers: 'You stiff-necked and uncircumcised in heart and ears!' (Act 7:51).

17 This verse introduces a description of the greatness of God who is a God of majesty and power. The Hebraic expressions used are superlatives to emphasise the uniqueness of Israel's God. In Revelation 19:16 Christ is depicted as riding on a white horse and on his robe and his thigh was written: 'King of Kings and Lord of Lords'. Three adjectives are used here of God: 'great', 'mighty' and 'awesome'. Together they emphasise his exalted nature, and two of them ('great and awesome') have already been used together in 7:21. The word 'mighty' has military overtones, as it is used of heroes in battle. It is probably employed here because of the idea of God as the one who fought for Israel and delivered them from the power of Egypt (see 1:29-31). The term is later a fitting expression for the coming messianic king (Isa. 9:6, 'mighty God'). The two further attributes of God ('shows no partiality' and 'accepts no bribes') are also the ones which his vice-regents, the kings of Israel, were also expected to display. His earthly representatives were not to be partial in judgment nor able to be 'bought' by bribery. These two principles were foundational for justice in Israel.

18-19 In Israel and the surrounding nations three groups of people were particularly liable to suffer injustice. They were the orphans, the widows and the strangers (or aliens) in the land. Later in Deuteronomy the three are again linked together (24:17). All of them were without the rights of others and without legal protection. God's compassion to these groups was to be matched by a corresponding response from Israel. In particular it is noted, God *always loves* the stranger (the Heb. uses the participle of the verb) and had displayed that love when he visited his people in redeeming grace when they were strangers in Egypt. His provision for the strangers continued throughout the wilderness experiences (8:2-4). Now his people were to reflect the same pattern of compassionate concern for the aliens in their midst.

20 The centrality of the LORD in the lives of his people is emphasised by the order of words in the Hebrew text. To bring this out the verse can be translated as follows: '*The LORD your*

God you shall fear; *him* you shall serve; and *to him* you shall
cleave; and *in his name* you shall swear'. The expressions are
very similar to those already used in 6:13 and 10:12 (see
commentary). The new idea introduced here in comparison with
these other passages is that Israel had to remain in close relationship
with the Lord. The Hebrew verb *davaq* is used in Genesis 2:24 of
the relationship between husband and wife and has already
occurred in Deuteronomy 4:4 as descriptive of the covenant bond.
Here it replaces the concept of love used in verse 12.

21 Because of what the LORD did for Israel he was the object of
the praise of his people (cf. Ps. 109:1, 'O God of my praise'). It is
preferable to take the expression in this way rather than the idea
that God's deeds were to be the object of praise by other people.
That idea is certainly present elsewhere (see Deut. 4:6-8) but the
focus here is on God as being the sole object of Israel's praise.
They had been eyewitnesses of the great and awesome deeds which
he had done as he redeemed them from their slavery and bondage.

22 One of the most striking deeds of the Lord, however, went
further back than the exodus. The promises to Abraham included
that of a large family and he did not waver at the promise of God
through unbelief but was strengthened in faith, giving glory to
God (Rom. 4:20). From Isaac the number increased until there
were seventy who went down into Egypt (Stephen in Acts 7:14
says that seventy-five people went down to Egypt, as over against
the seventy mentioned here and in Gen. 46:27 and Exod. 1:5. The
figure of seventy-five is taken from the LXX which omits Jacob
and Joseph from the list but includes *nine* sons of Joseph). The
contrast between the seventy and the size of Israel on the eve of
the conquest was dramatic. God had multiplied them as the stars
of the heaven in multitude, and so demonstrated in this way his
great and awesome deeds.

(viii) Obedience and Service (11:1-32)
Chapter 11 concludes the section which began with the Decalogue
in chapter 5 and which carries through an exposition of the first

commandment until the close of this chapter. Here in chapter 11 is a summary of what has gone before and also a transition to the exposition of the other commandments that is to follow. The central thrust of the covenant commitment is maintained. Obedience was necessary to the commands of the LORD if Israel was to occupy the land, and so see the fulfilment of another of God's promises to the patriarchs.

The chapter has a definite structure to it. Three requirements are set before the people (verses 1, 8 and 13), followed in each case by an illustration to enforce the lesson. The format is as follows:

1. *Requirement*: Love God and keep his commandments (verse 1)
   Illustration: Historical reminiscences from Egypt and the wilderness (verses 2-7)
2. *Requirement*: Keep all the commandments (verse 8)
   Illustration: The land flowing with milk and honey compared to Egypt (verses 9-12)
3. *Requirement*: Obey the commandments and love and serve the LORD (verse 13)
   Illustration: God's provision for them in the good land (verses 14-17)
4. *Summary*: A drawing together of the basic themes of chapters 5-11, together with a challenge to covenant obedience (verses 18-31).

1 The basic requirement was love for God, and the singular form of the imperative 'love' may be a direct quotation from 6:5. The other verbal forms from verse 2 onwards in the chapter are in the plural. Coupled with love is the need to keep the LORD's charge. The word 'charge', 'requirements', occurs only here in Deuteronomy and it comes from the same Hebrew root as the verb 'keep' ('keep his charge', Heb. *shamar mishmarto*). The combined expression reinforces the need for obedience to the LORD's demands in general. The following expressions appear to explain what constituted the charge. The Hebrew can be justly translated 'keep his charge, namely, his statutes, his judgments

and his commandments'. There could be no respite from loving
God or obeying his commands for it had to be carried out always
(Heb. *kol hayyamim*, 'all the days').

2-3 Many of those listening to Moses could still remember the
exodus, and his words are directed to them to recall the greatness
of God's deeds on their behalf. The appeal is to eye-witnesses of
the events (see verse 7), not to the adults and children who had
not seen for themselves or known personally the chastening of
the LORD. The syntax of the sentence in Hebrew is difficult and
the expression 'your children' (one word in Hebrew) is preceded
by the particle *'et* which normally designates the direct object of
the verb. Here as in 9:25, it is used to mark the subject. Doubtless
they knew about it by instruction, but they had not been participants
in the happenings of the exodus. The Hebrew word rendered
'chastening' or 'discipline' (*musar*) does not always carry the
meaning of punishment that chastening often implies in English.
It can carry the wider sense of instruction, and in later Hebrew it
carried the meaning of 'ethics'. The past years were years of
learning and instruction for Israel, which were to be put into
practice. The instruction was directed towards knowledge of God's
greatness and the manifestation of his mighty hand and his
outstretched arm. These are standard phrases in Deuteronomy to
describe the LORD's power which was used to rescue his people
from their slavery (see 4:34; 5:15; 7:19; 26:8). They also appear
as a phrase in extra-biblical texts to describe the activity of the
great king. The signs refer to the plagues which God had brought
on the Egyptians and their land and the other actions which he
performed to release his people. The signs were the proclamation
of events that culminated in the acts of the LORD involving Pharaoh
and his land.

4 The reference is to the destruction of the Egyptian army as
recorded in Exodus 14:21-31 and which features prominently in
the opening of the Song of Moses (Exod. 15:1-10). This is the
only explicit mention in Deuteronomy of the victory over the
Egyptian army, though it is implied in 1:30. The waters overflowed

(a rare Heb. word) the Egyptians as they pursued the Israelites and they were totally destroyed. The phrase at the end of the verse, 'to this day', has no significance for dating of the book. Rather, it simply expresses the definitive nature of the victory over the Egyptians. What had happened had finality, and Israel's redemption was complete.

5-6 The totality of the wilderness experiences was evidence of God's presence with his people and his miraculous intervention on their behalf. One event is singled out for particular mention, namely, the rebellion against Moses and Aaron recorded in Numbers 16. The contrast between the events of the exodus and this rebellion is striking, because attention is given in this way to both the grace and the judgment of the LORD. No mention is made here of Korah, who himself was killed but whose children escaped the judgment (Num. 26:9-11). On the other hand Zelophehad's daughters mention only Korah (Num. 27:3), while Psalm 106:17, 18 names only Nathan and Abiram but does speak of destruction by the earth opening up and the coming of fire from the LORD. The example is chosen to highlight what happened when Moses' authority was challenged, and the fact that the earth swallowed them up is parallel to what happened to the Egyptians at the Red Sea.

7 This verse connects back to verse 2. Speaking to the older members of the Israelite community Moses calls their attention to the fact that they themselves had been eye-witnesses. Those who had been present and observed the great redemptive act of the LORD (the singular is used to describe the whole exodus/wilderness experience) should respond all the more readily to God's present demand of love and obedience. Under the New Covenant the same connection is made between love and obedience (Jn. 14:15, 21).

8 The second requirement laid on the people is that of keeping the commandments which Moses was then giving to them. All his teaching (the Heb. has simply the expression 'all the commandment') was to be observed, and his authority to pass on as the covenant mediator the LORD's teaching was not to be challenged (cf. the reference in verse 6 to rebellion against Moses). Whereas in 4:1 observance of the Lord's commands is linked to life in the good land, here the connection is made with strength for the task ahead. The thought clearly goes beyond physical strength to the needed spiritual resolve to face the battles ahead in conquering Canaan. Later Moses encourages Joshua to have the same attitude as he assumes the leadership role (Deut. 31:6), and he in turn uses the same language as he addresses the people (Josh. 1:6-7). They were entering (or crossing over) into the land of Canaan and it was to be their permanent home. The thought of possessing the land is mentioned twice in the verse.

9 Implicit in this verse is the threat of expulsion from the land if they failed to keep the covenant requirements. To them and to their offspring the land was promised, but that did not mean that they would inevitably continue to possess it. In order to prolong their days in the land they needed to show continued obedience to the Lord. Otherwise they would be expelled from the land flowing with milk and honey (see the comments on 6:3 and 8:8) and come under the curse mentioned later in this chapter (verses 26, 28). What this curse would involve is spelt out fully in chapter 28 and expulsion from the land is made explicit (28:63-68).

10-11 A sharp contrast is drawn between the land of Egypt, which they left forty years before, and the land of Canaan which they were about to enter. In Egypt they planted their vegetables but they had to provide artificial irrigation. It does not seem that Moses was intending to denigrate the Egyptian practice which was to cut channels along which the water flowed. Rather he is pointing out that human achievement enabled food production in Egypt, whereas in Canaan they would be dependent on God's provision. The hills and valleys of Canaan were watered with rain from heaven. Coming into the land which God was giving to them required trust in him as their constant provider.

12 The land of Canaan had a special character in that it was a land for which the Lord cared. This idea is emphasised in three ways. First, God had a constant interest in it (in Heb. the participle of the verb *darash* is used). The same verb is used by Ezekiel with a negative to describe the condition of God's people without anyone to care for them (Ezek. 34:6). Secondly, the LORD's eyes were continually (Heb. *tamid*) upon it. Thirdly, no season of the year passed without God's tender care being shown to the land, for he looked after it from the beginning of the year to the very end of the year. The implication of all this was that God would show the same concern for his people as they inhabited the land.

13-15 The blessings of covenant obedience are further pressed upon the people. In the Shema (6:4-5) they had been commanded to love God with all their heart and with all their soul, while in 10:12 love and obedience to the LORD had been set forth again. What is surprising is that imperceptibly Moses' speech becomes a divine speech. This comes out first of all in the reference to 'the commands I am giving' in verse 13, but then becomes more explicit in verses 14 and 15: 'then I will give you ... and I will send grass' (in the Heb. text these two verbs, 'give' and 'send', are identical). Moses could be recalling words that God had spoken to him, or using words of promise that God had already given to Israel through him (Lev. 26:3-4: 'If you walk in my statutes and keep my commandments, and perform them, I will give rain in its season ... ', NKJV). Alternately, this could be another case, more common in the prophets, in which there is transition between 'he' and 'I' in a message from the LORD. There are several occasions in Deuteronomy in which Moses speaks but his message becomes imperceptibly the direct word of the LORD (see 7:4; 28:20 [see NIV margin]; 29:4-6). The promise is of rain in its due season, that is, when it was needed in preparation for planting the seed in October-November, and in February-March to bring the crops to full fruit. God's care over the land was such that every single Israelite (the suffixes attached to 'grain', 'new wine', and 'oil' are all singular) would find his/her needs met. This included the grass for cattle so that the people could eat and be satisfied. The conjunction of the verbs 'eat' and 'be satisfied' recalls the warnings already given in 6:11-12 and 8:12 of the dangers of satisfaction when they inherit the land.

16-17 Constant care was needed lest the people be enticed into thinking that one of the Canaanite gods had provided for their needs, especially concerning rainfall. Baal was supposed to be the god who controlled the rains which brought fertility to Canaan. Moses warns the Israelites that an ever present danger would be that their hearts would become open to seduction (the LXX takes the verb as *patach*, 'open', rather than the MT *patah*, 'seduce'), and they would soon serve and worship other gods. This was already forbidden (5:9; 7:3-5) but now receives renewed emphasis. Such turning away from the LORD would incur his anger and he would shut up the heavens, and the absence of rain would prevent the normal crop production. Thus the promised blessing would be turned into a curse because of their disobedience. This receives further expression later in Deuteronomy in the detailed section on blessings and curses (28:12; 28:20-24). It is hard to be certain if the reference to perishing quickly from the good land refers only to famine conditions which would be the result of God's withholding the rain, or it could be virtually a summary statement of the culmination of God's anger which would result in exile from the land. In the light of passages such as 4:26-27, this seems the better explanation.

18 This verse commences the concluding section of the chapter, and it also draws together the major themes of chapters 5-11. While it is not an exact repetition of 6:1-9 it draws heavily upon it, especially in verses 18-21. The whole teaching of Moses ('these words of mine') was to remain impressed on their hearts and souls. In summing up the basic instructions regarding the need for total commitment to God's laws Moses re-asserts material which has come earlier in his address including the directions that follow the Shema in chapter 6 (see the earlier exposition). The fact that they apply to all the people is made more definite by the use of the plural forms of the verbs here, whereas the singular is used in chapter 6. The order is also different and various verbal alterations occur as well. These include:

Deuteronomy 6	**Deuteronomy 11**
these words	these words of mine
shall be in your heart	you shall lay up in your heart
you shall teach them diligently (*shinnantam*)	you shall teach them (*limmadtem 'otam*)
your soul ... your might	your soul

Repetition of these instructions was both a further warning to them of the danger facing them with the Canaanites and a necessary reminder of their solemn duty before the LORD.

21 The motive for observing these commandments is the prolongation of their occupancy of the land of Canaan. This has already been impressed on them in 4:40; 5:16; 5:33; 6:2 and 11:9. Two different Hebrew words are used for 'land' in these passages (*'erets* and *'adamah*) without any significant alteration in meaning. Also, here for the first time instead of the normal phrase 'to prolong their days', it is said that 'the days of your children will be multiplied'. The reference to children points to the successive generations who would occupy the land (cf. 4:25). The expression 'like the days of the heavens above the earth' is similar to one in Psalm 89:29 which is parallel to 'for ever'. The expression may have been well-known to Moses and his hearers as a similar expression describing perpetuity has been found inscribed on a pottery jar from Egypt. The picture is of God's unchangeable faithfulness in regard to his covenant promise.

22-23 The injunction to obey repeats words occurring earlier in 6:17, while the summary of the LORD's command ('to love the LORD your God, to walk in all his ways, and to hold fast to him') reasserts the words of 10:12, 20. Israel's love to God had to be demonstrated constantly by obedience to his demands and by cleaving to him. The description of the impending dispossession of the occupants of Canaan has already been set out in 4:38 and 9:1, 4b-5. What is new is the addition of the sentence 'every place

on which the sole of your foot treads shall be yours' to the
description of the territorial boundaries of the promised land.
Joshua later appeals to this promise as he encourages the people
to proceed with the conquest of Canaan (Josh. 1:3). The allotted
territory had already been described in 1:8 and here it is given
again in slightly varied terms. The boundaries are the desert (south),
Lebanon (north), the Euphrates River (east) and the Mediterranean
(the west). These borders were only to be reached by the Davidic/
Solomonic empire. Some commentators consider that only three
boundaries are mentioned here because there is no preposition
before 'Lebanon'. However, in the parallel given in Joshua 1:4,
the preposition 'up to' (Heb. *'ad*) is inserted.

25 In the Song of Moses reference had been made to the reaction
of the original inhabitants of Canaan to the invading Israelites.

> Terror and dread will fall upon them.
> By the power of your arm
>   they will be as still as a stone,
> until your people pass by, O LORD,
>   until the people you bought
>   pass by (Exod. 15:16).

Earlier in 2:25 a similar statement is made as in this verse (using
the identical word 'dread' and a synonym of fear from the same
Hebrew root). The promise of God that the Canaanite nations
would not be able to withstand them also appears in 7:23-24.

26-28 Covenant commitment in the present and in the future
involved knowing the dual sanctions of blessing and cursing.
Moses draws attention emphatically to these aspects, commencing
the verse with an imperative of the verb 'to see' (Hebrew *ra'ah*).
First he speaks of the present, and then of a special ceremony of
covenant ratification at the mountains Ebal and Gerizim when
they actually come into the land. Later in Deuteronomy the present
and the future covenant ceremonies are given in greater detail
though in the reverse order (the future renewal in 27:1-26; the
contemporary covenant renewal in 28:1-29:1). The expression 'I
set before you today' has already appeared in 4:8 and will occur

again in 30:15 and 19 when the present covenant is renewed. It draws attention to the immediate choice that confronted God's people. Just as 'the land' (1:8) and 'this law' (4:8) had been set before them, so now the dual sanctions of blessings and curses are presented to them. The choice which the people would have to make was between these two – blessings and curses, life or death (30:15, 19). The blessing would apply if obedience was shown to the LORD 's commands. The verb translated 'obey' is actually the verb 'to listen' or 'hear', which often has the meaning 'hear and obey'. 'Curse' is mentioned here for the first time and it is presented as the direct contrast to the blessing. The conditions under which it would apply were twofold. In the first place if the LORD's commands were disobeyed then judgment would fall on the people. In the second place, and as a consequence of disobedience, the curse would apply if the people turned aside from the LORD's way and followed other gods. This whole section of the book is a reinforcement of the chief commandment and here at its close the folly of going after other gods is reinforced (cf. 6:14). In this context 'know' has a covenantal meaning, just as it has in Amos 3:2.

29 The scene of action changes now to the time of crossing over the Jordan into the land of Canaan. The thought of blessing and curse brings Moses to a preliminary description of a symbolic ceremony to take place between Mt. Gerizim and Mt. Ebal, situated just to the west of Shechem. A much fuller description of this ceremony appears later in Deuteronomy 27:1-26, while the actual historical description of it is given in Joshua 8:30-35. This is the first time Ebal and Gerizim are mentioned in the Old Testament and after the book of Judges they are never named again. Later Mt. Gerizim became the sacred site for Samaritan worship. It was so in New Testament times (cf. Jn. 4:20, 'this mountain') and remains so until today for the small Samaritan community that still exists. The proclamation of the curses from Mt. Ebal and the blessings from Mt. Gerizim was to be a dramatic way of emphasising the alternatives that were to dominate Israel's history in Canaan.

30 The detailed geographical description is surprising, but it may have been done to show that the place at which this ceremony was to occur was the very place where God had appeared to Abraham when he first came into the land of Canaan (Gen. 12:6). The description does not seem to fit the main route from north to south on the western side of the Jordan (the Heb. text says literally, 'Are they not on the other side of the Jordan behind the way of the setting sun?'). The location of Gilgal is also problematical, as there are at least three separate places by that name. One of them, situated a few miles south west of Gerizim may be intended. An alternative view, which has much to commend it, is that the Hebrew word *gilgal* in this verse is a reference to a Canaanite stone circle, a prominent Canaanite worship centre. Moses is therefore indicating that the invasion is going to bring Israel right into the heart of foreign religious territory. The use of the expression 'the terebinth trees of Moreh' supports this interpretation. This is the only time the plural (Heb. *'elonê moreh*) occurs in the Old Testament, and it appears to mean 'the oaks of prophecy'. Israel was to conduct a ceremony of blessings and curses at the very place where the people would come into direct conflict with Canaanite religion and false prophecy. There would be blessings if there was obedience to the voice of the LORD. If there was obedience to the idols of the Canaanites there would be curses.

31-32 The closing verses re-assert the central themes of this whole section of the book. Israel was about to cross the Jordan and enter territory which God had long ago pledged to give them. There is a ring of certainty in the words 'you will possess it and dwell in it'. The language of verse 32 is strongly reminiscent of 4:1, 5:31 and 6:1. When the land of promise was realised, obedience to all Moses' teaching would alone secure continued occupation of Canaan.

2. The Second Commandment (12:1–13:18)
('You shall not make for yourself an idol')
The exposition of the Second Commandment starts at this point, as Moses concentrates on how worship is to be maintained in its

purity when Israel comes into the land of Canaan. Israel was soon
to cross the Jordan and live among a people who had their own
beliefs and lifestyle. Interaction with the Canaanites was going to
pose great problems for the covenant people, especially in relation
to worship. There were superficial similarities between the worship
of Israel and that of the Canaanites (e.g., the presence of altars,
the use of the name 'Baal', the offering of sacrifices). Here Moses
sets out the things that are to be avoided by Israel, as well as
dealing with matters relating to the sanctuary and the provision of
food for eating. In addition, chapters 12-13 warn of the dangers
that will confront the people.

(i) Pure Worship (12:1-28)

The stress on the avoidance of heathen worship is brought out by
the structure of the chapter, in which heathen worship is dealt
with in verses 1-4 and again in verses 29-31. The whole pattern of
the chapter is as follows:

>   A No Heathen Worship (verses 1-4)
>   B   The Sanctuary
>   (a) Now (verses 5-7)
>   (b) In the future (verses 8-14)
>   C   Food for Eating
>   (a) Now (verses 15-19)
>   (b) In the future (verses 20-28)
>   A¹ No Heathen Worship (verses 29-31)
>   D   Conclusion (verse 32)

(i) Pure Worship (12:1-28)

(a) No Heathen Worship (12:1-4)

1 The opening words mark a new phase in the presentation, just
as a similar expression did at the commencement of chapter 6.
The statutes and judgements were divinely given, and they were
to be part of the instruction that was given to the people as they
went over into Canaan. They had to practise these statutes in

perpetuity in the land that God was to give them. There is a change
in the Hebrew expression here for the giving of the land, as
compared with 11:31. There the participle was used ('is giving'),
while here a prophetic perfect occurs ('shall have given'), which
throws emphasis on the certainty of God's gift of the land.
Possession of the land and obedience to God's statutes are closely
linked throughout this book.

2-3 Destruction of Canaanite places of worship comes first of all.
Israel had to realise that there could be no assimilation to the
religious practices of the Gentiles (Heb. *nations*) who then were
in possession of the land. These nations served their gods on high
mountains and hills, and under green (i.e. luxuriant) trees. High
hills were used as places of worship because the gods were thought
to inhabit them, and worshippers, in ascending the hill, were
considered to be nearer to the specific god. This is an addition in
comparison with the similar instruction in 7:5-6 (see the earlier
discussion). The instruction regarding breaking down the altars
and destroying the cultic objects is very similar to that in 7:5,
except that here there is added a reference to destroying the names
of the gods. 'Name' seems to be virtually equivalent to 'presence'.
There had to be total annihilation of false gods, because there was
only one presence to be acknowledged in the land, and that was
the LORD's.

4 The claim that the LORD made on his followers was that his
worship was exclusive. They must not worship him 'so', i.e. in
the same kind of way as the Canaanites. This instruction, repeated
in verse 31, was to set the pattern for the people, yet in their
subsequent history the people so often disobeyed it. The conflict
between the purity of the worship and assimilation to Canaanite
ways was to persist right through until the fall of Jerusalem.

(b) The Sanctuary – Now (12:5-7)
5 A contrast is stressed in the opening words – 'But the place
which the LORD your God chooses'. Mention has already been
made twice about 'places' associated with heathen gods (verses

2, 3). Now the true place of central worship for the people is said to be a place of God's choice. Earlier at Sinai an instruction had been given regarding making an altar of earth in every place where God's name was recorded (Exod. 20:24). The primary aim of that instruction was to link the worship of Israel with the abiding manifestation of God in the tabernacle. Here Moses establishes the command and promise of Exodus 20 under new conditions. He re-asserts that law. The people are to seek out and come to the place that God has chosen for his dwelling (the Heb. verb used is the one from which the Heb. word *mishkan*, 'tent', 'tabernacle', comes). At the present time they were to continue to seek the tabernacle, which would be located in one place out of all their tribes. The phrase, 'out of all your tribes', has been understood by some to mean that 'the place the Lord your God chooses' could mean various places contemporaneously. While it is true that alongside the central sanctuary worship was permitted at other altars, yet this phrase is best taken as referring to the *one* central place out of the tribes that the LORD would choose. God is said to put his name in that place for his dwelling. The place was going to be identified by the presence of the ark of the covenant within the tabernacle, and to it the people were to come.

6 The central place was to be where the Israelites brought their offerings, and in this verse seven distinct offerings are mentioned: (i) 'burnt offerings', that were totally consumed; (ii) 'sacrifices', of which the fat and blood belonged to God, but the flesh was eaten by the worshippers; (iii) 'tithes', the tenth of the produce of the land (see 14:22-29 for the fuller regulations); (iv) 'the heave offerings of your hand', a freewill offering of whatever the hand took up from the fields (or possibly personal offerings for occasions like birth or purification); (v) 'vowed offerings', which had been promised to the LORD; (vi) 'freewill offerings', gifts which were offered in sacrifice over and above those required; (vii) 'firstlings', the offering of firstborn from the herds and flocks (see 15:19-23 for further details of these offerings, and 26:1-11 for the ceremony of presenting the firstfruits).

7 There at the sanctuary they were to eat the specified portions of the offerings before the LORD. Because of God's provision for them, they were to eat with their families as an acknowledgment of his blessing. In everything to which they put their hands, they were to rejoice.

(c) The Sanctuary – In the Future (12:8-14)

8 This verse is an admission that everything was not right with the worship of Israel even before entry into Canaan. People were acting in accordance with their own desires, just as they were later to do in the period of the Judges (see the use of the same phrase, 'what is right in his own eyes', in Judges 17:6; 21:25). When they came into the land of Canaan this situation was not to continue: 'You shall not at all do as we are doing here today'.

9 The present situation would continue for a little longer, until the LORD brought them to the resting place and the inheritance that he was going to give them. The concepts of 'rest' and 'inheritance' are very important in Deuteronomy (for 'rest' see 3:20; 12:10; 25:19, and for 'inheritance', 4:21; 19:10; 20:16; 21:23; 24:4; 26:1). The people were to be brought into a place of rest by the LORD, and this would be at the same time an inheritance that would be granted to them. Both concepts were later to be taken over and employed as Christian terms in the New Testament (for 'rest', see Heb. 3:11-4:11; and for 'inheritance', see Eph. 1:11, 14, 18; 5:5; Col. 1:12; 3:24; Heb. 9:15; 1 Pet. 1:4).

10 These concepts are continued in this present context as Moses speaks about crossing over the Jordan and dwelling in Canaan. The act of giving the land was to be both the giving of an inheritance and the giving of rest to them. The 'rest' is understood primarily as rest from the surrounding enemies (see 25:19; Jos. 21:44: 23:1; 2 Sam. 7:1, 11; 2 Chron. 14:5). When they finally obtained the inheritance and the rest, they would dwell safely, the same idiom being used in 33:28.

11 In reference to the time when they become possessors of the land, Moses sets out the provision that the location of the ark will be by divine choice. First of all, it will rest in various centres such as Shiloh and Shechem, but then later Jerusalem will be the chosen site. As Psalm 132:13-14 expresses it: 'For the Lord has chosen Zion; he has desired it for his dwelling; "This is my resting place forever; here I will sit enthroned, for I have desired it".' As compared with verse 6, there are just five types of sacrifices mentioned here, and all of them, except the burnt offering, were eaten by the offerers. It is difficult to know why the word 'choice' has been used, for it seems to apply to the first four offerings mentioned. Perhaps it places emphasis on the fact that the offerings were to be the best.

12 Just as at the time when Moses was speaking there was to be rejoicing before the LORD (see verse 7), so later in the land of Canaan. The families, together with the servants and the Levites, were to celebrate joyfully as they brought the offerings. The Levite is designated as being he 'who is within your gates, since he has no portion nor inheritance with you'. Detailed legislation is to follow in 18:1-8 regarding the Levites. They were to dwell in towns that were allocated to other tribes.

13-14 Another of the frequent instructions to 'take heed' introduces the warning of verse 13. Burnt-offerings were not to be offered at any place that the Israelites saw. By 'place' is probably meant the Canaanite 'places' that have been condemned in verses 2-4. Just because their eyes saw a place (of worship or sacrifice), they were not permitted to proceed to offer at it. The exclusive place of offering for burnt-offerings had to be the place of the LORD's choice from among their tribes. There, and there only, these sacrifices were to be made, in accordance with the instructions that Moses was setting out for them.

(d) Food for Eating – Now (12:15-19)

15-16 This section does not deal with the offering of sacrifices but the preparation of meat for eating. The opening word 'however' (Heb. *raq*) has a concessive meaning here. In spite of the law which has just been set out, the Israelites are to be permitted to

kill for food anywhere in the land. Most English versions use the
word 'kill' to translate the Hebrew word used here (*zâbâh*), but it
is a technical word and probably the translation 'sacrifice' should
be maintained. If so, then this would help to explain later situations
such as the family sacrifice mentioned in 1 Samuel 16:5. Also,
the people are permitted to use gazelles or harts, i.e., it is not just
animals especially designated for sacrifice which may be eaten.
These animals are mentioned here for the first time in the Old
Testament. Moreover, the people themselves need not be ritually
clean in order to participate. The regulations dealing with ritual
cleanness and uncleanness are set out in Leviticus 12-15, and
consequently are not repeated here. As the people have desire
(Heb. 'in every desire of your soul'), so may they eat, according
as the LORD blesses them. The one restriction that is placed upon
the eating concerns the blood. In accordance with the law already
given in Leviticus 17:10-14, the blood was not to be eaten, but in
a ritual way poured out upon the ground. It symbolised the essential
principle of life, and so was in effect to be given back to the giver
of life.

17-18 This permission to eat meat anywhere in the land did not
extend to the eating of other products such as the tithe of the grain
or the firstlings of the herd or flock. These types of offering were
not to be consumed anywhere in the land, but only at the place
that the LORD chooses. This has already been made plain in verses
5-6 and 11, but it is now re-enforced here. The form of the
prohibition is an unusual one (Heb. *lo' Tûkal l^e*, lit. 'you are not
able to ... '), which occurs six other times in Deuteronomy (16:5;
17:15; 21:16; 22:3; 22:19; 24:4). As already set out (see verse
12), the eating was to be at the chosen place, and the whole
household and the Levite were to participate there.

19 The closing verse of the section again calls on the individual
Israelite (the verbal form is second pers. sing.) to take heed. This
time the position of the Levite is the object of the instruction. He
must never be forsaken 'as long as you live in your land' (Heb. lit.
'all your days upon the land'), a variant of the expression used

already in verse 1. The position of the Levite could be quite precarious, as he was dependent upon others for his support.

(e) Food for Eating – In the Future (12:20-28)

20-21 The new element that is introduced is the thought of the expansion of the land in the future, and the fact that the central sanctuary would be far off for many of the families. This extended territory was going to be a further gift of God ('when the Lord your God enlarges your border'), just as God had already said. The reference here may well go back to the form of the promise to Abraham regarding the land, but it also has verbal connections with Exodus 34:24. The ability to eat flesh was not going to depend upon proximity to the central place of sacrifice. Whenever there was need for meat, animals from the flocks and herds could be sacrificed, and used as food.

22 A similar regulation applies to this eating as did to the eating of wild animals like the gazelle and the hart (see verse 15). All, whether ritually clean or unclean, could eat of this meat.

23 Here, as in verse 16, the introductory word (Heb. *raq*) has a restrictive meaning: 'Only be sure that you do not eat the blood'. The reason for the prohibition is added: 'For the blood is the life; you may not eat the life with the meat'. This is basically a repetition of Leviticus 17:4, 11. The blood was regarded as symbolic of the life, and therefore it was not to be consumed.

24-25 The repeated prohibitions concerning the blood mark this out as a most important restriction (Heb. *lô' tôkal ... lô' tôk^elennu ... lô' tôk^elennu*). As with the earlier instruction (verse 16), the blood is to be poured out upon the ground. Here an additional incentive to obedience in this respect is given. Only if the people obey will it go well with them in the land and for their children after them. They must do what is upright in the LORD's eyes, not what is upright in their own eyes (cf. verse 8). Prosperity in the land could only be ensured by observing the statutes of the LORD. The intermixture of regulations and exhortation is a notable feature throughout Deuteronomy, and it marks out the book as being a treaty document rather than a legal code.

26-27 When things were consecrated to the LORD, then they were to be brought to the place God had chosen, and there the flesh was to be offered, and afterwards eaten by the worshippers. As with previous offerings mentioned in this chapter, the blood is to be handled in another way. Here it is made plain that the blood was to be poured out 'on the altar', a specification that is not given previously.

28 The stress on obedience is repeated, in terms which are almost identical with verse 25 (the Heb. words *'ad 'ôlâm*, 'forever', are added). The opening words of the verse are an unusual combination. They appear to be used deliberately to stress both the keeping and the obeying of 'all these words', by which is meant all that has preceded in this section.

(f) No Heathen Worship (12:29-31)
29-30 Part of the promise of the land involved action on God's part to remove those currently dwelling there. He was going to 'cut them off', using the same language that is used of disobedient members of the covenant community (cf. Gen. 17:14). The greatest danger for Israel was going to be attraction to the gods of the Canaanites. If they saw Canaanite worship they would ask, 'How do these people serve their god(s)?', and they would want to act in a similar way. The cause of Israel's downfall was ultimately going to be disregard for the instruction to remain separate from the Canaanites.

31 The chapter begins and ends on the same note. The LORD demanded exclusive worship, and one that was patterned entirely differently from the present practice of the Canaanites. The devotees to heathen gods in Canaan were involved with abominations as they sought to serve them, even burning their children in the fire. This was a practice in the Ancient Near East from around 2000 BC onwards, and the Old Testament mentions such offerings in connection with the god Molech. It may have been seen as an offering of the first-fruits to the LORD when children were dedicated to a particular god.

32 Emphasis falls on 'the word' that Moses was commanding the people. Earlier he has used the same expression in a similar warning passage (4:2), while in 5:22 he used the plural form 'words'. It clearly refers to the whole substance of the covenant document that he is setting before them. The first part of the verse addresses Israel collectively by using plural forms ('you', 'you shall observe'), but in the second part it particularises the instruction by reverting to the singular ('you shall not add', 'you shall not subtract'). In the extra-biblical treaties, there are examples of the prohibition, under a curse, of tampering with any of the stipulations of the treaty. Thus Esharhaddon of Assyria says in a treaty tablet: '(You swear that) you will not alter (it), you will not consign (it) to the fire nor throw (it) into the water, nor [bury (it)] in the earth nor destroy it by any cunning device, nor make [(it) disappear], nor sweep it away. (If you do) [may Ashur, king of the] gods who decrees the fates, [decree for you] evil and not good.' Here Moses prohibits any tampering with the divinely-given covenant requirements. The standard of belief and practice has already been set before them.

(ii) Dangers to the Faith (13:1-18)
There is a natural link between the opening of chapter 13 and the closing verses of the previous chapter (verses 29-31). The chapter divisions of the Bible are not original, and they often interrupt the flow of the text. The reference to worship at the central sanctuary leads on naturally to warnings against idolatry.

Another clear parallel with the secular covenants of the period occurs here. In many of them reference is made to possible incitement to rebellion. There was always the danger that a person would try and implicate a vassal king in a plot against his overlord. Once that position arose, the vassal had to act quickly and suppress that rebellion by military force.

Similar situations are covered in this chapter. Not only would turning to other gods be rebellion against the Lord of the covenant,

but idolatry as well. As such, the severest of penalties is set out as
a deterrent. Three possible areas of danger involved false prophets,
the family and any towns in which idolatry was practised.

(a) The Danger from False Prophets (13:1-5)

1-3 Later the general law regarding prophecy will be set out (18:9-
22), and the provision in these verses must be read in conjunction
with it. The Old Testament recognises the existence of true and
false prophets, as does the New Testament. Jesus warned of false
prophets who will deceive many (Matt. 24:11), and both Paul (Acts
20:29-31) and John (1 Jn. 4:1) give similar warnings. Moses
envisages a situation in which a prophet or a dreamer arises and
announces a sign or a wonder, as he seeks to get people to follow
other gods. There is no suggestion that the sign is in itself a false
one (cf. 2 Thess. 2:9). The difference between a sign and a wonder
is not very great. The sign is a visual demonstration to convince
people to do something, while the wonder is an event of a
miraculous kind. With the visual message, the prophet also brings
a verbal one: 'Let us follow other gods ... and let us worship/serve
them.' Such words did not accord with the word of the LORD, and
those who spoke such words must not be believed. They were
trying to entice Israel to follow other gods in place of the LORD.
Through such a situation the LORD was testing Israel to see if they
would prove true to his word. He wanted to know if Israel would
follow the command to love him with all their hearts, souls, and
minds (Deut. 6:5).

4 Throughout this verse the words 'him' and 'his' i.e., the LORD,
appear time and time again. Israel's obligation was to follow *him*,
fear *him*, keep *his* commandments, obey *him*, serve *him* and cleave
to *him*. Clearly a prophet's words had to be in agreement with
previous revelation. The contrast is made plainly between verse 1
and verse 4. On the one hand, a prophet would announce things to
the people. On the other hand, God had spoken and his commands
were to be observed. In later Old Testament books, illustrations
are given of the out-working of this principle. For example, Isaiah
warns the people not to turn to spiritists and mediums, but to the
law and the testimony (Isa. 8:19-20). Angry inhabitants were going

to kill Jeremiah when he predicted the destruction of Jerusalem. However, when the elders recalled that Micah had previously proclaimed the same message, he was saved (Jer. 26:1-24). Uriah the son of Shemariah prophesied similarly, and he was brought back from Egypt and killed (Jer. 26:20-23), while Ahikam was spared when he supported Jeremiah (verse 24).

5 Toleration could not be shown to such men, who were enticing the nation to commit treason against their covenant LORD. They were to be executed, so that the evil could be purged from among the people. Paul seems to echo the last part of the verse in his expression in 1 Corinthians 5:13: 'Expel the wicked man from among you'. To try and persuade others to repudiate the LORD's claim to full obedience was tantamount to rejecting the covenant itself. Their God is identified in accordance with the commencement of the Decalogue as the redeemer God who had brought them out of the Egyptian bondage.

(b) Danger from the Family (13:6-11)
The danger from close family relationships is illustrated by the lives of so many of the kings of Israel and Judah. The sorry influence of Athaliah as a wife and mother on Jehoram and Ahaziah respectively is a good example (2 Kings 8:16-27). In this section the danger of temptation to rebellion from within the family circle is dealt with, and it is depicted as coming secretly, not openly as in the case of the false prophet. Even in the close family, such rebellion was not to be tolerated.

6-7 Any close family member or a friend could easily be the means of enticing them to turn aside from the LORD. The invitation would be to go and worship 'other gods'. These gods are defined as those which their fathers had not known, gods of the people of Canaan from one end of the land to the other.

8 They had to be resolute in opposing such a person, and on no account must they yield to him or obey him. Because of the family relationship or close friendship there would always be the temptation to spare such a one. But it is stressed that no mercy should be shown and no attempt made to cover the sin that had been committed. The covenant commitment involved love to the LORD, even though it meant hating parents, brothers, wife and children (cf. Jesus' words, Luke 14:26).

9 Capital punishment was the only suitable penalty for a crime like this. Two different Hebrew verbs for 'kill' are used in this verse. The first one (*harag*) is the verb used in the Sixth Commandment (Exod. 20:13; Deut. 5:17), while the second one (*mut*) is the more common verb to use in this type of passage. The person to whom the approach had been made in connection with the rebellion had to be prepared to throw the first stone at the condemned person. For the fuller details of the judicial procedure involved here, see 17:2-7.

10 Two words are used to describe the penalty of stoning in the Old Testament. The one used here (*sagal*) is normally used of pelting with stones, as over against the other word (*ragam*) which applies to the action of communal stoning (see 21:21). The reason for the severity of the penalty is now given. Just as in the case of the false prophet (verse 5), the intended result of the enticement was to turn them aside from following the LORD. As in verse 5 the reason is that the seducer was trying to turn them away from their saviour and redeemer. This is a quotation again from the beginning of the Decalogue, and the fact that the reason and the citation are the same in both cases links the two crimes together.

11 Such an execution would also have a salutary effect on the whole of Israel. They would know what had been done, and this would serve as a warning to them should they be tempted to rebel also. Similar statements are also found at 17:13; 19:20; 21:21.

(c) Danger from the Town (13:12-18)
If a rebellion started from the work of a false prophet, or from a seducer in the family, this could lead to more serious problems if the whole community became rebellious. Now this matter is dealt with as the third danger facing the people.

12-13 Reports could arise of a town in which wicked men had encouraged the whole community to follow other gods. The Hebrew expression used here for 'wicked men' is 'sons of belial', occurring here for the first time in the Old Testament. This is not a proper name in the Old Testament, but it certainly became one in the later pseudepigraphical literature of the intertestamental period (in books such as *Jubilee*, the *Testament of Levi*, and the *Testament of Reuben*) and in the scrolls from the Qumran caves (the *Manual of Discipline*, the *War Scroll* and the *Damascus Document*). The expression is used in judicial contexts in the Old Testament (cf. Judg. 19:22; 20:13; 1 Sam. 25:17, 25; 1 Kings 21:10, 13) and also in connection with the enemies of kings (1 Sam. 10:27; 2 Sam. 21:1; 2 Chron. 13:7). Various derivations of the word 'belial' have been suggested, though none is absolutely confirmed. One common interpretation is to take it as meaning 'without profit', 'worthless', 'good for nothing', or another, as Jerome held, meaning 'without a yoke' and hence 'lawless'. A more recent suggestion is that 'belial' is an abstract noun in Hebrew denoting 'destructiveness'. If this is so, then 'the sons of belial' are those whose characters are destructive and evil. This certainly fits the context here, for it is used of men who incite a whole community to reject the authority of the LORD, and who substitute another god they have never known before.

14-15 If this happened, then the divine assessment of them was quite different from the estimation of their neighbours and kinsfolk. Careful and accurate investigations had to be carried out to be certain that this abomination had actually occurred. The term used for 'thoroughly' (appearing also in 17:4 and 19:18) is a very rare expression, as is the expression 'certain truth' (Heb. *'emet nacon*). The word 'abomination' used in verse 14 (NIV, 'detestable thing') is reserved in the Old Testament for actions which were abhorrent in the eyes of the LORD, especially the actions of the Canaanites. If a community followed Canaanite practices, then it could only expect to receive the same punishment. 'To put to the sword' is a military term (cf. Jos. 8:24; 10:28-38: 11:11f.; 19:47), while the word 'destroy' (verse 15) is connected with the word applied to the ban or curse on the Canaanites. The death penalty had to be carried out on both men and animals, so that the town given over to idolatry was completely destroyed. This legislation presupposes that the people as a whole would co-operate in the implementation of it, even if this entailed civil war.

16 Action had to be taken to gather the spoil or plunder together in the town square and burn it as a whole burnt offering to the LORD. The word used for the offering (Heb. *kalil*) is used elsewhere in setting out the sacrificial system of Israel (see Lev. 6:21-22). What remained was to be a ruined mound (Heb. *tel*) for ever. After Joshua the word 'tel' is only found in Jeremiah 30:18 and 49:2. The danger of breaching the ban was to be demonstrated later in the condemnation which came on Achan after his sin (Jos. 7-8).

17-18 The ban meant total destruction of everything, so that nothing was left over (the Heb. has, 'not a thing shall cleave to your hand'). To take anything would only lead, as in the case of Achan, to a continuation of punishment and to the maintenance of God's wrath. If obedience was shown to the instruction, then the LORD would turn from his wrath (cf. Exod. 32:12; Jos. 7:26; Jer. 4:8; and see the commentary on 4:24). The LORD's reaction to obedience is now stated in the reverse way. He will 'show mercy' and 'have compassion' on the people. Both these terms contain words which come from the same Hebrew root (*racham*), 'he will show mercy and be merciful', which stresses the gracious action of God to a sinful people. The other result of obedience to this direction would be that the LORD would increase the nation in numbers as he had sworn to the patriarchs. Already Moses had stressed that if the people were faithful, then the LORD would love them and increase their numbers (7:13; for the promise to the fathers, see Gen. 22:17; 26:4; and Exod. 32:13).

18 Only on condition of obedience would the LORD turn away from his anger and show mercy. His word had to be listened to and obeyed. In Deuteronomy the fulfilment of the promise of a large nation is said to be dependent upon Israel's obedience, with the prayer of Moses in 1:11 being the only exception. This verse forms an excellent conclusion to what has gone before, not only in the preceding paragraphs but the whole section (chapters 12-13) dealing with the application of the second commandment. The specification of the way of worship in the second commandment has been enlarged in these chapters to demonstrate the abuses of worship that the LORD will not tolerate. That commandment ends with the promise that the LORD shows mercy to the thousandth generation of those who fear him and who keep his commandments (5:10). The final verse of this section seems to be a conscious allusion to those words by its emphasis on keeping the LORD's commandments (cf. 'to those who keep my commandments', 5:10, with 'keeping all his commandments', 13:18).

3. The Third Commandment (14:1-29)
('You shall not misuse the name of the LORD your God')
This section commencing at 14:1 and extending throughout the chapter, is an exposition of the Third Commandment. As has been discussed already concerning this commandment (see commentary on 5:11), the intent of it is not only in regard to speech about God. Rather, it concerns living as the people of God and not bearing the character of God in a hypocritical way. Now a fuller discussion of those basic principles follows.

The contents of chapter 14 seem at first sight to be totally disconnected either with the third commandment, or with the immediate context here in Deuteronomy. However, two great principles underlie the exposition. First, there is the concept of the fatherhood of God in respect to Israel. At the time of the Exodus God claimed that Israel was his firstborn son, and so demanded that Pharaoh let him go (Exod. 4:22-23). Also God looked on the individual Israelites as his children (cf. 32:5, 19; Ps. 103:13; Isa. 1:2-4; Mal. 2:10). Secondly, as a consequence of this adoption, Israel had to follow a lifestyle in which they were called to be holy and dedicated to the LORD (Exod. 19:6). They had to demonstrate by their actions that they were indeed of the family of God. Both these principles are carried over and applied in the New Testament to believers today (cf. Gal. 4:4-7; 1 Pet. 1:16).

This chapter sets out, therefore, some of the requirements which Israel had to follow to show that she was a holy nation to the LORD. Not just his worship (chapter 12) or the threat of rebellion against him (chapter 13) were involved. Customs regarding mourning rites, dietary provisions, tithing and feasting were also part of the obedience of Israel to God's covenant requirements.

(i) Mourning Rites (14:1-2)

1a Old Testament believers had to bear the family likeness. They had to constantly remember that they were God's children. Once again the connection between Deuteronomy and Exodus is apparent. Or, to put it another way, the covenant document here re-echoes again the language and ideas of the covenant at Sinai and its surrounding events. The form of command is put here in the plural: 'You (pl.) are *the children* of the LORD'. More commonly in the Old Testament the singular 'son' is used of the nation of Israel (cf. Exod. 4:22). The use of the plural 'sons' brings home the responsibility of each member of the covenant community to live in this way. Both in life and in death the people of Israel were to be marked out as a separate people.

1b-2 In the face of death Israel was to behave differently from her neighbours. The plural form of address continues with instructions against heathen funeral rites. There were not to be any self-inflicted wounds, nor cutting of the lock of hair on the forehead. Lacerating oneself was an attempt to keep in touch with the dead, and plucking out of hair was another mutilation of the body associated with mourning. In both cases the forbidden practice was heathen in origin, but it was also a disfigurement of the body as something made in the image of God. Evidence from the ancient Ras Shamra/ Ugarit on the coast of northern Syria, suggests that these practices were part of a cult for the dead, in which it was not only the cutting of the body but the flow of blood which was important. In particular, letting blood flow may well have been a seasonal rite in connection with a Canaanite fertility cult. Now the focus changes to the nation collectively, and the form of address is singular: 'You (sing.) are a holy nation to the LORD'. Israel could never forget how distinctive was her relationship to the LORD. She had been chosen by God out of all the nations on the face of the earth, and had been made his special people. The language here is that of election to both privilege and responsibility. A unique standing before God ('his treasured possession') brought with it the responsibility to be 'a people holy to the LORD'.

(ii) Clean and Unclean Animals (14:3-21)

The provisions in these verses are a summary of the fuller details given in Leviticus 11, where the stress is also on the fact that Israel is a holy nation to the LORD (Lev. 11:44-45). The order in which the animals are mentioned is the same as in Genesis 1 – domestic and wild animals, fish and birds, and then insects. Several reasons have been suggested for the division into clean and unclean.

1. Hygienic reasons could dictate the prohibition in some cases, especially in regard to pigs and rodents.

2. Religious reasons appear to lie behind others. Some of the animals were sacred in heathen religions and therefore were to be avoided. Also, eating meat that had not been killed in the proper way (verse 21a) was not permissible, though strangers and foreigners could partake of it.

3. The connection with death may also have been an important factor. The cud-chewing animals rarely eat flesh, while many of those regarded here as unclean kill and devour other animals, or else feed on carcasses. Death, then, seems to be an overriding factor in the distinction between clean and unclean.

Perhaps the solution to the problem of the reason for this legislation is to be found in a combination of these suggested reasons. It may well be the case that there is also an element of arbitrariness in the choice of the various animals. Israel was pledged to obedience to her covenant LORD, and a test such as this was a reminder both of her distinctive character and the fact that she was to live by every word out of God's mouth (Deut. 8:3).

3 The singular form of address continues in this verse. There was to be no eating of detestable things. The use of this word 'detestable' is important, because it is a term linked with practices in Canaanite religious life which were not tolerated by the LORD (cf. the use of this term already in Deut. 7:25, 26; 12:31; 13:14). Its use here marks out what follows as being part of Canaanite worship, and therefore something in itself to be avoided by Israel.

4-5 There are some differences between Leviticus 11 and this section of Deuteronomy. The regulations in Leviticus are much more detailed, except in the case of the clean animals noted here. No mention is made of ritual slaughtering, as this has been covered already in 12:16, 23ff. The first three animals, the ox, the sheep and the goat, are all domestic animals. Cattle and the small domestic animals, male and female, formed the major part of the meat supply for Israel. But other wild animals were also permitted, as verse 5 specifies seven kinds of animals that provided allowable meat. These animals are not listed in Leviticus, but now that the people were familiar with them because of the wilderness journeyings or were going to come across them in the wooded hill country of Canaan, they are specified here. Some of these animals are difficult to identify, and the list is not complete. The presence of seven types is probably meant to indicate a representative sample of the much larger range of wild animals. The deer and the gazelle have already been mentioned together (12:15, 22) as permitted food. The wild goat, the ibex and the mountain sheep are only mentioned here.

6-8 Then follows the list of prohibited animals, together with the explanation of the reason on which the distinctions are made. This list also seems to be representative rather than comprehensive in scope, and it makes no mention of touching the unclean animals as is set out in Leviticus 11:24, 25, 28, 31. The two distinctions given are that the clean animals have split hooves, and also chew the cud. Verse 7 specifies the exemptions to this, as there were animals which chew the cud but do not divide the hoof, such as the camel, the rabbit and the coney. It has been suggested that the rabbit and the coney are excluded on hygienic grounds as they are disease carriers, though this does not explain the inclusion of the camel with them. This type of animal was ceremonially unclean for Israel. The pig was excluded for the opposite reason. It had a split hoof but did not chew the cud. It has often been thought that the prohibition against using pork was for hygienic reasons, but the addition of the prohibition against touching the carcasses of pigs strongly suggests that ritual considerations were also involved. In the ancient Near East pigs were used in cultic situations in Palestine, Babylon, Egypt, among the Hittites and in the Greek world. It was not a general custom but was restricted to special magical and mystery rituals. The eating of the flesh of pigs is noted by Isaiah as being associated with the eating of other unclean and abominable things (Isa. 65:2-5; 66:17).

9-10 From animals, the focus moves to fish. Those fish with both fins and scales could be eaten, but others were to be reckoned as unclean. The distinction seems to be between the free-swimming fish and those which burrow in the mud for their prey. This would include catfish in the Sea of Galilee and eels, rays and lampreys along the Mediterranean coast. Again, a hygienic reason may well have been behind this prohibition.

11-18 Next the birds are considered, with the opening comment being that any clean bird may be eaten. However, no definition of 'clean' is given. We are left to examine the list that follows and try to ascertain the underlying principle. A major problem is that it is very difficult to be certain about the identification of birds in this list. The first three names (eagle, vulture, black vulture) are the most certain, but even they may be broader in meaning than our English versions suggest. Most of these birds are flesh-eating (the exceptions are hoopoe and the bat), and therefore a hygienic explanation seems to be the best reason for their exclusion from the diet. The hoopoe and the bat are not flesh-eating, but probably their unclean habits justified their exclusion.

19-20 The legislation in Leviticus 11:20ff. has already dealt in a more specific manner with the matter of eating insects. Most four-legged insects were forbidden, except for certain kinds of the locust family. This ordinance here presupposes fuller knowledge of the laws relating to clean and unclean foods, for verse 20 does not indicate what constituted the class of clean winged creatures. The reference to 'any winged creature' (Heb. *'of,* verse 20) is broader than the word 'bird' (Heb. *tsippor,* verse 11) in meaning, and seems to be equivalent to the 'flying insects' of verse 19.

21a Eating of the bodies of animals that were already dead was forbidden. Clearly, the objection to this was not hygienic, as it was permissible for them to be given to a foreigner (Heb. *gêr*) or even sold to a stranger (Heb. *nokri).* The distinction between these classes was that the foreigner was a landless person who was commended to the kindness of the Israelites (Deut. 14:29; 16:11, 14; 26:11), while the stranger was not settled in Israel. He could have been temporarily in the land for commercial reasons, but he had no rights there. The body of the animal was perfectly acceptable for human consumption, but it had not been ritually killed in the appointed way (cf. Lev. 17:10-14 and the comment on Deut. 12:16). The idea was that it would be a pity if the body of a such an edible, clean animal was to be wasted when the foreigner was in need of food, and was not bound by the laws which directed the Israelites' behaviour. They were bound by their allegiance to their covenant LORD, and had to reflect the holiness that he demanded. 'Holiness to the LORD' was the basic motivation of their conduct.

21b The reference to cooking a kid in its mother's milk that occurs in this verse also appears in Exodus 23:19 and 34:26. There does not appear to be anything wrong with the practice in itself, except that what approximated to practices in heathen cults was to be avoided. The nearest parallel outside Israel is one that has been quoted from Ugarit/Ras Shamra in northern Syria in a text which contains the line: 'cook the kid in milk, the lamb in butter'. However, this Ugaritic text is itself problematical, and it does not refer specifically to 'the mother's milk'. If the Canaanites practised anything like this in their religion, then that was sufficient reason for it to be avoided by the Israelites. It may have been a ritual in which after the cooking the milk was sprinkled on the fields in a fertility rite. This prohibition still has relevance today for the Jewish people, in that it continues to provide the rationale for Jewish food laws forbidding meat and milk products being eaten together.

(iii) Tithing and Rejoicing (14:22-29)

Earlier in the Pentateuch tithing is dealt with in Leviticus 27:30-33 and Numbers 18:21-29, and here in Deuteronomy reference has already been made to the practice in 12:6, 11, 17. Later, further explanation is given of it (26:12-15). The earlier passages lay down the general pattern of setting aside a tenth of one's produce for the LORD. Here in this section four things are stressed.

1. The tithes were to be brought to the central sanctuary (verses 23-24).

2. If that place was too far away, then the tithe could be exchanged for money to buy food and drink (verses 24-25).

3. In God's presence they were to eat a portion of the tithe and rejoice (verse 26).

4. In every third and sixth year of the seven year cycle special provisions applied for storing the tithe, in order to provide for the Levites and the most needy groups in the society such as orphans and widows (verses 28-29).

The underlying principle was that there was a joyful recognition of God as the provider. The additional tithe reminded them that others who were not so well-off were to have their needs met out of the bounty of God's provision.

22 The practice of tithing (i.e. giving a tenth of one's produce) is referred to in general in Genesis 28:22, and in a royal connection in Genesis 14:20 (cf. for the later period 1 Sam. 8:15, 17). Here the emphasis is on the agricultural tithe, though mention is made of the firstlings of the flock and the herd in the next verse. The construction in Hebrew of this regulation is emphatic, 'You *must* tithe'. The last two words in the verse in Hebrew are simply 'year, year'. Presumably the meaning is that year by year they were to bring a tenth of the harvest of their fields.

23 The tithe is specified for the grain, new wine and oil. This tenth represented the total harvest, and the fact that some of it was eaten as a communion meal before the LORD was a recognition that it came from the one who had given the land to them and who was the source of the rich blessings they were enjoying. Presumably only a small portion of the tithe was consumed as part of this meal. These facts come to very clear expression later in the ceremony of bringing the firstfruits (see particularly 26:9-11). While there is no specific mention here of Canaanite practices, it does seem that the legislation has that in view throughout. The presentation of the tithe was in itself a denial of Canaanite fertility beliefs, for the ceremony had to be conducted at the LORD's sanctuary. Fertility practices such as the Canaanites used were not the reason for the bountiful harvests. The intention was that this practice would serve year by year to increase the people's reverence for the LORD. It had, therefore, a teaching function to perform as it strengthened the faith of the worshippers in the giver of the blessings.

24-26 Provision is now made for the situation when people were too far away from the central sanctuary and when the harvest was so abundant that they could not possibly bring the tithe itself. In this case they were to be permitted to exchange the tithe for money before they went to the sanctuary. They had to go with the money tucked in their hands to show that it was tithe money, and then to buy there whatever they desired – 'cattle, sheep, wine, and other fermented drink, or anything you wish'. The reference to the drinks is not to contrast wine with other non-fermented drink, but to contrast wine made with grapes with that made from other products such as honey and barley (the Heb. terms are *yayin* and *shekar*).

When they had made their purchases they were to eat before the LORD and rejoice in his presence. The essential fact was that the offerer and his family should eat joyfully before the LORD as an expression of heartfelt thanks for his blessings. Provision for the Levites and others was a secondary feature of the presentation of the tithe.

27 In their rejoicing the Israelites could not neglect the Levites, who had no territorial allotment, but dwelt in their towns (lit. 'in your gates'). This is a repetition of the principle already given in 12:12, 19, and which is going to be expanded further in 18:1-8. Presumably the share for the Levites had to be given to them where they were living, rather than at the central sanctuary. This sharing with the Levites was another way in which the Israelites were to remind themselves that God's blessings were not just intended for them personally. Thankfulness had to be accompanied by social responsibility towards the needy in their society.

28-29 Special provision is made for the tithes in years three and six of the seven-year sabbatical cycle. While the Levites shared in the other years in the distribution of the tithes, special provision was to be made for them in these years, and also for the other underprivileged – the aliens, the orphans and the widows. This inclusion of other needy people along with the Levites is a minor modification of the tithe law as already formulated. This is not to be thought of as an additional tithe, but rather a specific disposition of the annual tithe in these years. The whole tithe was to be brought to an accessible place in their towns (the emphasis is on 'all' to ensure that none of it was devoted to other purposes). The Levites and the other needy ones could come then to that place, eat and be satisfied. Obedience to this provision, like all the other regulations of the covenant, would bring with it blessing from the LORD. The post-exilic Israelite community pledged themselves to fulfil the demands of this law (Neh. 10:36-39), though in Nehemiah's absence they reneged on that pledge. Malachi 3:6-12 confirms this failure to honour the Lord's decrees, and he charges the people with robbery of their God.

4. The Fourth Commandment (15:1–16:17)

('Observe the Sabbath day by keeping it holy')

This chapter marks a transition to the Fourth Commandment of the Decalogue, with its concern for the structuring of time. The Sabbath law, a creation ordinance, but renewed in a specific form in the Sinai covenant, makes human time follow a pattern that was set at creation. After six days of work, there was a day of rest. All of life proceeded on this basic provision, and the sabbatical principle is extended here more widely, going far beyond the weekly Sabbath. The principle underlying the sabbatical year and the year of jubilee stem from the basic law for the Sabbath.

Here in Deuteronomy the sabbatical law is varied, especially in relation to the motive for keeping the command. Whereas in Exodus 20:8-11 the reason for keeping the command is God's creative activity, in Deuteronomy the reason is redemption from Egypt (Deut. 5:12-15). When we come to this present section of Deuteronomy, not only do we get the structuring of time, but the concept of redemption appears strongly, thus echoing the theme of Deuteronomy 5:15. The redemption motive comes in here first of all in 15:4-18. It is not mentioned explicitly, but is clearly implied in the reference to the LORD giving the land of Canaan to Israel. It becomes explicit in verse 15: 'Remember that you were slaves in Egypt and the LORD your God redeemed you. That is why I give you this command today'. The Israelites were to act in a certain way towards their slaves in recollection of their nation's experience of slavery and redemption. Similarly the law of the firstborn was enunciated when they were brought out of Egypt (see Exod. 13:2, 11-13; cf. also Num. 3:11-13). When the section in chapter 16 that contains the provision for the three great pilgrimage feasts is considered, the redemption theme is present very clearly. It features in 16:1, 3, 6, in relation to the Passover, and in 16:12 in relation to the Feast of Weeks. There is no explicit mention of it in relation to the Feast of Tabernacles, though in the legislation earlier in Leviticus it is said that living in tabernacles was necessary so that future generations would know what their forefathers had done when the LORD brought them out of Egypt (Lev. 23:43).

(i) Compassion to Needy Brethren (15:1-11)

The reference in chapter 14:23 to the firstborn is renewed at the end of this chapter. But first there is discussion of two other topics, cancellation of debts and the release of slaves. In each of the three sections of this chapter the same general pattern is followed, as so often in this book:

1.	verse 1	General Law – Debts
	verses 2-11	Exposition
2.	verse 12	General Law – Slaves
	verses 13-18	Exposition
3.	verse 19	General Law – Firstborn
	verses 20-23	Exposition

Every seven year period in the whole cycle of the Jubilee system was marked by abolishing debts owed by fellow Israelites. In Exodus 23:10-11 and Leviticus 25:4 provision is made for letting the land lie fallow in the seventh year. The poor were free to help themselves to the produce during that year, which was regarded as a Sabbath of rest to the LORD (Lev. 25:4).

1 Every seven years there was to be a release. The Hebrew word used here (*shemittah*) comes from a root that means 'to let fall'. In Exodus 23:11 it is applied to leaving land fallow, while here it is applied to the remission of debts. The question of whether the intention is a permanent remission or simply a one year moratorium on repayment, has often been discussed. The former seems to be the case. The year of release and the Jubilee year belong together as part of the same symbolism. What took place in the year of the release was carried a stage further at the Jubilee when there was restoration of personal freedom and also recovery of property that had been alienated. The context supports this interpretation, because the legislation comes in conjunction with the law relating to the release from slavery. Hence the idea seems to be clearly something of a permanent, not temporary, nature in the way of cancelling debts.

2-3 Verse two commences with an introductory statement, 'This is how it is to be done' (Heb. lit. 'this is the word of the release'), with the same pattern being followed in 19:4. The release is declared to be the LORD's release (cf. similar declarations regarding the Passover [Exod. 12:11] and the Sabbath [Exod. 16:25]). Every loan given to a fellow Israelite had to be set aside forever. The distinction between fellow Israelites and foreigners is emphasised. The latter was not a sojourner (who was integrated into Israelite society) but a foreigner passing through Israel on business or only residing temporarily there. In both verses 2 and 3 specific mention is made that the debt of a 'brother' had to be cancelled. While the language of verse 2 is stated in the third person, that of verse 3 is in the second person, which makes the instruction a personal responsibility of every Israelite.

4-5 The existence of poor in the land (verse 7) is not contradicted by these prior verses. The ideal remained that if there was full obedience shown to the LORD's commands in the land of Canaan, everyone should have plenty. The land was being provided as an inheritance from the LORD and if Israel would only listen carefully to his voice there would be a rich abundance for all. Listening to the voice of the LORD is the same as holding to the law of Moses.

6 The LORD would certainly bless just as he had promised, and Israel, if obedient to him, would be economically independent of other nations. It would be providing capital to other nations rather than needing to borrow. The verb 'rule' (Heb. *mashal*) only occurs here in Deuteronomy. In the context it is not military imperialism that is in view but economic prosperity and independence.

7-8 The reality had to be faced, however, that owing to Israel's foreseen disobedience, the poor would always be present. Wherever they might encounter a poor Israelite in any of their towns, they were to show a generous spirit. They were not to harden their hearts or be tight-fisted (the Heb. idiom is 'you shall not close your hand'). That this was not almsgiving is made plain by verse 8. Whatever the poor man needed was to be lent to him, but on a pledge which required later repayment (the Heb. verb is the same one which has already been used in verse 5).

9 No Israelite was to have the wicked thought (lit. 'a word from belial', cf. 13:13) that he would not lend because he would soon lose his money as the seventh year was approaching. While the full significance of 'belial' is unclear, it clearly denoted something that was bad or evil. In these circumstances the poor person could appeal to God and it would be reckoned as a sin in his eyes. It is not said explicitly that such a sin would be punished but that is clearly the implication of the passage.

10 The call to generosity is repeated, with the added instruction that such giving must not be accompanied by a bitter spirit. The provisions might have seemed onerous were it not for the emphasis on God's provision for the people. The Israelites, if obedient to this and God's other provisions, would be blessed in all their work and activity.

11 The final verse in this section is an acknowledgment of how imperfectly the system would operate due to human sin and greed. Jesus' words in connection with his anointing in Bethany, 'The poor you will always have with you' (Matt. 26:11; Mark 14:7), are probably a use of this verse in Deuteronomy. The responsibility towards the poor and needy is strikingly emphasised in the Hebrew text by the repeated use of the second masculine singular suffix 'your' – 'your hand', 'your brothers', 'your needy', 'your poor', and 'your land'. Each individual Israelite had to show obedience and meet the needs of those in want.

(ii) Freeing of Slaves (15:12-18)
The seventh year of service was to be marked by freeing both male and female slaves. Any Hebrew slave who had entered voluntarily into an arrangement with a master was to go free. The fact that the Israelites had been set free from their slavery was to be the motivation for setting their own slaves free (verse 15). The experience of redemption, which they remembered weekly in the

observance of the Sabbath, was the pattern that they were to follow in regard to their slaves. Moreover, liberal provisions had to be given to a freed slave, so that he was not sent away only to suffer hardship. Not every slave would want to go free. In some cases freeing a slave would be an act of extreme cruelty, as for example in the case of an old slave or one without family. Hence a slave who wanted to remain with a master whom he loved would have his ear pierced as a sign of life-long servanthood (see the provisions in Exod. 21:2-6, and in connection with the year of Jubilee, Lev. 25:39-55). Paul's reference to himself as bearing the marks of the Lord Jesus seems to be an allusion to this practice (Gal. 6:17).

There are very few passages in the Old Testament that provide illustrations of the application of this law. The most helpful passage is undoubtedly Jeremiah 34:8-22, in which Jeremiah quotes the law after slaves had been set free and then taken into captivity again.

12 The connection with the preceding section is most probably the idea of debt. Having spoken of those who require a loan, Moses now turns to those who have sold themselves into slavery. The terms used in this verse clearly define the nature of the slavery. The issue is slavery involving fellow Israelites. It concerns 'your brother, a Hebrew man or a Hebrew woman'. In what follows no further details are given in the case of a female slave, but certainly the general principles are stated in a way that could easily be applied to the release of female slaves.

The seventh year was to be marked by granting freedom to a slave so that he or she could go free. In the earlier Babylonian law code of Hammurabi the period of service was set at three years, with freedom coming in the fourth year. Two further conditions affecting slaves have also to be considered in connection with the provision here. First, the law in Leviticus 25:40-41 allowing for release of slaves in the time of Jubilee was a supplementary provision that allowed for release if the Jubilee came before the seventh year. Secondly, there was another option open to the slave and that was acceptance of voluntary life-long service of his master (Exod. 21:5-6; Deut. 15:16-17).

13-14 Provision is now made to ensure that slaves did not have to endure repeated periods of slavery because of poverty. Any slave sent away was not simply to be given freedom. Rather, he had to be provided with as much as he could carry. Provision from the three basic elements of rural produce – the flock, the threshing floor and the winepress, were to be laden on him. Just as they had been so blessed by the LORD, similarly they had to 'bless' the departing slave by giving him liberal provisions.

15 The first part of this verse, 'Remember that you were slaves in Egypt', is a direct quotation from the Fourth Commandment in its Deuteronomic form (Deut. 5:15). This was to be the motivation that prompted the Israelites to act compassionately to departing slaves. They had to think back to their experience and recall the LORD's redemption. The verb used here (Heb. *padah*) is used in Deuteronomy to indicate Israel's release from slavery in Egypt, but it is used elsewhere of the release of slaves in general (Exod. 21:8; Lev. 19:20) or of redemption of the firstborn (Exod. 13:13, 15).

16-17 When the year of release came a slave might not wish to go free, and two reasons for such feelings are given. On the one hand, there might be such affection between the slave and his master's family that he desired to stay with them. On the other hand, he might recognise the abundance in his master's home (Heb. 'that is good with him') and not want to go out to a more precarious lifestyle. In such cases piercing the ear with an awl was a judicial action and resulted in a symbolic sign of what had transpired. The slave had voluntarily chosen to remain in service to his master until death. He was in those circumstances to be a perpetual slave (Heb. *'eved 'olam*) and this term does not seem to have been a derogatory expression. The same regulation applied to female servants. The piercing of the ear was probably followed by attaching a tag to the ear, thus designating this slave as different and probably in a preferential position within the household.

18 The instruction here applied to verses 12-15 and to verses 16-17. A slave owner was not to think himself deprived when a slave went free, for he had had the labour of that slave for six years. Several versions translate the Hebrew word *mishneh* as 'double': 'his service to you these six years has been worth twice as much as that of a hired hand' (NIV). It is true that it can be translated as 'double', but it also can mean 'a copy' (Deut. 17:18; Josh. 8:32). Here and in Jeremiah 16:18, however, it means 'an equivalent'. The idea was that the slave had worked without payment and he had therefore discharged his debt because he had saved the master six years of wages. The section ends with the assurance of the LORD's blessing if there was obedience to his commands (cf. 4, 6, and 10).

(iii) The Law of the Firstborn (15:19-23)

19 The law has already been given to Israel (see Exod. 13:11-15; 22:29-30; 34:19-20; Num. 18:15-18). Now there is a re-assertion of it, especially as it relates to the central sanctuary. The situation as it concerns the firstborn male is dealt with here, and only in regard to cattle and sheep/goats. As is customary in Deuteronomy, the law is stated as a general principle and then an exposition provided of it. The firstborn, i.e. the first calf, kid or lamb produced by an animal, was to be consecrated to the LORD. The calf was not to be used for ordinary work, while the lamb was not to be shorn.

20 A new aspect of the legislation is the provision for the eating of the firstborn in the presence of the LORD. In this way attention is drawn to the provision of the central sanctuary and of the requirement that certain religious functions be fulfilled there. Presumably the intention was that the animals be slaughtered when fully grown, and this on a yearly basis (Heb. 'year by year'). The precise time is not indicated, and possibly the sacrificial meal took place at any of the three great pilgrimage feasts. The fact that the priests and their families also shared in it (see Num. 18:15-18) is similar to the provisions for the tithes (see 14:23-27).

21 No animal which had a serious flaw could be used in sacrifice (see 17:1, and Lev. 22:17-25). That general principle is here applied to the firstlings. The firstborn were dedicated to the LORD and the prohibition only applies to eating them in a sacrificial meal.

22-23 No restriction is placed on the eating of the blemished animals in the towns, i.e. other than at the central sanctuary. This is in accordance with the principle already set out in chapter 12:15-28 and is another indication of concern to enunciate fully the basic concepts set out in that chapter. A corollary to this would presumably be that the requirements of verse 19b did not apply to blemished firstlings. However, the rule concerning the blood still held true (see 12:16, 23-25). It could not be eaten but instead had to be poured on the ground.

(iv) The Pilgrimage Feasts (16:1-17)

This section concentrates on the great feasts of the year, when Israel had come to the place that the LORD would choose and there celebrate before him. The references here to this 'place' (verses 2, 6, 11, 15, 16) again makes clear the connection with the appointment of the central sanctuary set out in chapter 12. The place to which pilgrimage would be made was the place where the tabernacle was located. Each of these feasts was dependent upon the events surrounding the exodus and related in various ways to the redemption that God accomplished at that time. This is made plain in verses 1, 3, and 6 for the Passover, in verse 12 for the Feast of Weeks, while Leviticus 23:43 does the same for the Feast of Tabernacles. Directions for the observance of each of these feasts had already been given earlier in the Pentateuch (see Exod. 12, Lev. 23, and Num. 28-29). Our knowledge of the early calendar used by Israel is very limited. Only four of the names for months occur in the period before the exile. They are as follows:

Abib	March/April	Exodus 13:4
Ziv	April/May	1 Kings 6:1, 37
Ethanim	September/October	1 Kings 8:2
Bul	October/November	1 Kings 6:38

Even these forms are re-named in the references after the exile, while the other eight months are also given. Outside the Bible the only thing that approximates to a calendar is the 10th century BC inscriptions on a limestone tablet found at Gezer. It was probably a school-boy's exercise, and it lists the agricultural activities of the year in a rough chronological order.

(a) The Passover (16:1-8)

The first of the feasts was the Passover, which took place in the month of Abib (equivalent to our late March/early April). The first Passover was an anticipation of God's deliverance of his people from the final plague in Egypt. Subsequent celebrations were intended to recall the specific event by which Israel was redeemed from Egypt. The Passover underwent some minor changes. Looking ahead to settlement in the land of Canaan, Moses had already made provision for the presentation of the first sheaf of the harvest at Passover time (Lev. 23:11). Here in this passage further changes take place (see especially verses 2, 5-6) in relation to the type of animal and the place at which the festival was to be observed.

All the symbolism of the Passover (including the unleavened bread and bitter herbs) pointed back to the exodus. But like all the other sacrifices its inbuilt imperfection pointed forward to a far fuller Passover to come. While John the Baptist's words, 'Look, the Lamb of God' (Jn. 1:29) have no exact parallel in the Old Testament, they seem to be modelled far more on the idea of the Passover lamb than any other lamb. The connection between the Passover and its fulfilment in Christ comes out in the merging of the Passover with the first Lord's Supper. Paul made the link explicit when he speaks of Christ as our slain Passover Lamb (1 Cor. 5:7-8).

1 The month of Abib was marked out as a special month by the observance of the Passover. It was to be kept as a feast to the LORD (cf. the similar language in reference to the Sabbath, Exod. 16:25; and the year of jubilee, Deut. 15:2). The word 'passover' comes from a verb which is only used seven times in the Old Testament. The best explanation is that the verb as used in Exodus 12 denotes that God 'leaped over' the houses of the Israelites. The noun was then taken as the designation of the feast that recalled the event. It was in the month of Abib that God brought out his people from their slavery in Egypt. Their leaving the land of Egypt is emphasised, as well as the haste with which they departed ('by night', cf. Exod. 12:29-31).

2 Two new specifications occur in this verse as compared with the earlier legislation. First, the type of animal to be used is now said to be from either flock or herd. The two and a half tribes in Transjordania were already rich in cattle (see Deut. 3:19), and this may have been to make special provision for their circumstances. Secondly, the sacrifice was to begin at the place at which God recorded his name (see Deut. 12:4-7). Thus the feast was henceforth to be kept at the central place of worship. This was to replace the original manner, set out in Exodus 12:3, in which each man had to slay a lamb for his own family.

3 The Passover sacrifice could not be eaten together with leavened bread. Instead, for seven days unleavened bread (Heb. *massot*) had to be used. It is described as 'bread of affliction', i.e. bread which reminded them of their hard labour in Egypt when they did not have the time to make other bread which required longer preparation time. For all time they had to remember the manner of their departure from Egypt. They had gone out in haste. The Hebrew word for 'haste' (*kippazon*) is only used in Exodus 12:11, Isaiah 52:12 and here. It means something more than just haste. Rather it is hurry along with fear or trepidation. The manner of their departure was to be recalled every time they used the unleavened bread.

4 No remaining leaven was to be found in any Israelite territory for seven days. The animal was to be sacrificed in the evening, on the first day (the RSV and NIV render 'on the evening of the first day', but the Hebrew text does not support this). The intention clearly was to limit the observance to *one* evening. In this way the uniqueness of the Exodus experience would be maintained in the annual celebration.

5-6 A distinction is made in regard to the location of the sacrifice. It could not take place within any town gates of the inheritance that the LORD was giving them. Instead, the sacrifice was to take place at the central sanctuary at twilight (cf. Exod. 12:6, Heb. 'between the evenings'). The head of the family was to sacrifice it (*you,* second pers. sing., Exod. 12:5, 6), while the priest's duty was sprinkling the blood.

7-8 The slaughtered animal had to be cooked and eaten at the sanctuary. After the night-time feast the people would return to their tents. Clearly this did not mean 'return home' but go back to their temporary lodgings which they occupied during the festival week. A more detailed specification of verse 3 is given in verse 8. For six days they had to eat unleavened bread, and then the seventh day was a solemn, concluding festival day to the LORD. The word used here for this solemn assembly is first used in Leviticus 23:36 of the Feast of Tabernacles. The fact that this week ended with a solemn festival day in which no work was done makes the parallel with the week ending with the Sabbath much clearer.

(b) The Feast of Weeks (16:9-12)
This festival took place seven weeks after the day following the presentation of the first sheaf at the Passover. Hence the name of it in Greek was later called 'the fiftieth [day]', 'Pentecost'. It marked the completion of the harvest, and so it was primarily a feast of thanksgiving. Everyone had to give voluntarily in proportion to the blessings that God had bestowed upon them. This feast also served as a special means of providing for the Levites, the foreigners, the orphans and the widows. The motivation for keeping it was identified with the Passover (cf. verse 3 and 12).

9 Instructions for this feast (also called the 'Feast of Harvest' [Exod. 23:16] and the 'Day of First Fruits' [Num. 28:26]) have already been given with more detail in Exodus 23:16; 34:22; Leviticus 23:15-21; and Numbers 28:26-31. Those given here are less precise, but are intended to stress that this feast is also one to be celebrated at the central sanctuary. The seven weeks would be calculated from the second day of the Feast of Unleavened Bread (the first day was a Sabbath). The interval between Passover and Harvest festivals was to allow the pilgrims to return home, complete the harvest and then come back to the central sanctuary again.

10 The English term for 'Feast of Weeks' does not bring out the fact that this was another pilgrimage occasion. The Hebrew word *chag,* like its Arabic counterpart *hajj,* has that implication. There was no stipulated amount to be brought as an offering. Instead it was intended that there be a voluntary gift in accordance with the blessing of the LORD. The word the NIV renders 'in proportion' only occurs here in the Old Testament. In the context, and in comparison with verse 17, it means an equivalent measure.

11 The Feast of Weeks was another celebration at the central sanctuary, and it was meant to be a joyous occasion. With thanksgiving the people were to enjoy the good gifts which were the product of the land that the LORD their God had given them. It involved the whole family, including servants, and it was an occasion for sharing with the Levites and the most needy in the society (the alien, the fatherless and the widows).

12 The unhappy condition of Israel in Egypt was to be a marked contrast with the joyful celebration of this feast. The harshness of their slavery (cf. verse 3) was to be recalled as they celebrated. This reminder would emphasise the wonder of their redemption and reinforce the need for obedience to these decrees.

(c) The Feast of Tabernacles (16:13-15)

Almost six months after Passover, Israel had to live in temporary huts or tents for seven days. This was to remind them of their camping in the wilderness. It came at the end of the year's agricultural activities (September/October), and it was a happy occasion of communal thanksgiving. Shiloh was the centre of this festival during the period of the judges (Judg. 21:19-23), and it was doubtless there that Elkanah went for his annual visit (1 Sam. 1:3). Once more the location is emphasised (verse 15) as well as the fact that the needy had to be remembered too (verse 14). This is the only feast to which the prophets make reference when describing the ultimate ingathering into the kingdom of God (Zech. 14:16-19). It is chosen in that context because it celebrated the sovereign provision of God (in the wilderness, and annually in the harvest), it involved even the 'foreigner' or 'alien', and because it was the annual occasion in which the covenant was re-read in the hearing of the people (Neh. 8:14-18). Zechariah uses the concept to depict the Gentiles coming within that covenant and worshipping the King, the LORD Almighty (Zech. 14:16).

13-14 No precise dating is given here for the feast that marked the close of the agricultural year. The detailed legislation relating to it is given in Exodus 23:16; Leviticus 23:33-43; and Numbers 29:12-38. The celebration started on the fifteenth day of the seventh month (Lev. 23:34). The name 'tabernacles' comes from the Hebrew word *sukkot* that denotes the huts or booths which were used during this festival. The derivation of the custom was that by God's command the people were to reproduce the type of lifestyle they had experienced after coming out of Egypt (Lev. 23:39-43). Like the Feast of Weeks, this was a joyful time as they celebrated the 'ingathering' (as it is called in the legislation in Exod. 23:16) along with family, servants, Levites and the needy.

15 This third feast detailed in the chapter is also specifically a celebration at the central sanctuary. The seven days of festival are provided for because (Heb. *ki*) the LORD is the one who blesses the harvest and the manual work that they put into their agricultural pursuits. The final clause is best taken as a main sentence: 'therefore you shall rejoice'. Annually the people had to acknowledge from whom their blessings came and consequently a joyful spirit was to permeate their seven feast days.

(d) Summary (16:16-17)

16-17 The obligation on all the men in Israel is reinforced in these words. At least three times in the year they had to appear before the LORD at the central place of worship. That women were also present is clearly stated in verse 11 and 14. The repeated mention of the place which the LORD will choose in the legislation in this chapter reinforces the provisions of Chapter 12. A central sanctuary was going to be important for the unity of the nation. The basic principle of appearing before God was that no one could come empty-handed (see Exod. 23:15 for the same restriction). Bringing a gift was in itself an acknowledgment of the source of their bounty and of the LORD's liberality to his redeemed people.

5. The Fifth Commandment (16:18–18:22)
('Honour your father and your mother')

The focus now moves to the implications of the Fifth Commandment, and this section expounds the principles of the authority structures contained in it. That more than just honour and respect *to parents* was intended is shown by the fact that the commandment was given to *adults*, not *children*. There was a more general principle embodied in it of respect for all whom God placed over his people. In this section attention is given to institutions already in existence or yet to come which would manifest God's rule over the lives of his people. Israel was not a secular state, but rather one in which religious beliefs affected every aspect of life in society. The main topics to be covered are judges and judicial procedures, kingship, priesthood and prophecy.

(i) Righteous Judges (16:18-20)
God's law had to be administered with absolute fairness. All the judges and officials had to be impartial in their actions, and therefore no bribery could be tolerated. Appointment of judges had already taken place much earlier, in order to ease Moses' burden. Exodus 18:17-26 details the way in which the advice of Moses' father-in-law Jethro was followed and the judges were appointed to decide the simpler cases. Moses already referred to that in his opening speech recorded in this book (Deut. 1:9-18). The serious cases were still brought to Moses for adjudication. Now it is envisaged that judges will be appointed in every town. Probably selected from the elders, they were to act where the legal position was quite plain. For other cases, where judicial inquiry was necessary, a higher court was appointed (17:8-13). Breach of their provisions would bring about their failure to continue in the land, for they had to follow justice alone (verse 20, lit. 'justice, justice you shall follow').

18 The wording here is stronger than simply 'you should have judges and officials'. It is: 'you shall *appoint*', i.e., judicial appointments were to be made by a central authority. The distinction between 'judges' and 'officials' is not clear. It could be that the 'judges' made the decisions which were then carried out by the 'officials'. Or, the 'officials' could have carried out a wider role in ruling rather than just a restricted judicial function. In all towns the Israelites were to occupy, they were to appoint these officers. This new arrangement of towns forming the tribal divisions was to replace the previous one of appointment over tribal divisions. The task of the officials is administering 'true justice' (NEB; Heb. *mishpat tsedek*). God demanded that those responsible for the judicial procedure in the theocracy act like himself, for righteousness and justice were declared to be the foundation of his throne (Pss. 89:14; 97:2).

19 Three things are specified as forbidden. The first is that justice was not to be turned aside (Heb. *natah*). Justice was not to be denied to any one (cf. Amos 2:7 and 5:12). Secondly, there was to be no respecting of persons and allowing favouritism to influence judicial decisions. Thirdly, bribery was not to be permitted, again following the pattern of God himself (Deut. 10:17). The explanation given is almost the same as that in Exodus 23:8 with the exception of the replacement of 'wise' for 'those who see'.

20 The whole existence of the state depended on the right administration of justice. If the Israelites wanted to live and to inherit the land of Canaan then the appointed leaders had to pursue justice. The repetition of the word 'justice' has the effect of saying, 'Pursue justice exclusively'. The authority behind the operation of laws in Israel had to be the fact that they were divinely given.

(ii) The LORD the Sole Authority (16:21–17:1)
These verses may seem to be out of place in this section, but this is not the case. Moses mentions two transgressions that the judges must take special heed to avoid. First, the authority of the LORD must not be replaced by any idolatrous source of supposed revelation. To set up a Canaanite Asherah or pillar would be doing

what God hated (16:21, 22). Secondly, the judges had to be careful that any sacrifice in connection with the administration of justice came under the same rule as worship. No deformed animal was to be offered, for God had to be honoured in legal matters as much as in general worship (17:1).

21 This section, which is closely connected with both the preceding and the following sections, commences with a negative. This is followed by two more in the following verses, so that these three parallel those in verse 19. Here the prohibition relates to setting up any Asherah pole beside the LORD's altar. The Hebrew text has literally, 'Do not set an Asherah, any tree/wood, beside the altar ....' It is possible this means two separate, though closely connected, cult objects, or, as NIV has it, a designation of the Asherahs of whatever wood from which they are made. No object of Canaanite worship could be brought into such proximity to the LORD's altar, whether that altar was central or local.

22 In Canaanite religion, alongside the feminine Asherah, there was a pillar which was the corresponding masculine cult object. Like the Asherah, the pillar was not just an object of worship but also a means of obtaining verdicts in judicial procedures. In the Ugaritic texts Asherah is called 'Asherah of deposits, Asherah of oracles'. Israel was to have no other source of authority other than the LORD himself. The concluding phrase in this verse probably applies to both prohibitions. The use of the verb 'hate' is not so much a feeling but a choice. It is here a legal term (opposite to 'love') which can mean to 'reject' or 'break relations with' (cf. Judg. 11:7).

17:1 The third prohibition has reference to Canaanite worship practices. Clearly the offering of blemished animals was an acceptable practice with the Canaanites, but rejected by the LORD. Any animal with a bodily blemish or mutilation was unacceptable. This is declared to be an abomination to the LORD, using a term reserved for the LORD's condemnation of Canaanite actions (see 7:25; 12:31; 18:12; 22:5; 23:18 and 25:16).

(iii) Rules Affecting Judgement (17:2-7)
A concrete case is cited to illustrate how carefully justice is to be administered. The particular case is breach of the covenant by turning to idolatry.

2 The phrase, 'to do evil in the eyes of the LORD', is frequently used in the historical books of the Old Testament to show how God evaluates actions of men. In particular it is used of his displeasure with idolatry and it became a standard expression to describe departure from his norms (cf. 2 Kings 3:2, 8:18, 14:24, 17:17). To show the seriousness of the offence the technical phrase for violation of the covenant is used, while later (in verse 5) the phrase 'this detestable thing' (NIV 'this evil thing') is employed. The same subject is dealt with elsewhere in Deuteronomy in 4:15-24 and 13:1-18.

3 Entry into Canaan was to expose the Israelites to fresh attractions to idolatry, but to bow down to the heavenly bodies would mean worshipping what God had created rather than God himself. Such worship was in the forbidden zone (for fuller discussion on idolatrous worship, see the comment on 4:15-31).

4-5 However, if the information concerning the alleged crime came to the officials, whether by direct report or perhaps by circumstantial rumour, a full investigation was to be made of the offence. Gender was not to deter the administration of justice, for in the Hebrew text twice it is specified that an offending man or woman is to be executed. The expression 'this detestable thing' is a term which is used to describe many different kinds of things that were offensive to God. But it is used specifically of idolatry, so much so that 'detestable [thing]' can be used as a synonym for 'idol' (Isa. 44:19) or even for a specific pagan god (see the use of it in 2 Kings 23:13 where it refers to Milcom, the god of the Ammonites). There was to be no secret accusation or punishment, for the sentence of death was to be carried out by stoning at the city gate. This is where Stephen suffered martyrdom (Acts 7:58), and pre-eminently where Jesus, the holy and righteous one (Acts

3:14), suffered 'to make the people holy through his own blood' (Heb. 13:12).

6-7 The provision regarding having more than one witness re-inforces what has already been said in Numbers 35:30. There should be no irresponsible accusations, for in addition to having two witnesses, these witnesses must be prepared to take up the first stones. The intention is clearly to exclude malicious accusations and to ensure that witnesses were prepared to initiate the execution process.

(iv) The Supreme Tribunal (17:8-13)
Just as in the wilderness difficult cases came to Moses (Exod. 18:13-27), so also when Israel was settled in Canaan would there be provision of a supreme court. This was clearly not meant to be a court of appeal, but one to which cases too difficult for the local judges would be taken (verse 8).

8-9 The general principle is that if problem cases could not be solved satisfactorily at the local level, then they could be referred to a central tribunal which met at the central sanctuary. The types of cases which required referral to this tribunal were complex cases in which it was hard to determine whether an accident had taken place, or whether there was deliberate intent to cause harm or even death. The fact that the meeting place was the sanctuary emphasised that God himself was the supreme judge. Both priests and judges were to be involved.

10-11 The judgments of this central tribunal had to be accepted as from the LORD himself. In Exodus 21:6 and 22:8, 28 the judges are actually called 'gods' in the Hebrew text (cf. also the use of the same term for the Gentile rulers in Ps. 138:1). Covenant regulations require implicit obedience. Later in Israel's history the king would exercise this authority in settling difficult cases.

12-13 The illustration is now given of what should happen if there is wilful disregard of the judgment which has been made. Such action is contempt (notice the use of the noun in verse 12 and the verb from the same root in verse 13), and the flagrantly disobedient citizen is to be put to death. This was so that anyone else who had thoughts of flouting the decisions of the tribunal would be warned concerning the consequences of being contemptuous.

(v) The Law of the King (17:14-20)

Ultimately the time would come when Israel would desire a king. That desire would not be in conflict with the fact that the LORD is the great king, nor out of keeping with the earlier references to kingship (see Gen. 17:6, 16; 35:11; 49:10). Just as in the extra-biblical treaties where the choice of a king by a vassal state was regulated, so Israel had to follow divinely prescribed rules. The coming king must be from within the covenant nation itself and be designated as king by the LORD (verse 15). The regulations here are another assertion of the principle that the whole of life had to be governed by God's covenant provisions.

14 The felt need for a king would arise in the land that the LORD was giving his people Israel. When Israel had taken possession of it and become established there, then the question of the appointment of a king would arise. The motivation would be that Israel would want to be like the other nations around her. This was precisely the reason given by the people in the time of Samuel when they requested a king (1 Sam. 8:20).

15 The first of four basic conditions relating to the king is given in this verse. God must designate the king, and he could only be appointed from within Israel. This ruled out any non-Israelite coming to the throne. A similar provision is made in respect to the office of prophet (Deut. 18:15).

16 The second condition is that the king must not multiply horses, i.e., horses for warfare. If Israel really trusted in the LORD then there would be no need for vast military preparations. Other nations put their trust in their battle array, but Israel was called to trust in the LORD (Pss. 20:7; 147:10-11).

17 The third condition is that the king must not follow the practice of heathen kings in acquiring a harem or great riches. Both would lead away from obedience to the LORD. The violation by Solomon of these provisions stands out in later history (see 1 Kings 10:26-29; 11:1-8).

18 The fourth condition is that the king had to have his own copy of the covenant document, just as with secular treaties when each vassal king had his own copy of the treaty document. While this could refer just to this section on kingship, it was more likely that it refers to the whole text of Deuteronomy. This copy was to be made from the official copy kept by the priests. How carefully this provision was kept is unclear, but certainly at the coronation of Joash, Jehoiada put the crown on his head, presented him with a copy of the covenant, and proclaimed him king (2 Kings 11:12).

19-20 The purpose of this regulation was twofold. On the one hand, the covenant was to give constant direction to the king in his personal life. On the other hand, it was to have practical application to the life of the nation. The effect of reading on the king's own life was to produce deeper reverence for the LORD and to preserve him from pride. Towards the nation the effect would be that the king would observe all the requirements of the law, not turning to right or left (a common Old Testament expression to denote not turning from a straight path). The threat is given that disobedience to this requirement would lead to judgment in the form of the removal of the king and his successors from the throne of Israel.

(vi) Priests and Levites (18:1-8)
This section deals in summary form with the provision for the Levites. The details have to be read alongside the far fuller provisions set out in Numbers 18, where in addition to the matter of their support, the duties of the priests are made clear (especially verses 1-8). Reference has already been made in Deuteronomy 12:12, 19 and 14:27-29 to the provision for the Levites. Once more regulations are being made for a new situation that will arise

because of settlement in the land. In this section it is the rights of the Levites that are stressed.

1-2 A distinction is made between the whole tribe of Levi and the priests. The latter had to come from among the Levites, but not all the Levites were automatically to serve as priests. The text suggests that the non-priestly Levites had a subordinate role to fulfil. The fact that the Levites had no territorial possession (they were excluded from the tribal allocation of land), was no disadvantage to them. They were to live from the special offerings made to the LORD, and from the fact that they had the LORD himself as 'their inheritance'. This phrase comes from Numbers 18:20 and has already been used in Deuteronomy 10:9. The special relationship they had with the LORD and the responsibilities they were given more than compensated for the lack of land. However, it is clear that some priests did own land (see Jer. 32:7ff.) and even the present passage suggests that a priest could benefit from the sale of family property (verse 8).

3-4 This list has to be read in conjunction with Leviticus 7:32-34, Numbers 18:11-12, and Deuteronomy 14:22-29. It is more detailed than the other passages as it sets out some of the things that the Levites were to receive from the three yearly tithe. It is not clear how much in addition they would receive, though they could also produce some of their own needs from the restricted pasture lands that they were allocated around their towns (Num. 35:2-8).

5 The Levites were not acting on their own initiative but because of God's choice of the family (the Heb. text has the pronoun 'him', whereas NIV inserts 'them'). Just as with kings (Deut. 17:15) and with prophets (Deut. 18:15), so were the Levites acting because God had set his favour on the family line. Their task was to stand and minister, i.e. serve at the place of worship, on behalf of the people.

6-8 Provision is made for the case when a Levite desires to come to the central sanctuary. No restriction is to be placed on him, and he is not be discriminated against as he takes his place among his fellow Levites. He is to receive an equal share with them, even though he might have money that came from the sale of ancestral properties (verse 8). The tasks at the sanctuary are not specified, but clearly the Levites had a teaching role to fulfil as well as functioning at the altar (see Deut. 33:10; Mal. 2:3-6).

(vii) The Voice of Prophecy (18:9-22)
One of the greatest dangers that Israel would face in Canaan would be to try and seek messages from the LORD in false ways. The Canaanites had a variety of practices that were used to direct them in decision making. But these practices were simply various forms of the occult, and as such were detestable to God, who was going to provide a special way of declaring his will to the people.

9 Once again mention is made of the fact that possession of the land of Canaan was to be a divine gift to Israel. Upon entry there, Israel was to be confronted with practices which were 'detestable' in God's sight. Other things already mentioned in Deuteronomy which came within this category were idolatry (7:25), human sacrifice (12:31), eating animals that were ritually unclean (14:3-8) and offering defective animals (17:1). No imitation by Israel of these detestable practices was permissible.

10-11 The list in these verses is the most comprehensive summary given in the Old Testament of practices relating to sorcery and divination. The first one ('sacrifices his son or his daughter in the fire') appears to have been more than simply child sacrifice. Twice elsewhere it is referred to in connection with divination (2 Kings 17:17; 21:6) and as the expression occurs here along with other terms that clearly fall within the category of divination, it must be given that meaning here also. It amounted to some form of trial by ordeal or magical test. It is linked with worship of the Ammonite God Molech in 2 Kings 23:10 and Jeremiah 32:35. The next three practices relate to various forms of divination. 'Divination' could be carried out by means of various devices, such as shaking out arrows from a quiver (Ezek. 21:21), while 'sorcery' involved reading signs (such as the configuration of the clouds) to achieve a message or create apparitions. The person who interpreted 'omens' used devices like a cup as a means of revelation (cf. Gen. 44:5), or by observing the actions of others (1 Kings 20:32-33). The next two practices were concerned with some form of magic. 'Witchcraft' was probably carried out by cutting up herbs to make a drink, or by other signs intended to prevent danger. 'Spells' could be cast to try and bind people to a particular course of action, with the use of curses to impel them to act in a certain way. The three final terms relate to spiritism. The 'medium' attempted to communicate with the dead, and references elsewhere in the Old Testament suggest that they made strange sounds (Isa. 29:4). The early Greek translations call them ventriloquists. The most obvious biblical example of a medium is the witch of Endor (1 Sam. 28:3-19). The 'spiritist' was a person who claimed supernatural knowledge and so asserted dominance over others. The final term relating to the one who 'consults the dead' seems from Isaiah 8:19 to be a general term for those who attempted to achieve messages from the dead.

12-13 The judgment of verse 9 is repeated in an emphatic way. All these practices were abominable to the LORD, and were placed in the same category as idols (see 7:25-26). Moreover, the abominations were the reason why the Canaanites were being dispossessed of the land, and the time was fast approaching when the sin of the Amorites would be full (see Gen. 15:16). In contrast, Israel had to remain 'blameless' before the LORD. In this context blameless means 'upright' or 'lacking in defilement'. Entanglement in any of these practices was a contradiction of Israel's status as a holy people to the LORD (7:6).

14 Israel had to seek God's will in his appointed way. Those who were his children had to follow his ways rather than imitate the children of false gods. The manner in which it is stated draws attention once more to the separation of God's people from the Canaanites.

15 In contrast to heathen ways, God was going to provide what the people had requested back at Horeb. They had wanted someone to stand between themselves and God and declare his message. Now God was going to give them an on-going source of knowledge of himself, mediated to them by the prophets. The Hebrew word for prophet is probably borrowed from one of the other Semitic languages, and its meaning must come from its use within the Old Testament. Its use in Exodus 4:10-17 concerning the appointment of Aaron to speak on Moses' behalf, shows that its basic meaning was 'spokesman'. The qualification that the prophet would be like Moses is important. Future prophets would have to live godly lives, show the same faithfulness in ministry, and carry out their task with the same devotion and self-sacrifice as Moses. The closing chapter of this book recognises that no other prophet could exactly fulfil Moses' role (Deut. 34:10-12). Those called by God would be from within Israel ('from among your own brothers'), safeguarding the people from Canaanite practices. Attentive listening to the prophets' messages was equivalent to listening to God himself. In later times, when Israel broke the covenant bond, one of the punishments was the absence of a prophetic spokesman (1 Sam. 3:1; Ps. 74:9).

16-17 When they gathered at Horeb the people were afraid, for they feared they would die (Exod. 20:18-21). They did not want to hear God speaking directly to them, or to be confronted with fire again. Instead they wanted a mediator to stand between themselves and God. This would be particularly so when Moses and Joshua were dead. Coming generations would need an individual or an institution to carry on the task of conveying God's revelation, and the desire of the people met with God's approval.

18-19 The promise is given of a spokesman (or spokesmen) whom God would raise up to speak in his name. Such a person had to come from within Israel, and would fulfil a role similar to that occupied by Moses at that time. His messages would not be original, for they were to be given to him by God. This meant that any rebellion against such messages was to be treated seriously, and God himself would call to account those refusing to listen to *his* words (cf. the allusion to verse 19 in Luke 11:50-51).

20 So serious was false prophecy in God's eyes, that anyone who attempted to speak in the name of some other god, a false god, was to be executed. In making such announcements a false prophet was assuming authority which he did not have.

21-22 In the minds of the people the question would quickly arise, 'How can we tell if someone is really God's prophet?' These verses assume that the person is a prophet speaking in God's name and that he makes predictions which are verifiable in his lifetime. If the predictions do not come to pass, then that prophet is not a genuine spokesman for the LORD, and the congregation need not fear him. This is an assertion in other words of what Balaam had earlier said: 'God is not a man, that he should lie, nor a son of man, that he should change his mind. Does he speak and then not act? Does he promise and not fulfil?' (Num. 23:19).

This passage (verses 9-22) relates to both the succession of prophets in the Old Testament and to the coming of Jesus as the great prophet. Taking up the role of a prophet did not depend upon coming from a family of prophets (cf. Amos 7:14). Rather, it was by God's call that a person assumed that function. The apostle Peter made it plain that Jesus was the ultimate fulfilment of this passage (Acts 3:22-23).

6. The Sixth Commandment (19:1–22:8)
('You shall not murder')

All the institutions of Israel were regulated by God's rule over his people. It is not surprising, therefore, that regulations affecting the true administration of justice should be set out in detail. In particular this section as an application of principles behind the Sixth Commandment has a broader focus than 'murder'. Probably both murder and manslaughter are involved in the prohibition in that commandment. Some of the provisions in this section are given briefly, and seemingly without a great deal of connection with each other. However, in this chapter there is an expanded reference to the places of asylum and the law affecting witnesses, separated by a reference in verse 14 to the prohibition of altering boundary markers and so defrauding a neighbour.

(i) The Cities of Refuge and Legal Procedures (19:1-13)

Though the cities discussed in this section are not called cities of refuge here (cf. Num. 35:6ff.), clearly they are to be identified with the earlier provision first stated in Exodus 21:13-14. Numbers 35 contains a fuller statement of the regulation. At the end of the historical prologue in chapter 4 of this book, Moses' appointment of the three cities of refuge on the eastern bank of the Jordan is mentioned (4:41-43; Bezer, Ramoth-Gilead and Golan).

1-3 These opening verses specify the setting aside of three more cities on the west bank of the Jordan when the conquest is completed. Once more stress is placed on God's provision of the land for his people (verses 1-2), and the fact that Israel was to occupy houses and towns that had been Canaanite possessions (see 6:10-11). The principle stated in verse 3 is clearly that the cities had to be evenly distributed and with ready access to them. Just as provision had already been made for decentralised slaughter of animals (12:15), so now the right of asylum is made possible away from the central altar. That the cities ultimately set aside were Levitical cities and that the practice was closely tied to the life of the high priest (Num. 35:25) highlighted the fact that these cities were really extensions of the altar. Joshua 20:1-9 spells out the actual allocation of the cities, when Kedesh, Shechem and Kirjath Arba (Hebron) were added to the three cities already designated east of the Jordan.

4-7 The intention of the provision is set out. It did not apply to a murderer, but to someone who unintentionally caused a death. The fact that in the expression 'the man who kills another' the same Hebrew verb occurs as used in the Sixth Commandment shows that the English word 'murder' is too restricted a translation. Clearly the Hebrew verb could include both murder and manslaughter, as the elaboration of the principle shows in this context. The illustration is given (verse 5) of a wood-gatherer, whose axe head flies off and kills a bystander. In this case there was no prior hatred of the victim, and so the offender could flee to one of the appointed cities. This law enabled such a person to have a fair trial, and prevented 'the avenger of blood' from taking the law into his own hands. This term could refer either to a close relative or to an appointed representative of the elders. The lost life of a relative had to be paid for with the life of the one who had killed. Numbers 35:22-28 sets out the regulations which would apply in the case of accidental manslaughter. The NIV phrase 'without malice aforethought' (verse 4) is an English legal term to describe the absence of predetermined thought to commit a particular crime, especially that of murder.

8-10 Further allocation of cities of refuge was to be permitted if the territory occupied by Israel was enlarged. This assumes that the six for which provision had already been made (three on the east and three on the west of the Jordan) would be insufficient. However, there is no recorded evidence that the number of the cities of refuge was ever raised to nine. Perhaps the explanation lies in the way the provision is phrased here: 'If the Lord your God enlarges your territory ... and gives you the whole land ... because you carefully follow all these laws I command you today ... then you are to set aside three more cities'. The provision for these three additional cities depended upon full obedience by the people, and seeing that this never occurred, the provision was never put into effect.

11-13 These final verses dealing with the cities of refuge make it plain that there was to be no abuse of this right of asylum. A murderer could flee to a city of refuge but the elders of his own city could extradite him, so that justice could follow at the hands of the avenger of blood. In this example there was a predetermined plot to commit murder, yet justice had to be done. The murderer could find temporary safety in a city of refuge, and before he could be convicted at least two witnesses had to come forward (Num. 35:30). Human sentiment had to be set aside (cf. the use of the expression 'show no pity' in 7:16 and 13:8), and the death of the murderer was regarded as a cleansing ritual for the land which had been defiled by the shedding of innocent blood (Num. 35:33). The only examples we have of the practice of asylum in the Old Testament are recorded in 1 Kings 1:50-53 and 2:28-34, where the place of refuge is the altar and not within a city of refuge. Perhaps this way of seeking asylum is presupposed in the references in the Psalms to God as the 'horn of my salvation' and to the words of Jesus in Matthew 23:35.

(ii) Tampering with Evidence (19:14)

14 Inserted between two longer provisions is this brief reference to removing a neighbour's boundary marker. In Assyria there were large stones which set out the boundaries of properties allocated by the king, and on which curses were inscribed (cf. Deut. 27:17), though these stones were not actually situated on the land. Each Israelite's property was to be marked, and no removal of the markers could be permitted. The land had been gifted by the LORD, the great King, and so such an offence was in reality against him. A conspicuous example of breach of this provision is the case involving Ahab and Naboth (1 Kings. 21:1-26; 22:37-38). What made Ahab's crime so serious was that his action was intended to rob Naboth not only of his land but of his 'inheritance'. The law here is repeated in a very similar form in Proverbs 22:28 and 23:10, and it is clear that other breaches of the ordinance occurred (Hos. 5:10).

(iii) False Witnesses (19:15-21)

15 No sentence could be imposed unless two or three witnesses came forward. Numbers 35:30 specified that capital punishment could only take place if there were witnesses. This law is also referred to earlier in Deuteronomy in regard to murder (see the commentary on 17:6-7), but now the same rule is applied more generally.

16-20 If a false witness turned up, then this was one of the difficult cases which had to be referred to the central court (see 17:8-13).

Making the disputants stand 'in the presence of the LORD' is defined by the phrase which follows: 'before the priests and the judges who are in office at the time'. These officers were representatives of the LORD, and they had to investigate the crime and carry out any penalty. After thorough investigation such a false witness was to suffer the same judgment he sought on the other man.

21 Once again the people are reminded that mere human sentiment had to be set aside, for the law of retaliation had to apply – an eye for an eye, a tooth for a tooth (see Exod. 21:23ff.). That law was intended to ensure that the punishment fitted the crime, and did not go beyond it. In other words, it prevented harsh vengeance and guaranteed justice. The law of retaliation comes into Jesus' Sermon on the Mount (Matt. 5:38-42). As with the other contrasts in that chapter ('You have heard ... but I tell you') our Lord was not contradicting the Mosaic law. He was correcting the legalistic interpretation which the Pharisees had adopted. In this particular case he is setting aside the idea of unlimited personal vengeance. A Christian is encouraged to suffer loss rather than act in a vindictive manner.

(iv) The Wars of the Lord (20:1-20)
This section on warfare has to be set against a wider background, as the opening verse indicates, and it must also be linked with other laws about warfare which follow in succeeding chapters (21:10-13, 23:9-14, and 24:5). When God brought his people out of Egypt, it was proclaimed in the Song of Moses that 'the LORD is a warrior; the LORD is his name' (Exod. 15:3). He manifested his mighty, saving power in all the events surrounding the exodus. The Song of Moses stresses the fact that God was able by his might to deliver, and that he did so to fulfil his covenant love (Exod. 15:13).

This deliverance out of the slavery of Egypt was the precursor of other battles during the wilderness journey and the approach to Canaan. The earlier historical prologue in this book made it plain that the battles were not Israel's but the LORD's (see 1:30, 42; 2:24-25; 3:2-3). It is not surprising, then, that a record was kept of the Wars of the LORD (Num. 21:14). If the rest of that verse depicts God as the divine warrior sweeping through Moab, even greater point is added, as the Israelites were being reminded yet again that their victories in battle were really because they were the LORD's battles.

Two other points need stressing. The first is that going into battle was the LORD's decision. If the people went contrary to his expressed will and entered into battle on their own, disaster followed (see Deut. 1:42-45 for the account of the defeat at the hand of the Amorites). Secondly, the fact that the spoil taken in battle was completely dedicated to God (Deut. 7:24-26) highlighted once again the fact that the battle was the LORD's, and he had the right of possession of the things captured. Achan's infringement of the rule led to paralysis of the army when the invasion of Canaan was underway (Jos. 7:1-12).

(a) Preparation for Battle (20:1-4)

1 Past experience should have taught Israel the basic lesson that victory could only be achieved by the LORD. What happened in the Exodus from Egypt set the pattern, and Israel was to remember constantly what God had done for his people. If God called them to battle, then fear was not to dominate their thinking. By 'presence of the LORD' is probably meant the ark of the covenant, the symbol of the divine presence (see Num. 10:35; Jos. 3:1-6; 6:1-14, 1 Sam. 4:3-8).

2-4 The role of the priest at the time of battle is significant. He had the task of addressing the army and encouraging them in their God-given mission. He himself was not to accompany them into battle, but rather he had to consecrate them to the mission to which the Great King had called them. The words he spoke were intended to encourage the troops with the reassurance that God's presence should banish apprehension or fear as they faced battle.

(b) Exemption from Service (20:5-9)

Not until much later under David was there a standing army in Israel. At this earlier period there were no professional soldiers, though there were officers who appointed commanders (verse 9). In preparing for battle certain regulations had to be fulfilled, including observance of ritual laws (Deut. 23:9-11). Also the quality of the army mattered more than its size, if God's power was to be acknowledged as the real source of victory. This truth was to be reinforced powerfully in the story of Gideon and the three hundred men (Judg. 7).

5-7 The first three exemptions all have humanitarian motives behind them. They all point to the fact that it was God's intention that his people enjoy life in the land he was giving them. If their trust was in him, then military concerns were not to be a major concern. The first case is that of a man who has built a house but not yet 'lived' in it (verse 5). While various English versions use the verb 'dedicate' here in this verse, there is no available evidence that it was an Israelite custom to dedicate a new house. A builder of a new house should have the opportunity to live in it, rather than dying in battle without ever experiencing the pleasure of life with his family in the new home. The second case involves someone planting a new vineyard (verse 6). In this example the exemption from military service would extend for several years. After a vineyard was planted, it was left for three years without reaping a crop. Then a year of dedication to the LORD followed, before the fruit could be eaten in the fifth year (see Lev. 19:23-25). Until that stage was reached that man was not to be conscripted into the army. The final humanitarian example (verse 7) is the case of a man betrothed to a woman but not yet married. He is to be allowed to stay at home and marry. There was a further extension of this application in that a newly-married man was given at least a year at home (24:5).

8 The final exemption falls into a different category. While the previous ones had mainly humanitarian motives behind them, this one had a psychological one. The priests had already encouraged the people not to be fainthearted or afraid (verse 3), but the officers were to further trim the ranks of those who lacked absolute commitment to the LORD's battles. The timid and fainthearted could easily cause disaffection in the ranks, and so the opportunity was given of returning home. Everyone going into battle had to be fully convinced that the LORD was going to give the victory. The principle here was utilised in the time of Gideon, when the opportunity was given for the fearful (using the same word as here) to turn back before the army went into battle with the Midianites (Judg. 7:1-3).

9 Clearly there was no standing army at that time. The officers may well have been drawn from the ranks of tribal officials, and one of their tasks was to appoint additional leaders for the impending battle.

(c) Treatment of Enemy Cities (20:10-18)

A distinction was to be made in the treatment of enemy cities. Those outside the boundaries of the promised land could be offered an opportunity to enter into a covenant arrangement with Israel. However those cities which fell within the boundaries of Israelite territory were under the ban imposed by God, and the army was to destroy them totally.

10-11 A foreign city was to be offered the opportunity to enter into a covenant arrangement, and for its people to become vassals. To 'make an offer of peace' (verse 10) was the same as making a covenant proposal, as later Old Testament passages show (cf. 2 Sam. 10:19; 1 Kings 20:18; 1 Chron. 12:17-18). If such a city accepted the proposal (Heb. lit. 'answer in peace'), then the covenant was established and the people in it were forced to give involuntary, unpaid labour to their new masters. The application of this regulation is seen in the Israelites dealing with the Gibeonites. They tricked the Israelites into thinking that they were a distant city (Josh. 9:3-6) and so they made peace with them. The NIV obscures the Hebrew idioms in Joshua 9:15. Other translations such as the NKJV show that making peace was equivalent to making a covenant: 'So Joshua made peace with them, and made a covenant with them to let them live ....' The incident which follows in Joshua 10:1-15 shows further evidence of the nature of this treaty of peace when Israel came to the rescue of the Gibeonites. They were the servants (i.e. the vassals) of Israel and they had a right to appeal for help (verse 6).

12-15 If the offer of a covenant was refused, then the city was to be attacked. When God gave them victory over such a city the men were to be killed, but the women and children were to be spared. The goods plundered from it were not to be destroyed, but available for use by the Israelites (verse 14). The point is reinforced in verse 15 that distant nations were to be treated in this way, whereas a different rule was to apply to the nearby nations, such as the six nations noted in verse 17.

16-18 Within the territory allotted to Israel no pity was to be shown and total destruction was to occur (see comment on Deut. 7:1-6). No temptation was to remain which could allure Israel into practising the detestable practices of the Gentile nations and consequently bringing them into a position of sinning against their God. The ultimate judgment of God on sin and unbelief applied quite logically in the process of the conquest of the promised land.

19-20 To find instructions regarding preservation of fruit trees in time of war in this place in the book has struck many commentators as strange. However, this does not appear strange when we realise once more that this section (20:1–22:30) is an exposition of the Sixth Commandment. Human life lived under God's lordship is in view, and these laws regarding trees fit in admirably with the humanitarian concerns expressed earlier in this chapter. There is also a marked contrast expressed here between current practice in the Near East and the standard expected from God's people. During a long siege there would be the temptation to denude the area of all trees in order to facilitate the building of ramps, ladders and other military equipment. Non-fruit trees could be used for these purposes, but the fact that a battle was raging could not permit unlimited destruction of all trees. God had given the land for the sustenance of human life and even in times of acute need the natural environment had to be respected. The rhetorical question, 'Are the trees of the field people, that you should besiege them?' (verse 19) adds even greater point to the law. A city composed of sinful humans could be attacked, but innocent trees were to be left to provide food for current and future generations. Later in Israel's history the Israelites (at God's command through Elisha) did destroy trees in violation of this provision (2 Kings 3:19, 25).

(v) God's Law in Life and Death (21:1-23)
This chapter continues some of the general themes of the preceding sections. Here there is concentration on the rights of individuals, and procedures are set out for action where rights have been abused. The chapter opens and closes with reference to the land which God was giving them (verses 1 and 23), a theme which comes up constantly throughout the book. The readers had to be reminded often that they were God's people living in God's land.

(a) A Case of Unsolved Murder (21:1-9)
A special provision existed when a murder was committed by an unknown assailant. The elders from the nearest town had an obligation to carry out a ritual which in effect was a mock execution. This involved an animal and objects which were considered ritually clean and suitable for this ceremony.

1-2 The case described here could either be murder or manslaughter. Presumably the slain body was found by someone passing by who then reported their find. Representatives of the central authority (elders and judges) would measure the distance to the nearest town, which would then accept responsibility for the purification ritual. The need for purification is made clear by reference to the fact that the crime occurred in the promised land, 'the land the LORD your God is giving you to possess'. It was holy land, sacred soil, and therefore cleansing of the land had to follow.

3-4 The language used in these verses makes it plain that this is not the description of a sacrifice. It is the village elders, not the priests, who carry out the procedure. The word used for the killing of the heifer (Heb. 'araf) is not the normal word used for slaying a sacrificial animal (Heb. *shachat*). Specific stipulations were set out for the ritual. The heifer used was to be one which had not been used as a work animal, and therefore it was 'holy'. The place was a rural valley, unused for crops, and which had a flowing stream passing through it.

5 It is unclear what role the priests played in the ritual (see comments on verse 7). However, just as they were involved in passing judgment in difficult cases (17:8-9), so they were required to participate in this type of case as well.

6-9 Actions and words combine to teach the principles behind the ritual. The breaking of the neck of the heifer showed that the crime deserved punishment. The washing of the hands signified purification and it was also a declaration that the community were innocent. It is unclear who were to make the declaration, but certainly the words in verse 7 allow for it to be done by the priests. The Hebrew text simply says: 'they shall answer'. It is possible that the priests made the declaration and the elders repeated it or responded to it. It was a declaration that they had no part in the crime, and a plea that God, who had shown marvellous grace to Israel when he redeemed them from Egypt, would again act in grace towards them. Probably also the idea was implicit that if the whole nation was punished, then God's purpose in bringing them out of Egypt would be nullified. While it is not specified, presumably if the person who committed the offence was ever found he would be dealt with in accordance with Deuteronomy 19:11-13.

(b) Marrying a Prisoner of War (21:10-14)

At first sight it appears strange that this section comes within an exposition of the Sixth Commandment. It does, however, serve to link the earlier regulations dealing with warfare and homicide (20:1-20; 21:1-9) with the following section concerning wives and children. Moreover it is related to general questions affecting life (cf. verse 14 which in Heb. says that the wife can be let go 'for her life', and the later reference to the execution of recalcitrant children, verse 21).

10-11 Further provision is made in the case of foreign cities, i.e. those outside of Canaan (cf. the earlier comments on 20:10-18). If the LORD gave his people victory in battle, a girl taken as a prisoner of war could be chosen as a wife.

12-13 Four conditions are set out before the marriage could take place. The girl's hair was to be cut, as were her nails. She had to change out of the clothes she was wearing when captured, and she had to be allowed a month to mourn her parents. All these things represented a break with her past life. As the hair symbolised life, it had to be cut (perhaps not shaved completely but merely trimmed), while nails of hands and feet were to be cut as a sign of purification (cf. 2 Sam. 19:24). The removal of the old clothes can be compared with the washing of clothes after uncleanness (see Lev. 11 and 15) and those of the Levites before their installation to office (Num. 8:7). The period of mourning is also connected with her new status. She had to mark the break with her old life by observing a month of mourning (Heb. 'a month of days') so that she was demonstrably separated from her previous heathen life. Mention of her parents seems to imply that this is a case of an unmarried woman still living with her parents.

14 Such a wife had to be afforded certain rights should divorce take place. Doubtless the usual divorce procedures set out in chapter 24:1-4 would apply. Though such a wife had once been a captive or slave, yet she could no longer be treated like one. No more could she be sold as a piece of property, but she had the right to go wherever she desired.

(c) The Rights of the FirstBorn (21:15-17)
Again it may seem at first that this section is unrelated to the sections dealing with warfare. But loss of men through death in battle often resulted in polygamy, with all its resultant problems. Here the main concern is over the father's favouritism displaying itself in displacing the firstborn son. For the first time in the Bible the principle is stated that a firstborn had to be given double inheritance rights. Presumably this meant that if there were seven

sons, the estate was divided into eight portions, and the firstborn son received two of them.

15-17 The case described here is probably an extreme example, in which one wife is loved and another unloved. When the husband came to designate inheritance (equivalent to making a will) he could not show favouritism to the son of the wife he loved. Instead he had to follow the normal practice and so allocate to the oldest son of the unloved wife his rights as the firstborn. The reason given for this is that the firstborn was 'the first issue of his [procreative] power'. That is, the firstborn son was a sign of a man's ability to produce children, and so that son was given special recognition when it came to property distribution.

(d) A Rebellious Son (21:18-21)

The reference to the death penalty (verse 21) brings this section within the wider grouping of passages relating to the Sixth Commandment. It sets out the extreme penalty in the case of an utterly rebellious adolescent child, though there is no evidence in the Old Testament that this penalty was ever applied.

18-19 Several important principles are given in these verses. The power of parents was limited in the case of an adolescent who blatantly disobeyed, with them not having the right of life and death. They could not take the law into their own hands, and they could only take their son to the elders after parental rebuke and discipline had been disregarded. The expressions 'take' and 'bring' suggest that the son in question was still an adolescent, not an independent adult.

20-21 The parents had to make their accusation before the elders, adding now the further charge that the son was a profligate and a drunkard. These two sins are brought together elsewhere (cf. Prov. 23:20-21), and they mark out the self-indulgence of the offender. The crime of such a person was so serious, because it was not just disobedience against the parents but against the whole covenant structure of Israel. If it was allowed to continue covenant life would be threatened. Hence execution was the prescribed penalty in order that the evil might be purged (for the use of this expression see 13:5; 17:7, 12; 19:19; 21:9; 22:21, 24; 24:7). In addition, such a penalty would serve as a strong deterrent for any other rebellious youths.

(e) Accursed of God (21:22-23)

22-23 The closing verses of the chapter do not deal with crucifixion, but impaling on a tree after execution. This was common in a variety of forms in the Near East in biblical times, and there are various cases in the Old Testament (see Jos. 8:29; 10:26; 2 Sam. 4:12; Lam. 5:12). This supplementary act was to make a public spectacle of the executed criminal in order to serve as a deterrent to others. However, speedy burial had to take place of such an accursed body lest the land be defiled. In Galatians 3:13 Paul quotes this verse in which he declares that Christ became a curse for us. Just as the dead person is called 'God's accursed' here in Deuteronomy 21:23, so Christ hung on the cross as a condemned and executed criminal. In that way he was publicly displayed as being the curse of God for our sins. The references to Jesus' death by Peter in Acts 5:30 and 10:39 are probably also allusions to this passage.

(vi) Humanitarian Acts (22:1-8)

The opening part of this chapter (verses 1-12) contains a variety of laws applying both general principles and specific obligations. Nowhere in Deuteronomy is the command 'You shall love your neighbour as yourself' (Lev. 19:18) repeated expressly, but clearly the spirit of that command pervades so many of the general laws in this book.

There are two difficulties about this section.

1. At times it is hard to see the connection that exists between various laws. There is a sudden transition from laws dealing with helping a brother (verses 1-4) to transvestism (verse 5), from humanitarian laws affecting the protection of mother birds (verses 6-7) and building protective parapets around the house

roof (verse 8), to regulations relating to planting, ploughing and clothing (verses 9-12). In general they appear to be further extensions of the principle of life embedded in the Sixth Commandment.

2. In regard to several of the provisions it is hard to be sure of the basic reason underlying them. They are stated in few words and the cryptic form has no explanation attached to it.

The opening verses amplify what was given earlier in Exodus 23:4-5. Not only had the legal requirements to be met, but the spirit of them had to be applied to general cases in which a brother's property (here especially his animals) might suffer loss. The word 'brother' clearly does not mean 'neighbour', but rather 'covenant brother', 'a fellow Israelite'. To take it in this way is essential, as verse 2 specifies that the brother may live a long way off, or be unknown. Covenant life had to express both love to God and to one's fellows. The regulations here go beyond Exodus 23:4-5 in provision for care of a lost animal (verse 2), in specifying other property in addition to animals (verse 3), and providing help to a neighbour in difficulty (verse 4). The repeated 'Do not ignore it' (verses 1, 3) required intervention in situations rather than absolving oneself of responsibility for the needs of others (cf. the actions of the priest and the Levite in Jesus' parable of the Good Samaritan, Luke 10:30-35).

5 For men and women to interchange clothing (or other things associated with either sex) may seem comparatively harmless. But this involves an attempt to blur the basic sexual differences built into God's created order, as well as having overtones of other practices that could not be tolerated. In the ancient world such interchange of clothing was associated both with types of homosexuality and also with particular forms of heathen worship. That these latter aspects are in view seems confirmed by the way in which the practice is described as an abomination, linking it with other detestable Canaanite religious practices (see Deut. 7:25 and 18:12).

6-7 The case given in these verses extends God's care over his creation to other than domestic animals. While intrinsically there would be nothing wrong in taking both young birds and the mother, yet to do so would be an abuse of God's provisions for future human food needs. Also to do so may reflect a disrespect for motherhood in general, and so be related to the Fifth Commandment (Deut. 5:16), especially as the explanation is the same in both cases ('so that it may go well with you and you may have a long life'). Thoughtful provision had to be made for the food supply of future generations.

8 The provision concerning the building of a parapet around the roof shows the general concern for human life. So much of family life was conducted on the roof (including entertainment) that this was both a wise and a necessary precaution for the protection of people against possible injury or death. Other Near Eastern law codes (such as the earlier Code of Hammurabi) had similar provisions. No mention is made of penalties for breach of this provision, but the similar law in Exodus 21:33-34 makes payment of compensation obligatory.

7. The Seventh Commandment (22:9–23:14)
('You shall not commit adultery')
It is only in 22:22 that reference is made to adultery in the whole of this section, yet the focus is on expounding the seventh commandment: 'You shall not commit adultery'. This sin was known as the 'Great Sin' in the ancient Near East (see the comment on Deut. 5:18). The marriage relationship is frequently used throughout the Old Testament to illustrate the covenant bond between God and his people. To prove false to that bond was a form of adultery, and the people had to aim at keeping themselves from any action that resembled adultery. Hence instructions are given regarding inconsistent behaviour that would show that the unique bond with the LORD had been broken.

(i) Prohibitions for Farming and Clothing (22:9-12)
A religious reason is given for the prohibition in verse 9, while

the background for others might also lie in practices that were common among the surrounding peoples. Some of the rules are difficult to explain because of the lack of stated reasons for their observance, but is probable that several factors are involved. This would mean that the major reason for their presence here in Deuteronomy would be to assert the distinctiveness of God's people even when it came to agricultural practices and clothing. A further reason may well be that these practices served as a teaching function in Israel. That is to say, in observing them the Israelites would have constant reminders that they were different from other nations, and just as they kept distinct certain things in life, so they had to keep themselves distinct as a holy people to the LORD.

9 Just as Israel was the LORD's vineyard (see Ps. 80:8-19; Isa. 5:1-7; Jer. 12:10) which was to be kept undefiled, so in their agricultural practice the Israelites were not to grow other crops along with grapes. The mixing of crops was a well-known Egyptian practice, and in addition to being a distinctive people the Israelites had to avoid any action that might attract them back to the life experienced while in Egypt. The reason given is a religious one. If the prohibition was disobeyed, then both the crops and the produce would have to be regarded as dedicated to the LORD. This does not necessarily mean that the crops would have to be taken to the sanctuary (see NIV margin), but that no use could be made of them by the people.

10 There is no suggestion that this prohibition is based simply on the incompatibility of using the ox and the donkey together for ploughing. The ox and the donkey were set apart in that one was clean and the other unclean (see the earlier distinction of clean and unclean animals in Deut. 14:3-8 and more fully in Lev. 11:1-47). The important principle was that these types of animals had to be kept separate, just as Israel had to avoid any temptation to syncretism. Paul clearly understood the text in this way as he shows by his use of it in teaching that believers and unbelievers should not be yoked together (1 Cor. 6:14-18).

11 Clothing of mixed material was also prohibited. Just as the linking of dissimilar animals would be a sign that the people were failing to make clear that they were God's people, so utilising different materials in a garment would symbolise failure to maintain covenant distinctiveness. This same instruction appears in Leviticus 19:19, where it and the prohibition of sowing mixed seed in a field come in the midst of a passage in which God proclaims his lordship over Israel sixteen times ('I am the LORD [your God]'). It is only in this verse and in Leviticus 19:19 that the Hebrew word translated 'wool and linen woven together' (NIV) or 'mixed stuff' (NKJV) occurs, and it is almost certainly a foreign word, possibly of Egyptian origin. Again, a simple act was symbolic of deep commitment to be the covenant people of God.

12 The fourth instruction in this section is a positive one. The cloak, which was worn as a garment in the daytime and used as a blanket at night, had to have tassels on the four corners. The fuller legislation regarding it is given in Numbers 15:37-41. It also comes in a passage that re-asserts both the need for holiness and the claim that the redeemer made over his children (Num. 15:40-41). The tassels, which included a blue thread in them, were meant to remind them at all times that they must obey the LORD.

(ii) Laws Relating to Marriage (22:13-30)
The remainder of the chapter is taken up with applying fundamental principles to some specific cases affecting betrothed or married couples. The earlier part of the chapter has in general been dealing with God's concern for the created world. Now the attention focuses on one of the specific creation ordinances: marriage.

There are difficulties in explaining within the Mosaic legal system all the content of passages such as this. This is partly because certain facts, which may have a bearing on our understanding of the laws, are unexplained in the text. For example, Deuteronomy 22:28-29 does not indicate the status of the man seducing a virgin. He could be married, unmarried, or engaged to another. There is also the difficulty of explaining why the law dealt in conspicuously different ways with cases that seem to be analogous. A sexual relationship between an unmarried man and a married woman was punishable by both being put to death (verse 22), but no penalty is set in the law for a sexual relationship between a married man and an unmarried woman. The absence of specific cases within the Old Testament means that we do not have sufficient information on the application of the laws to be able always to draw out the full implications of the legislation.

However, some general principles may help to guide us in understanding this passage better.

1. Once more the covenant relationship between the LORD and Israel forms the theological background for the relationship between husband and wife. The symbolical aspects of marriage may well have dictated severe penalties for sexual offences.

2. It is clear that wider issues were at stake rather than just the sexual relationship between two people. Offences were not just against another party, but against the society as a whole. This is made clear by the instructions in verse 18 to 'the elders of the city' and in verse 21 to 'the men of the city'. Through the offences the structure of society as a whole was being attacked because of an attack on the basic institution of the family.

3. Broader issues still seem to be involved. The family was the means of passing on the knowledge of God, and also the channel through which inheritance of the promised land was effected. This latter fact helps to explain the presence of polygamy in Israel for it served to protect the lines of inheritance (see the later discussion on levirate marriage in Deut. 25; cf. also Ruth 4:5-6). Conversely, adultery was a disruption of the line of inheritance, and this comes out markedly in the case of the penalty for the promiscuous girl in verses 20-21. She was guilty of bringing disorder into the father's line, and hence the punishment takes place 'at the door of the father's house'.

13-17 The first case presented is one where a man makes a false accusation against his new wife, having come to detest her (Heb. *sane'*, 'hate'), which may mean not only an emotional response but physical rejection. Two possible explanations of this case can be made. The more common one is that this is a case of a man accusing his new wife of not being a virgin when he married her. This is a slanderous accusation that brings disrepute to the woman (verse 14), and which her parents reject strongly. They bring out the blood stained cloths which the bride had retained from the wedding night as evidence that she had been a virgin prior to marriage. The second explanation would be that the husband is accusing his new wife of being already pregnant when the marriage took place. In this case the parents in producing cloths would be asserting that she was still menstruating when married, and therefore the accusation of pregnancy was false. It is hard to be certain which explanation is better, as both are plausible in the context. As the word translated 'virginity' in verses 15 and 17 may well indicate simply 'a woman of marriageable age', the second explanation is probably the better one.

18-19 Whichever explanation is adopted of verses 13-17, the false accusation brings the punishment of a fine of a hundred shekels of silver. This was a very large penalty to impose, clearly with the intention of preventing false accusations being made against newly-wed wives. The fact that David later bought Araunah's threshing floor and oxen for only fifty silver shekels (2 Sam. 24:24) gives some indication of the nature of the penalty. The money was paid to the woman's father because of the defamation of his daughter's character. In addition, the man was forbidden to divorce his wife at any time in the future. While nothing is said about the situation in the marriage for the wife in such circumstances, it gave her security which she would not have had if she was divorced.

20-21 If the man's accusations are proved to be true then punishment appropriate to the offence would be applied. The offence is said in verse 21 to be 'a disgrace in Israel' (Heb. *nᵉvalah*), which is an expression used for disorderly conduct in general, but specifically of immoral acts (cf. its use in connection with the rape of Dinah [Gen. 34:7] and the rape of Tamar [2 Sam.

13:12-13]). In Jeremiah 29:23 it is used of adultery with a neighbour's wife. The execution was to take place by stoning at the door of the father's house, since the woman was guilty of a sin that affected the line of descent in her father's family.

22 Adultery by a man with a married woman was to result in the execution of both of them in order to remove the evil from the people (note the use of almost identical phrases at the end of verses 21 and 22). In this case the presumption was that there was no coercion involved. No mention is made of the marital state of the man, but the woman, though married, seemingly consents to the sexual relationship. If the couple are discovered (Heb. 'found lying with a woman'), then both are to be put to death.

23-24 The next case is one where within a town a man sleeps with a betrothed girl. At the gate of the town both are to be executed, but for different reasons. The girl is to be punished because she must have consented to the act, for if she had cried out then someone in the town would have heard her. The man is to be punished because he violated a betrothed girl, and therefore his action is regarded as if he had committed adultery with a married woman, the 'wife' of one of his fellow Israelites.

25-27 This next case is different, not only in that it contemplates a rural setting instead of a town, but force is involved. The Hebrew text says 'if he seizes her and lies with her', which the NIV rightly translates as 'rapes her'. Only the man was to die, because the girl had not committed any offence, since if she had cried out nobody would have heard her. A comparison is made to the similar case of unwitnessed murder. In both of these cases there may well have been indications of intent to commit the offence, and even in the absence of witnesses the offender was to be found guilty.

28-29 The law envisages another situation in which the seduction of an unbetrothed girl takes place. While the NIV and many other versions treat both this case and the previous one as rape, yet the terminology is different. In verses 25-27 rape is described by using the verbs 'seize' and 'lie with'. Here the verbs are 'grab' and 'lie with', followed by the expression 'and they are discovered'. The differences seem to point rather to seduction. If the couple are discovered, then the man is obliged to marry the girl, he is prevented from ever divorcing her, and in addition he has to pay the sum of fifty silver shekels to the girl's father. To have paid the money to the girl would have brought it back within his control, and it probably represented the equivalent of a bride price. No mention is made of the feelings of the girl in having to live in this marriage relationship, but it provided economic security for her in a situation wherein she might never find a husband if this marriage did not take place. In Exodus 22:16-18 provision is made for the girl's father to refuse to give her in marriage.

30 The final situation envisaged in this series of regulations concerns a man marrying his father's wife. The expressions used here, including 'wife' and 'he must not dishonour his father's bed', allow for several possibilities. 'Wife' could be either the man's mother, or more probably his step-mother, but no mention is made of whether the father was still alive. In Hebrew, the expression to dishonour the father's bed, is literally 'to uncover his father's skirt.' Especially in Leviticus 18 and 20 it refers to proscribed sexual activity. Another factor may possibly be in mind. The son and heir would take over his father's wife and concubines, and in this way lay claim to all his father's property. Hence this law links in with the earlier ones on inheritance rights (21:15ff.) and its form (not 'if ...', but 'a man shall not take ...') links it with the ones that follow (23:1-9).

(iii) The LORD's Assemblies (23:1-28)
The opening portion of this chapter has two sections that contain homogeneous material. The latter part has a collection of miscellaneous laws. The opening verses (verses 1-8) form a unit because of their form. Instead of using the casuistic or descriptive style ('if ...' or 'when ...') they employ the proscriptive one used in the Ten Commandments ('you shall not ...'). From verse 9 the text reverts to the descriptive form.

For the first time in Deuteronomy the full expression 'the assembly (or 'congregation') of the LORD' is used in verses 1-3. Previously mention was made of the day of the assembly (9:10; 10:4; 18:16), but now specifically the covenant people gathered before him are denoted as the LORD's assembly. The people whom God had called out to be a kingdom of priests and a holy nation are regarded as his congregation. From the Hebrew word for assembly (*qahal*) has come the New Testament concept of the church. The word used by the LXX to translate the Hebrew *qahal* has even come into English (Gk. *ecclesia*, cf. 'ecclesiastical', or the title of the biblical book 'Ecclesiastes'). The apostle Peter merges together various Old Testament passages as he sets out the continuity of the church concept in the New Testament era (1 Pet. 2:4-10).

Certain persons were excluded from participation in the outward manifestation of the LORD's assembly. That is to say, some people, while living within the covenant community, were not permitted to take part in the formal assemblies.

1. At that time, eunuchs were disallowed from sharing in the formal life of the people (**verse 1**). The reference is most probably to males who had undergone self-mutilation rather than to those who were accidentally castrated. The practice of castration was known in surrounding countries, and in some it was practised with religious significance. Hence, in Israel no man with deliberate genital mutilation was permitted to associate with the assembled worshipping community. Isaiah depicts a day coming when eunuchs will be given an honoured place in God's kingdom (Isa. 56:4-5), while the New Testament records a notable case of the inclusion of an eunuch among the early believers (Acts 8:26-40).

2. The next category to be excluded is called in the Hebrew text *mamzer* (**verse 2**). The word only occurs once again in the Old Testament in Zechariah 9:6. It seems to be something more than illegitimacy that is in view. Various suggestions have been made, such as that these were born of an incestuous relationship, or, if a link is made with verses 17-18, that they were the

children born to cult prostitutes. The reference in Zechariah 9:6 may well give the best clue, as it refers to the mixed population of Ashdod. Here the word could well refer to children born of mixed parentage. Any child of a Hebrew-pagan marriage would be excluded until the tenth generation, which probably means 'for ever', as the number ten was symbolic of completeness.

3. No Ammonite or Moabite was ever to come before the LORD in the solemn assembly (**verses 3-6**). There may well be a link with verse 2 in that both these tribes were descendants of an incestuous union (see Gen. 19:30-38). Two other reasons are also given. They failed to provide for the Israelites on their journey to Canaan as they travelled through the desert, and because the Moabites (possibly aided by the Ammonites, though this is not mentioned elsewhere) hired Balaam to pronounce curses (Num. 22-24). The warning of Genesis 12:3 ('whoever curses you I will curse') was thus being fulfilled, as God turned the curses of Balaam into blessings for Israel. The reason for this is expressly stated to be God's continuing love for Israel (verse 5). Not only had God chosen Israel in love (7:7), but his constant provision for them was a sign of his continuing love. The reference in verse 6 is clearly to the prohibition of entering into any treaty arrangements with the Ammonites and Moabites, the Hebrew text using two of the words which are frequently connected with covenant ('peace' and 'goodness'; cf. the use of 'goodness' in 1 Sam. 25:30; 2 Sam. 2:6; 2 Sam 7:28; and 'peace' in the full expression 'covenant of peace' in Num. 25:12; Isa. 54:10; Ezek. 37:26). This passage was read aloud to the people in Nehemiah's time after the Exile and formed the basis for a general exclusion of all foreigners from God's assembly (Neh. 13:1-3).

4. Somewhat less stringent requirements applied to Edomites and Egyptians (**verses 7-8**). The Edomites were related in that they were descendants of Esau. The Israelites' attitude to the Egyptians had to be governed by the fact that they themselves

had been aliens in Egypt, and at least initially they had been shown favours by the Egyptians. After three generations those of these groups who believed and were committed to the covenant could enter the assembly. Time was needed to ensure that immigrants were truly one with the covenant community in their faith and obedience.

(iv) Hygienic Toilet Requirements (23:9-14)

The regulations revert now to the casuistic style ('if/when ... then ...'), and this section complements what was set out earlier in chapter 20 regarding battle conduct. It deals with two specific situations, from which broader application must have been made to a variety of related matters. This is stressed by the general direction of verse 9 and the later reference to the holiness of the camp (verse 14).

9 This verse adopts one of the standard Hebrew expressions for going to war: 'When you go out ... against your enemies ....' Some expression is normally added such as 'to war' (Deut. 20:1). Here the concern is with the situation within the camp, and the soldiers are warned to guard themselves against any impure act in relation to sanitation.

10-11 The first example concerns something that takes place during the night. The customary explanation is to link it with Leviticus 15:16-17 and explain it as a seminal discharge. However, the language is different in the two passages, and it fits this context better to understand it as urination within the camp itself. Because of tiredness or laziness a soldier would not go outside the camp to relieve himself. He was to be banished from the camp until evening, when after appropriate ritual washing, he could return.

12-13 The second case is that of defecation. Provision had to be made for a designated place outside the camp. The Hebrew word used for 'place' is simply 'hand', which can in a few places in the Old Testament designate a side or place (see 1 Sam. 4:8; Deut. 2:37) or it can be used to describe an ordinance or a prescription (see especially Ezra 3:10). It has been suggested that the figure of a hand may have been used in biblical times as a pointer, just as we continue to do today. The place was definitely outside the camp, as the Hebrew text of verse 12 emphasises by using the word 'outside' twice ('Designate a place *outside* the camp, and you shall go there *outside* [the camp]'). Provision was also to be made for the appropriate tool to be available for digging a hole and burying excrement.

14 The explanation for this careful attention to sanitary details is because of the presence of the LORD in the midst of the camp. He walks about the camp (a phrase used of God's presence in the garden of Eden, Gen. 3:8), which may relate to the presence of the ark of the covenant in the midst of the camp. This would give the camp its holiness, and also indicate that if the military attack was undertaken with his approval, then he would deliver his people from their enemies. From Numbers 10:35 we know that whenever the ark set out Moses prayed: 'Rise up, O LORD! May your enemies be scattered; may your foes flee before you'. The holiness of the covenant bond had to be reflected even in physical cleanliness and hygiene, lest the LORD take note of their breach of his stipulations ('see anything indecent among you') and turn himself away from them.

8. The Eighth Commandment (23:15-24:7)
('You shall not steal')
There appears to be a shift here to the exposition of the Eighth Commandment with discussion of the rights of possession and matters relating to theft. This applies even to the verses dealing with divorce (24:1-4) and kidnapping (24:7), for in these there was metaphorical theft of life (Heb. *nefesh*) in the former and physical theft in the latter. Whereas the seventh commandment is concerned with purity, the eighth commandment is concerned with the preservation of what is proper in the various spheres of life. Clearly the two commandments are thematically close, so much so that some have suggested that in Deuteronomy they are being discussed together. However, when examined closely the various

cases cited all deal with an aspect of respect for property, whether it be God's (23:15-16; 23:21-23) or man's (23:24-25; 24:6). Newly weds could not be 'stolen' from one another, no more than millstones could be separated.

(i) Various Regulations (23:15-25)

15-16 Following discussion of the military camp in verses 9-14, another case is taken up which may well have arisen more often during military campaigns than at other times. On occasions slaves would escape from other countries and find their way into Israelite territory. Three things are specified concerning them. First, while other countries in the Near East had laws regarding the return of slaves, and these laws occurred in several extra-biblical treaties, Israel was not to follow this practice. To do so would imply that she was in a covenant relationship with foreign nations. Secondly, the runaway slave could choose for himself where he was going to live in Israel and make his living. There was no specified geographical areas for the foreigners. Thirdly, such a slave was not to be oppressed in any way. The Israelites had to remember that they were recently oppressed slaves themselves in Egypt, and hence they were not to mete out similar treatment to other slaves.

17-18 Temple prostitution, both male and female, was rife in the Near Eastern religions. No Israelite was to engage in such activity, even though the terms used here (Heb. q^edeshah, qadesh, the female and male terms respectively) come from the Hebrew word for 'holy' or 'sacred'. Little information is given in the biblical text regarding them. Asa expelled the male shrine prostitutes from the land (1 Kings 15:12), and his son Jehoshaphat got rid of those who remained (1 Kings 22:46). From extra-biblical texts it is clear that sexual intercourse with these temple prostitutes was related to the whole understanding of fertility for family, herds and crops. The Hebrew word used for 'male prostitute' in verse 18 is the derogative expression 'dog' (Heb. kelev), which is echoed in Revelation 22:15. The money earned by such abominable practices could not be used to pay a vow, for such payment was out of gratitude for God's gracious gifts to the recipient.

19-20 Regulations regarding how to treat a poor brother Israelite were set out in the Book of the Covenant (Exod. 22:25), and expanded further in Leviticus 25:35-38. Interest was not to be charged to a fellow Israelite, though it was lawful to charge a foreigner. If one was in need, his brothers had to provide for him. The principle behind this regulation was that all the members of the covenant family had been provided with the land by God, and as they obeyed him they would be blessed in all their activities in it. A foreign trader did not stand in a similar relationship, and so he could be charged interest. The general principle is applied by Paul in Romans 13:8-10 in that the debt we owe to one another as Christians is to love one another, which is the fulfilment of the law.

21-23 A vow was not obligatory, and failure to make one was not a sin (verse 22). However, once a vow was made performance of it was required by God, and non-fulfilment of it would be regarded as a sin. Any solemn commitment of this kind to the LORD had to be kept. Just as the LORD of the covenant spoke words which he would fulfil, so his people had to mirror that commitment to a promise made. When they made a vow freely (or willingly) in response to God's gracious dealings with them, they had to honour it.

24-25 While property rights were recognised, a traveller could satisfy his thirst or hunger from the crops of a fellow Israelite. However, he could not carry anything away in a basket, for that would be an abuse of the privilege and it would be an act of theft. While there is a humanitarian aspect here, the stress is on respect for the property of others. The practice of meeting hunger in this way persisted through to New Testament times (Matt. 12:1-8). The Pharisees took exception to what Jesus' disciples did, not because of the practice itself (for it is clear that the disciples were genuinely hungry in that they ate the corn), but because it was done on the Sabbath day.

(ii) Divorce and Re-Marriage (24:1-4)
Two situations in which divorce could not take place have already been given in 22:19, 29. Now the opening verses of this chapter

give specific legislation on divorce. No other Old Testament passage contains such detailed references to it, and later passages in both Old and New Testaments depend upon it (e.g., Isa. 50:1; Matt. 19:7; Mark 10:3-5).

Careful examination of the passage lessens some of the problems traditionally surrounding it.

1. The regulation does not make divorce mandatory in the situation mentioned. Rather, the emphasis is on the fact that if a woman is divorced and then marries another man, under no circumstances can the original husband re-marry her.

2. Modern translations of this passage (such as the NASB, NIV, and NKJV) make it clear that the description of circumstances in verses 1-3 is followed by the consequences as far as re-marriage is concerned in verse 4. The consequence is not the second part of verse 1 ('he writes her a certificate of divorce').

3. This passage is therefore consistent with the rest of biblical teaching that while in the Old Testament period divorce was not given divine approval, yet it was both practised and tolerated (cf. Matt. 19:8; Mark 10:5-6).

4. The ground given in verse 1 (Heb. *'ervat davar*, 'something indecent') as the reason for the divorce need not necessarily be adultery. Trivial reasons, which later appeared in rabbinical writings, are not sanctioned by this passage. Capital punishment was prescribed for adultery and that certainly does not apply here. The action could well be something of a shameful nature (most probably in connection with sexual relations) which did not constitute adultery.

5. The certificate of divorce was a wise provision to safeguard the woman's rights and to give her legal protection. In addition to the use in verses 1 and 3 of a technical term for a divorce document (Heb. *sefer k^eritut*, lit. 'a certificate of cutting off'), the Hebrew verb for divorce occurs three times in these verses.

6. The reason for the prohibition on re-marriage is because of the shameful thing that had been done (verse 4). In the text, no

explanation is given of this reason. If the first divorce was not for adultery, then the second separation would be regarded as such, as the wife was leaving one man and wanting to marry another (in this case her first husband). Even though the second marriage was now finished, there could be no return to the original relationship. The woman would have become detestable in God's sight. This view stands in contrast to the way in which most English versions make the act detestable ('That would be detestable' NIV) rather than 'she would be detestable'.

7. Finally, care had to be taken to preserve the purity of the marriage relationship, lest abuse of it bring defilement upon the land (cf. the similar expression in 21:23).

(iii) Various Social Laws (24:5-22)

Following the section on re-marriage there is a collection of laws, all of which relate to various aspects of social life. Only the first one has any direct connection with the opening verses. While continuing to expound the Eighth Commandment, the strong humanitarian stress is also maintained. The covenant family, redeemed from slavery and bondage in Egypt, had to show special concern for the under-privileged and those prone to be down-trodden. Hence three times in this section there is the call to remember the experiences in Egypt and God's redemption of his people (verses 9, 18, 22).

5 Earlier in 20:7, exemption was given from army service to a betrothed man. Now it is specified that a newly-married man is given relief from any form of military service or other public duties for one year. This was a recognition of the place of marriage and the home in the structure of society. A man was to rejoice in the wife of his youth (cf. the similar language in Prov. 5:18). The new relationship had to be in existence for a year before military or other service was imposed on the husband.

6 Interest was not to be charged to a fellow Israelite (23:19) but in some circumstances possessions could be taken as security for a

loan. Every house would have a pair of millstones, but their daily food supply depended on them. Hence the prohibition on their use (even of the upper one) in connection with a loan.

7 A very pointed application of the Eighth Commandment is now made. Within Israel there was to be no kidnapping. All stealing was forbidden, but stealing a person by force was the worst form that such stealing could take. It involved the taking and use of someone for personal gain, and the verb 'treat as a slave' implies degrading and oppressive treatment. Capital punishment was to be inflicted on anyone who carried out such an act of kidnapping, which was a denial of human dignity and the freedom of individual life.

9. The Ninth Commandment (24:8-25:4)
('You shall not give false testimony against your neighbour')
The major idea behind the Ninth Commandment is fairness, and this flows through into the exposition of it. To obey this commandment meant to think and act fairly towards the possessions and dignity of one's fellows. Hence attention is drawn to matters of concern relating to justice, impartiality and false witness.

At first sight it seems incongruous to deal with leprosy under the rubric of the Ninth Commandment. The interpretive clause is found in the words: 'Remember Miriam!' (24:9). Because of her attitude and actions Miriam was afflicted with leprosy. There could be no more serious case of libel than hers.

(i) Remember Miriam (24:8-9)
8-9 Detailed provisions are set out in Leviticus 13-14 in connection with leprosy. Here the command is given that great care was to be taken to follow the instructions that the LORD had given through the priests concerning this matter. The term translated leprosy in our English Bibles (Heb. *tsara'at*) was considerably broader in scope than simply a skin disease, as it included things like mildew on clothes and walls. The role of the priest, acting as the public health officer, was to distinguish between benign conditions and

the form of leprosy known today as Hansen's disease. The reference to Miriam's experience is to show the consequences of disobedience and the way in which God used leprosy in her case as a judgment (Num. 12:9-15), just as God did so later with Uzziah of Judah for usurping priestly functions (2 Chron. 26:21).

(ii) Just Treatment of the Debtor (24:10-13)

10-13 Further instructions are given relating to items taken as security (see also Exod. 22:26-27). When taking something as security for a loan certain rights of the debtor were still to be respected. His house was not to be entered, and the man himself had to select the item he would give as a pledge. Nor could his garments be kept overnight. The implication is that the man in question was very poor if all he had to give as security is a cloak. In an extra-biblical text found south of Tel Aviv there exists a complaint to a governor against an official who kept a farm worker's cloak overnight. The rule was clearly breached at times in Israel (Amos 2:8; cf. Job 22:6). The fact that the cloak had to be returned each morning would be a constant reminder of the debt. Observing this provision would bring thanks from the debtor and would be reckoned as a righteous act before the LORD.

(iii) Just Treatment of the Hired Worker (24:14-15)

14-15 The rights of hired workers are to be safeguarded, and an employer cannot take advantage of them, whether they are native Israelites or foreigners. There is to be no oppression of the needy, and each day their wages are to be paid at sunset to enable them to buy food and the other necessities of life. If there is a case of oppression, then appeal can be made directly to God, and the community as a whole can be judged guilty of sin. James 5:4 refers to this provision and the cries of the reapers are said to have reached the ears of the Lord Almighty.

(iv) The Principle of Individual Responsibility (24:16)

16 For specific sins there is no family or corporate responsibility. Rather, a person is responsible for his own crimes, and capital punishment is to apply only to him. King Amaziah later applied this law (and it is quoted in the account) when he executed those who had killed his father, yet spared their children (2 Kings 14:5-6). Ezekiel also expounds the principle in chapter 18:1-32 as he speaks out against false ideas of inherited guilt. He depicts three generations – the first righteous, the second rebellious, the third righteous. The last man is not to die for his father's sins for 'the soul who sins is the one who will die' (Ezek. 18:20).

(v) Justice for the Oppressed (24:17-22)

17-22 The recollection of redemption from slavery in Egypt was the oft-repeated motive for Israel's actions. It occurs twice in this section (verses 18 and 22). Redeemed Israelites had to recall God's gracious intervention on their behalf and acknowledge the fact that all they now possessed was from his hand alone. Special attention had to be given to the aliens, the fatherless and the widows, the groups in Israelite society who were most easily oppressed. Two specific areas of responsibility are mentioned. First, justice had to be applied uniformly throughout Israelite society, including all situations involving these groups. The expression used here (Heb. *natah mishpat*) is clearly a technical term for perverting justice (in addition to this passage see its use in Exod. 23:6; Deut. 16:19; 27:19; 1 Sam. 8:3; Prov. 17:23; Lam. 3:35; Amos 2:7). Secondly, provision had to be made for their food supply. They had no land themselves, but yet they have to share in the bounty of it. When harvesting fields, olive groves, or vineyards, care had to be taken that they were not stripped bare. Sufficient had to be left so that the needy could come and find provision for their needs too. Ruth's experience is a graphic illustration of the principle in action (Ruth 2:1-23).

(vi) Justice in Corporal Punishment (25:1-3)

25:1-3 Strict rules had to be followed for administering any corporal punishment to a fellow Israelite ('your brother', verse 3). Even a criminal had rights that had to be protected. After due legal process the judge had to be present when the punishment is inflicted. This was to ensure that the due penalty, and nothing more, was exacted, and done in such a way as to preserve the dignity of the offender. Excessive beating would mean that a man is being treated like an animal, and hence his dignity would be taken from him. Forty lashes was the limit, and in Jewish practice this was later restricted to thirty-nine to make sure the limit was not accidentally breached. In New Testament times this practice was still followed, and Paul notes how on five occasions he received this punishment for witnessing to Christian truth (2 Cor. 11:24).

(vii) Justice for Workers (25:4)

4 The words of this verse are familiar because they are quoted by Paul in 1 Corinthians 9:9. He argues that those who labour in the Gospel are to be given a fitting response in material terms. After quoting these words about the ox, he asks a question which requires a negative answer. 'Is it about oxen that God is concerned [in this passage]?' This points us in the direction that the original intent of this passage was not to teach about kindness to working animals but to state a principle about human labour and reward. This view is strengthened by the fact that the passage comes in a section here in Deuteronomy dealing with inter-personal relationships, and it has the ring of a proverbial saying about it. Thus it is similar to English expressions such as 'a willing horse' or 'an old dog'. Paul's application is therefore entirely in keeping with the original force of the saying, and his use of it again in 1 Timothy 5:18 reinforces this interpretation of the context here.

10. The Tenth Commandment (25:5–26:16)

(*'You shall not covet ... anything that belongs to your neighbour'*) The last commandment is the broadest both in its intent and application. In its Deuteronomic form (see comment on 5:21) the verb 'covet' conveys the idea of mental processes, thus prohibiting even patterns of thought that might lead someone to commit an offence. Hence in the case of weights it is not only the *use* of false ones, but their *possession* that is prohibited (25:13-16).

The section on firstfruits and tithes (26:1-15) may seem an inappropriate conclusion to the Tenth Commandment. When viewed as the cure for covetousness this apprehension disappears.

The Israelites individually had to come annually before God, making confession of his grace, and bringing their gifts willingly to him. In this regard Paul encourages a similar attitude in Ephesians 4:28 when he says: 'He who has been stealing must steal no longer, but must work, doing something useful with his own hands, that he may have something to share with those in need'.

(i) Levirate Marriage (25:5-10)

5-7 In certain restricted circumstances a brother-in-law (Latin *levir*, 'a husband's brother', hence the English technical term 'levirate marriage') was expected to marry a brother's widow in order to ensure that his brother's name was continued in Israel. The practice goes back to patriarchal times (Gen. 38:8) and was known in other Near Eastern societies, and is still practised in some modern ones today. This was not to be regarded as a breach of the tenth commandment since it was the opposite of coveting another man's wife. Instead, it was a way of building up a brother's family. The practice receives here further regulation. Clearly it is an extended family situation that is in view, for the woman is expressly forbidden to marry outside the family. If the brother-in-law she married was himself already married, then polygamy is in view. Just like divorce (Matt. 19:8), polygamy is a concession to human sinfulness, and it served to preserve family inheritance. This is made clear here by the reference at the beginning of verse 5 to the fact that the brothers were living together, i.e. they were occupying the same property. Inheritance came through the husbands, and through sons who inherited from them. The son born to the woman in a levirate marriage would ensure that the father's name was continued. In that society there was no greater threat than that a man's name could be blotted out from Israel.

8-10 The application of the principle of the levirate marriage was not automatic, for a man could refuse to marry. In this case there was to be persuasion by the elders and if the refusal was maintained a ceremony was held which involved public humiliation of the man. One of his sandals was removed, he was spat on by the woman, and his family was given a name to indicate the community's disapproval of his action ('the family [Heb. *bet*, 'house'] of the unsandalled'). The removal of the sandal indicated that the man was forfeiting any right to his brother's property, while spitting in the face was an act of contempt. The book of Ruth helps to illustrate some of the principles involved in this present passage, but it is not strictly parallel. In the case of Ruth, Boaz was not the brother-in-law but a distant relative, there is no stigma on the man who does not wish to marry her, and the ritual of removing the sandal is different.

(ii) A Threat to Progeny (25:11-12)

11 The next case to be dealt with is that of a woman stopping a fight. A wife, in attempting to stop an attacker beating her husband, could use various means but not seize his private parts. The severity of the penalty points to some reason beyond sheer modesty. There was the danger that the man would be injured and be unable to bear children. If this was the reason it would provide an immediate connection with the preceding passage, which dealt in another way with the problem of lack of children. However, the penalty suggests that the reason could also be connected with the fact that the male organ of reproduction carried the covenant sign of circumcision. The woman's action was in complete disregard of that fact, so that the punishment is severe in line with the threat of the cutting off from Israel of disloyal covenant servants (Gen. 17:14). The punishment also involved mutilation, so that there was a similarity between the covenant sign and the penalty.

(iii) Dishonest Weights (25:13-16)

13-16 Honesty in trading is also demanded. Just as the law has to be administered with complete honesty (16:18-20), so also buying and selling have to be regulated by strict principles of ethical standards. To have two different sets of scales and measures was very tempting for a merchant. It was serious because it involved dishonesty before God and it was a way of defrauding others for personal gain. While the possession of the different scales and measures is not a sin in itself, yet they could easily encourage the sin of covetousness to become blatant action. It is apparent from later passages in the prophets that this regulation was often disregarded (cf. Amos 8:5). The threat is once again given of the removal from the land if there is disobedience to God's laws. The statement in verse 16 is at first sight surprising, because the expression 'for the LORD your God detests anyone who does these things' (Heb. *to 'avat yhwh*, 'an abomination to Yahweh') is used mainly of Canaanite practices. However, the phrase is always used in Deuteronomy along with a demand for exclusive worship of the LORD, so that the neglect of or disobedience to regulations was an act of treachery against the covenant.

(iv) Remember Amalek (25:17-19)

17-19 The renewed expression of the law of love to others in the previous verses is now coupled with another way in which love to God is to be expressed. These verses form a transition between the long exposition of the Decalogue and the covenant renewal that follows. They refer to historic events in the desert, while also pointing ahead to life in the land of Canaan. The actions of Amalek were to be remembered for ever and the Israelites were to execute God's judgment upon them. The regulation here reiterates the presumption concerning the Amalekites given in Exodus 17:14-16. Even then there was a forward look to what Joshua would have to do when Canaan was invaded. The general reference in verse 17 to what Amalek did to Israel refers to specific major incidents (such as that recorded in Num. 14:39-45, cf. Deut. 1:42-44) and also to repeated attacks from the rear on stragglers (verse 18). The reason for Amalek's attitude to Israel was a religious one: 'they had no fear of God' (verse 18). This is confirmed by the reference in Exodus 17, where it is best to translate verse 16 as, 'Because a hand was against the throne of the LORD, the LORD will be at war against the Amalekites from generation to generation' (see NIV footnote). There was no spiritual reverence of the living God in their hearts. Their actions displayed their basic antagonism, and their cursing of Israel was to have as its consequence God's curse upon them (Gen. 12:3). Rest in the land of promise involved obedience to all of God's commands, and hence the section ends with the words: 'Do not forget!'

(v) Thanksgiving for the Land (26:1-15)

This chapter forms the conclusion to the covenant stipulations which began at chapter 6. The focus is still on possession of the land and God's requirements for his people in it. Regulations are given for the presentation of some of the firstfruits to the LORD, and the giving of the tithe in the third year. The concluding verses are both a declaration of God's lordship over the people and a reminder of their obligation as God's treasured possession to fulfil carefully all his prescriptions for them.

(a) Presentation of the Firstfruits (26:1-11)

1-2 Israel was constantly reminded that the land into which they were coming was God's special provision for them. It was an inheritance from him. When settled there, in thankful acknowledgment of God's grace in giving them the land, they would have to make a token presentation of the firstfruits from it. Some items were to be placed in a basket and brought before the LORD at the central sanctuary. While the text does not specify it expressly, the point of the ritual seems to have applied not only to the initial harvest in Canaan but to each successive one as well.

3-4 The man bringing the offering had to declare before the priest that he had come to the land that God had sworn on oath to his forefathers to give to Israel. Probably the priest performed certain actions and spoke specific words, both of which were repeated by the offerer, though the brief nature of the account leaves some doubt concerning the ritual. The priest was to take the basket and set it down before the altar.

5 Central to the whole procedure was the confession that the offerer was to make (verses 5-10). It was not a creed in the sense of a full acknowledgment of Israel's belief in the living God. Rather, it was a confession restricted to some important facets linked with a new religious celebration, and it reaches its climax in verse 10. In a solemn declaration before the LORD, the offerer had to acknowledge: 'My father was a wandering Aramean'. The 'father' is clearly Jacob, as the rest of the verse makes plain. It is somewhat strange that he is called an Aramean, though he married Aramean

wives (Leah and Rachel) and lived in Aram-naharaim during the
period of the birth of his sons (Gen. 29-32, and see also Hos.
12:12). The adjective 'wandering' translates a Hebrew participle
which can mean either 'perishing' (i.e. dying) or 'wandering'.
The latter idea would fit the circumstances of Jacob's life, for he
wandered from Canaan to Paddan-Aram, back to Canaan and then
finally to Egypt. It was as a man about to die that Jacob in old age
went down to Egypt. Yet in the context the former idea seems
preferable. From his small family of seventy, God brought to
fulfilment his promise of the large family which would become a
great nation (see Gen. 46:26-27; cf. Acts 7:14 where in his defence
Stephen refers to the seventy-five members of Jacob's family,
following the LXX version of Gen. 46:27 and Exod. 1:5 which
omitted Joseph and Jacob but included *nine* sons of Joseph).

6-7 The second aspect which the confession stressed was the
condition of the people while in Egypt. They were in abject slavery,
mistreated by the Egyptians, and forced to work in harsh servitude.
Out of their situation of toil and oppression they cried out to the
LORD their God and he heard their prayer.

8-10 The third and final aspect of the confession was the reference
to God's redemptive power and his provision of the land of Canaan.
He had displayed his power ('with a mighty hand and an
outstretched arm'), and had performed signs and wonders before
the Egyptians and his people Israel. He had brought Israel to the
banks of the Jordan and they could look across and see the
bounteous land he was giving them, 'a land flowing with milk
and honey' (for discussion of this phrase see page 20). The climax
came in the last declaration: 'And now I bring the firstfruits of the
soil that you, O LORD, have given me'. This was an
acknowledgment that it was the LORD, not Baal the fertility god of
the Canaanites, who was the provider, and therefore it was fitting
that the offerer set the basket down before the altar and worshipped
the LORD. Just as in the extra-biblical treaties an act of homage
was required of a vassal, so in Israel covenant servants made their
homage in word and deed before their sovereign.

11 From the produce of the land the Levites and the foreigners were also to be fed, and hence they too were to share in the joyful celebration of God's gracious provision.

(b) The Giving of the Tithes (26:12-15)

12 The second ceremony would come in the third year of occupation of the land (two years later than the initial firstfruits ceremony). It would take place not at the central sanctuary but throughout the Israelite settlements. Those dependent upon others for their food supply, especially the Levites, foreigners, orphans and widows, were to be remembered at this time (see the fuller provisions in 14:22-29, particularly verses 28-29).

13-15 As in the previous ceremony there was to be a formal declaration before the LORD (probably following some ritual as with the firstfruits), along with a prayer for God's blessing on the people and the land. The declaration included an acknowledgment that everything God required had been done, and that nothing was eaten or removed while the offerer was ritually unclean or involved in any proscribed religious practice. The Israelites fasted while mourning (Ezek. 24:15-24), and they did not give offerings to the dead. The practices referred to here were clearly pagan Canaanite rituals. The word 'mourning' only occurs elsewhere in the Old Testament in Hosea 9:4 where it clearly relates to pagan rituals. It is clear from verses 16-19 that this declaration was tantamount to a renewal of covenant vows. The prayer for continued blessing of the people and the land (verse 15) was a fitting recognition of the source of the prosperity they would enjoy. The earlier legislation (14:28-29) had set the pattern – obedience, then blessing. Now the declaration of obedience (verses 13-14) is followed appropriately by the petition to the LORD for his continued blessing. The same pattern is reflected also in Malachi's call to the people after the Exile (Mal. 3:10-12). The declaration of obedience was discontinued in the intertestamental period by John Hyrcanus (High Priest 135-104 BC).

11. Covenant Commitment (26:16-19)

16-19 After listening to the covenant requirements the people had to pledge themselves in a solemn ceremony of allegiance to their God. At Sinai, following the reading of the Book of the Covenant, Israel made that pledge (Exod. 24:7), and now in the plains of Moab a fresh pledge is required. Moses draws the stipulations of this book to a close by reminding Israel of the required response, which would be formally given before the LORD (29:9-15). There is no mention in the text of an actual ceremony, but it is presupposed by the wording. The actual words echo much of the language that has been used earlier in this book, both in what is said about the people's commitment to the LORD (verses 16-17) and his declarations and promises to them (verses 18-19). They summarise the unique relationship that God established with Israel as his chosen people, and the obedient response that was demanded from a people who were consecrated to his service. He had chosen them out of all nations to be his treasured possession (Heb. *s^egullah*, Exod. 19:5-6; Deut. 7:6; 14:2) and they were marked out as a separated or holy people to him. The final verse notes the high responsibility which had been committed to Israel, who was greatly exalted above every other nation. The combination of 'praise, fame, and honour' (verse 19) was a standardised formula for highest renown (cf. Jer. 13:11 and 33:9). While the missionary purpose of God's choice of Israel is not spelt out expressly (cf. 4:3-8), it is implicit in the description which is given. In the New Testament this becomes explicit in the application of Old Testament terms relating to Israel to the church (1 Pet. 2:9-12).

D. RE-AFFIRMATION OF THE COVENANT (27:1–30:20)

1. Future Covenant Renewal in Canaan (27:1-26)

A new section of the book commences at this point. The stipulations having been set out in detail, the closing verses of the previous chapter have provided a transition from exposition of the law to allegiance to the LORD. The people have now to commit themselves by solemn oath to him, and provision has to be made for the continuity of the covenant after Moses' own death. In both of these aspects the text here in Deuteronomy has close parallels with the extra-biblical treaties, in which curses, blessings and succession arrangements play a prominent part.

Succession arrangements were important in the Ancient Near East. When a king felt his death was imminent, he made his vassals swear an oath of allegiance to his designated heir. Then, following his death, another oath of commitment was taken to the new king. This two-stage process is apparent in the biblical text. Moses and Joshua formed a dynasty, with Joshua having earlier been set apart by the direct command of God (Num. 27:18-23). The covenant was to be renewed prior to Moses' death (see chapters 29-32), with Joshua being explicitly linked with Moses in this transitional period (see especially 31:1-23; 32:44-47). But provision had also to be made for a fresh covenant renewal once the people had entered Canaan. Just as threats and promises, curses and blessings, played a major part in extra-biblical covenants, so they did in both of these covenant ceremonies.

The whole of chapter 27 (with the exception of verses 9-10, which relates to the present experience of the people in the plains of Moab) concerns symbolic renewal of the covenant when the Israelites have entered the land of Canaan. The proclamation of blessings and curses from Mount Gerizim and Mount Ebal has already been referred to (11:29-30), and the historical account of the actual ceremony is given in Joshua 8:30-35. The site was probably chosen because of its ancient associations with the patriarchs, for Shechem (modern Nablus in the Palestinian territory in the West Bank), situated at the eastern end of the valley between two mountains, was where both Abraham and Jacob had built altars (Gen. 12:6-7; 33:18-20). There also the bones of Joseph were ultimately to be buried (Jos. 24:32).

(i) The Altar on Mt. Ebal (27:1-8)

When the crossing of the Jordan had taken place and possession of the land (in principle at least) was a reality, three things were required of the people. They had to erect stones on which the law would be displayed; they had to erect an altar on Mt. Ebal; and then to offer sacrifices.

1-4 The fact that the elders along with Moses give the command emphasises the idea of succession of leadership that runs through these final chapters of the book. Moses has not been referred to in the third person since 5:1, but the use here seems to set off the covenant renewal ceremony from the law and its exposition in chapters 5-26. The people were solemnly charged to keep all the commandments that had been given, and to look ahead to the soon approaching time when they would be over the Jordan. They are instructed that large plastered stones are to be set up with the law (or some suitable portion[s] of it) written on them. There is no specification of the number of stones or their size. The reference to 'all the words of this law' could be just to the Decalogue, or else it could include much more of chapters 5-26. Such a method of displaying important instructions was typically Egyptian, not Mesopotamian. Writing the law in this way would both be a symbolic demonstration of its binding nature on the covenant people, and also a reminder of its character as a witness against them if they were disobedient (see Jos. 24:26-27).

5-6a In addition to the stones, an altar was to be erected on Mt. Ebal. The fact that this instruction was given shows that the law concerning the central sanctuary was not meant to forbid other sites absolutely, providing that the LORD chose those places. It is a striking fact that Mt Ebal, from whose slopes the curses were to be spoken, was chosen as the place of sacrifice. Perhaps Ebal was selected to show that God was able even on the mount of cursing to remove the sins of his people and restore them to his fellowship.

The Samaritan text of the Pentateuch substitutes 'Gerizim' for 'Ebal' here, but this was doubtless to connect this site with it as the later Samaritan place of worship. As in the law in Exodus 20:25, here too no dressed stones were to be used for the altar. This prohibition may have some connection with the fact that suitable iron tools for stonework were almost exclusively in Philistine control. At any time, especially for things connected with their worship, the Israelites were not to be dependent on those outside of the covenant bond. Archaeologists have discovered an altar on Mt. Ebal, but though the location and dating of the site seem to fit, no inscription or other definite evidence was found to link it with Joshua's altar.

6b-7 Two kinds of sacrifices were to be offered. The first were the burnt offerings, which were completely consumed by fire, and which symbolised the entire consecration of the offering to God. The second were the peace or fellowship offerings, which were normally offered in conjunction with other sacrifices, as here. They symbolised the fellowship of peace between the LORD and his people. As on Mt. Sinai the renewal of the covenant was to be marked by this ceremonial feast, which was a recognised way by which ratification of covenants took place.

8 The reminder regarding the nature of the writing on the stones is important. It had to be very clearly done, so that some one could read it to the people before they entered into the ratification ceremony. Intelligent understanding of the covenant's demand was essential before the ratification ceremony took place (cf. the New Testament stress on using the renewed mind in offering ourselves as sacrifices to God, Rom. 12:1-2). This is emphasised by the fact that in the account of the fulfilment of these provisions it is said that Joshua read to the people 'all the words of the law' (Jos. 8:34-35).

(ii) The Proclamation of the Curses (27:9-26)
9-10 Before setting out the curses the people are reminded that they were even then God's people. The call for silence is repeated

elsewhere in the Old Testament at the climax of certain religious ceremonies (Neh. 8:11; Zeph. 1:7; Hab. 2:20), though the word used in verse 9 only occurs here in the Old Testament. It calls the people to silence in order that they can give undivided attention to the words which follow. At first sight the initial statement by Moses and the Levites seems out of place. They say to the people: 'You have now become the people of the LORD your God.' Several times already in this book the claim is made that Israel is the redeemed people of God (see e.g., 4:20; 9:26). However, at each successive covenant renewal the people had to make that confession anew as they pledged allegiance to the LORD. That allegiance was not only to be in words but also demonstrated in obedience to the commands and decrees which had been promulgated through Moses.

11-13 The actual ceremony in the valley is then portrayed. The people were to be divided into two tribal groups of six. The sons of Leah (4) and Rachel (2) were to stand on Mount Gerizim and pronounce the blessings. It is noteworthy that Levi is included in the list, because the Levites were an integral part of Israel and their privileged position did not prevent them from being identified with the other tribes on this occasion. However, because Ephraim and Manasseh are combined under the name of Joseph, the list is still only six. The sons of concubines Bilhah and Zilpah (in addition to Reuben and Zebulun, sons of Leah) were to stand on Mount Ebal and proclaim the curses. Several factors about the curses should be noted.

1. There were twelve curses (corresponding to the number of the tribes) and the sins were chosen to reflect God's total demands on the people. All the curses relate to sins that are condemned elsewhere under the Mosaic law.

2. The form of the successive statements, each starting with 'Cursed', links the fate of the covenant breakers with that of the serpent (Gen. 3:14). Those who commit sin are identified in judgment with their father the devil (Jn. 8:42-47). Nowhere is the actual content of the curse expressed here.

3. This ceremony was in essence an oath-taking, as the people reaffirmed their covenant allegiance. They had to listen as the Levites recited each curse, and then they had to respond with their 'Amen' ('So be it'). While the Levites were represented in the tribal groupings, they also had the priestly function of reciting the curses and the blessings.

4. The element that links these particular sins together appears to be secrecy (cf. the use of the phrase 'in secret' in verses 15 and 24). Even when men could not see the particular sin committed, and it went unpunished, yet in God's sight it was known and it was reckoned as rebellion.

5. The final curse, with its all-embraciveness, reminds the reader that the others were representative examples, but each part of God's law was to be obeyed.

6. While six of the tribes were to stand on Mount Gerizim to bless the people, there is no list of blessings corresponding to the curses (as there are in the next chapter). This is probably because what transpires here is an oath-taking, not the reciprocal blessings and cursings mentioned in verses 12-13. We know from Joshua 8:33 that the people stood on both sides of the ark of the covenant as it was carried by the priests. Probably the ark symbolised both the presence of the LORD and the blessings that his presence brought to the people. The emphasis here, however, is clearly on the oath-taking.

14-15 The Levites were required to recite the curses in a loud voice. Even if not all the people were able to hear in that particular geographical setting, yet the proclamation was necessary. To each of the curses 'all the people' were to respond with the 'Amen'. While the full procedure is not set out, it is quite possible that each tribe in turn had to make their formal affirmation. The first curse is the longest of the twelve. It virtually brings together the first two commandments in forbidding anything to take the place of the LORD, such as carved or moulded images which would be worshipped in secret (Heb. *basater*). As frequently elsewhere in the Old Testament, this phrase 'in secret' is used of covert, evil activity. While outwardly professing to belong to Israel, such a person was secretly linked with an alien god.

16 Disrespect for parents and others in rightful authority (see the discussion relating to the scope of the Fifth Commandment, 5:16) is next addressed. The Hebrew verb used means to make little of something, and so it is the very opposite of the positive verb 'honour' which is used in Exodus 20:12 and Deuteronomy 5:16. In this case the actual form of the curse is already given in Exodus 21:17: 'Anyone who curses (the Heb. verb is one used in Deut. 27:16, a synonym for the one used here) his father or mother must be put to death.'

17-19 These three verses all deal with malpractices in relation to truth, which have a bearing on the whole covenant community, not just the offended individuals. The first is a case when a boundary marker (or something like the Assyrian *kudurru*-stones, see the commentary on 19:14) was surreptitiously removed. This action in effect was aimed at defrauding a neighbour of his rightful property. The second case is the treatment of a blind man, leading him out of the way. Like the example mentioned in Leviticus 19:14 (putting a stumbling block in front of a blind man) there seems to be a wider principle at stake. Not only could there easily be deceitful dealing with such a person, but because of his blindness there would be no possibility of identifying the offender. The covenant encouraged justice to all, and therefore there is a curse on those who act deceitfully to defraud one of the most vulnerable groups in society. The third group likewise comprises those who had no one to defend them – the alien, the orphan and the widow. They might have no way of redressing an offence in law, and therefore an offender could take action against them imagining that he would be immune from any legal penalty.

20-23 The following four curses all relate to sexual offences. The first of them, sleeping with his stepmother, has earlier been condemned (22:30). Bestiality had been forbidden in the Book of the Covenant (Exod. 22:19). It was so serious because it involved man, created in God's image, having intercourse with animals, which were a lower order of creation. It was, therefore, a total rejection of God's purposes in creation. Moreover, it was a pagan practice in which people thought they could attain union with the deity symbolised by the animal. This would help to explain its presence in the Book of the Covenant alongside prohibition of sacrifice to any pagan god (Exod. 22:19-20). The third sexual aberration was intercourse with a step-sister or half-sister. Israel would have been familiar with the incest practised among the royal family in Egypt. Nowhere in the Mosaic law is there direct prohibition of relationships with a full sister, but clearly that was understood to follow from a regulation such as this. The final one in this group is the curse on a man having a sexual relationship with his mother-in-law, already prohibited in Leviticus 18:17 and 20:14.

24-25 These two cases relate to murder, and therefore a breach of the Sixth Commandment. While the first of them merely says 'strikes' (Heb. *makkeh*) his neighbour, the context makes it plain that it is not just manslaughter that is in view (hence NIV 'kills his neighbour'). The second one presupposes someone accepting a bribe to murder an innocent person. The act of accepting the bribe was a serious offence in itself, whether or not the planned action was carried out. The person accepting the bribe would not do so unless he thought that his action would remain unknown, for otherwise he would not be able to profit from the bribe he received.

26 The final curse is a general one, directed to failure to uphold in practice all the commands of the law. The law was not an abstraction, but it was meant to be obeyed. Moses knew by experience the tendencies of the people to depart from it (cf. e.g. the breaking of the Sinai covenant, Exod. 32-34), and the long list of curses in the following chapter reinforces this view of human, sinful nature. This appears to be why the curse aspect dominates over the idea of blessing in these two chapters. This curse, with its all-inclusiveness, reminds us that the others are representative examples, but that all of God's law was to be obeyed. Paul quotes this verse in Galatians 3:10 to show that peace with God cannot come through *our* obedience to the law. It comes only through Christ who 'redeemed us from the law by becoming a curse for us' (Gal. 3:13).

2. Blessings and Curses (28:1-68)

The previous chapter has set out the procedure for renewing the covenant when the Israelites entered into Canaan. Now attention comes back to the immediate circumstances in the plains of Moab. Israel is reminded by Moses both of the blessings that God has promised to an obedient people and the curses that will follow disobedience.

The pattern in this chapter has its parallels in the extra-biblical treaties. They contain pronouncements of curses and blessings which gods involved in the oath-taking ceremony would dispense in accordance with the deserts of the covenant servants. When the covenant was made at Sinai curses and blessings were included in the Ten Commandments (Exod. 20:2-17), and also expanded later in the Book of the Covenant (Exod. 23:20-33). Leviticus 26 contains both blessings and curses, while in Deuteronomy they occur in the Ten Commandments (Deut. 5:6-21), at the conclusion of the exposition of the First Commandment (Deut. 11:8-32), and principally here in chapter 28.

Before looking at the blessings and curses another comment should be made. In chapter 27 the future procedure at Mount Ebal and Mount Gerizim, with matching sets of six tribes, is described. It seems that the matching sets of six blessings (verses 3-6) and six curses (verses 16-19) in this chapter (28) must be connected with that same division of the tribes, even if the later procedure was not followed in the plains of Moab. Certainly Joshua 8:34-35 specifically mentions the reading by Joshua of the words of the law (the blessings and the curses) and this would seem to embrace Deuteronomy in that reading.

(i) The Blessings (28:1-14)

1-2 The opening words tie in with the conclusion of chapter 26 (verses 18-19). Israel was exalted over the other nations by God's sovereign choice, but such a position of renown entailed obedience to the LORD's commands. If they showed due obedience then promised blessings would flow to them. This emphasis on obedience reappears in verses 9, 13 and 14. God's covenant would not be abrogated, but the enjoyment of the covenant blessings would depend upon obedience on the part of the people. Even in judgment the covenant would stand. Israel in exile was reminded that there was a temporary separation between God and his people but no divorce (Isa. 50:1), and with deep compassion God would restore his bride (Isa. 54:5-8).

3-6 In verses 3-6 there are six successive phrases in the Hebrew text that all start with the word *baruch*, 'blessed'. They cover the fullness of blessing that will come in the various relationships of life, the paired opposites expressing the totality of life. The curses in verses 16-19 correspond to these six blessings, except that the third and fourth are interchanged, and the expression 'the fruit of your cattle' is omitted. Blessing is promised in both urban and rural life (verse 3), extending to the fertility of both people and animals (verse 4) and the provisions of daily sustenance (verse 5). The final statement of the six expresses the prospect of divine blessing on the totality of life (verse 6). Two of the expressions used in verse 4 have already occurred in the blessings stated in 7:13 ('the calves of your herds and the lambs of your flock', see commentary on that passage). Perhaps the language was again used deliberately to reinforce the point that the LORD, not Baal, was the God who provided the fertility for his people and their animals.

7-14 The exposition of the blessings that follows in these verses is a free development of the basic statements. It has a definite pattern to it, as the various items are introduced in a given order, and then the order is reversed. This chiastic pattern is as follows:

A	foreign relations (verse 7)
B	domestic affairs (verse 8)
C	the covenant LORD (verse 9)
C¹	the covenant LORD (verse 10)
B¹	domestic affairs (verse 11, 12a)
A¹	foreign relations (verses 12b, 13)

Conflict was going to be a constant experience for Israel throughout her history. She would have to conquer Canaan and then maintain her presence there. Some of the attacks would be minor excursions by small neighbours, while other ones would be attacks by major countries in the region. If obedient to the LORD, Israel would find that attacking nations would flee in disarray (verse 7). Internally, Israel would enjoy many blessings, so that the land which was God's gift would abound in food. All the activities of the people would be productive, and it would be indeed a land flowing with milk and honey. The mention of fertility may well have been to remind Israel that the LORD was the provider for Israel, and no recourse to fertility rites such as those practised by the Canaanites was necessary or permissible (verse 8). The central core in verses 9-10 shows that the vital concern of Israel had to be her relationship with the LORD. She was his holy people, and his possession ('his holy people', verse 9; 'called by the name of the LORD', verse 10). That was the central aspect of the covenant relationship, and if that was overlooked then disobedience would quickly and easily follow. In verses 11-12a the theme of temporal blessings in the land promised to the patriarchs again features prominently. The subject of provision of abundant rain has been dealt with in 11:13-18 (see commentary). Here it is said that God opens his 'storehouse' (a word more usually used of treasuries), which is reminiscent of the way in which Psalm 104:3, 13 speaks of the outpouring of rain from God's upper chambers. External nations come back into focus in verses 12b-13. Israel was to achieve economic independence among the nations (see comment on 15:6), exercising a leadership role among the nations ('the head, not the tail'; see the same idiom reversed in verse 44 and cf. Isa. 9:15-16). For this to happen, sole allegiance had to be given to the LORD, and this is expressed positively in terms of obeying him and following his ways (verse 13b). The negative expression of it comes in verse 14 with the warning against turning aside to or serving alien gods. The phrase 'to turn aside' is a common Old Testament one for departing from God's commands (see the use of it in the story of the golden calf, Exod. 32:8), and virtually becomes a technical term for a breach of the covenant bond.

(ii) The Curses (28:15-68)

As with the extra-biblical treaties, the section on curses is far longer than the section on blessings. The perversity of human nature in transgressing God's laws was taken into account, just as the negatives in the Ten Commandments ('You shall not ...') are addressed to sinners. This whole section points to the inevitable consequences of disobedience. Even when renewing the covenant Israel was faced with the dreadful prospect of experiencing God's curses rather than his blessings.

Several characteristics of this section stand out.

1. It commences in parallel with the blessings:

> 'If you fully obey ... these blessings will come upon you ... You will be blessed ... ' (verses 1-3).
> 'If you do not obey ... all these curses will come upon you ... You will be cursed ... ' (verses 15-16).

The same areas of life are in view and disobedience will bring the exact reverse of the blessings. This becomes clearer as the chapter progresses, for so many of the curses simply reverse the earlier blessings (cf. verses 15-19 with verses 1-2; verses 23-24 with verse 12; verse 25 with verse 7; verses 25, 37, 46 with verses 1, 9-10; verses 43-44 with verses 12b-13a; verse 45 with verse 2).

2. The severity of the curses should have reminded Israel of the true nature of disobedience, as a forsaking of the living God and repudiation of his covenantal demands. When the Book of the Law was found during Josiah's reforms he recognised the nature of the curses (2 Kings 22:13), as did Jeremiah when he was told to go and proclaim to the people the curse of the covenant. His response was: 'Amen, LORD' (Jer. 11:5b).

3. Throughout the curses there is the recurrence of the same ideas, such as disease or defeat before enemies or exile. This is partly because the pictures of the future given here are not in chronological sequence but are parallel to one another. This marks out this list of curses as different from those in Leviticus

26, where it is clear that there is a progressive sequence in the curses (cf. Lev. 26:14ff., 'But if you will not listen to me → then I will do this to you → If after all this you will not listen to me, I will punish you for your sins → If you remain hostile towards me → I will multiply your afflictions').

4. As with the previous section, after the six rhythmic curses (verses 16-19) comes the general expansion of the curses. There are six divisions here (verses 20-26, 27-37, 38-48, 49-57, 58-63, 64-68). The first theme and the fifth begin with diseases and end with exile, while the fourth and sixth are solely devoted to siege and exile. That event would be the ultimate verdict on the disobedient covenant people because it would show that the promises to the patriarchs had been reversed by the sin of Israel – no longer a large nation but one scattered among the nations, no longer a blessing but rather a thing of derision, no longer in possession of their own land but driven into exile.

The later Old Testament history depicts the infliction of these curses on Israel. The prophets warned of the coming doom in terms drawn from passages such as these (cf. Isa. 5:26ff. where the description of the impending Assyrian invasion seems to echo Deut. 28:49ff.). Exile, desolation and finally the destruction of Jerusalem in AD 70 meant that Israel had reaped to the full the consequences of her own folly and disobedience. Messengers were sent time and again, but Judah 'mocked God's messengers, despised his words and scoffed at his prophets until the wrath of the LORD was aroused against his people and there was no remedy' (2 Chron. 36:16).

15 The presentation of the curses commences with an introduction identical in style with that which introduced the blessings (verses 1-2). The only changes are the negative ('if you *do not* obey'), the addition of the words 'and his decrees', and the substitution of 'curses' for 'blessings'. The NKJV version preserves the parallelism closer than does the NIV. This parallelism is important because it reinforces the point that Moses was setting out the dual sanctions of the covenant for the people, blessings or curses. Soon he was to express it also in terms not only of blessing and cursing but of life and death (30:19-20).

16-19 The six curses simply speak of the reversal of the very things that had been spoken of in the list of blessings (with the minor changes already noted; see comment on verses 3-6). Living in the good land of Canaan would turn out to be a disaster for Israel if there was disobedience to God's instructions for them. Covenant privilege would not insulate them from God's judgments.

20-26 The curses are traced back directly to God's action because of the way in which the people would 'forsake' him. This verb is used over a hundred times in the Old Testament as a term for breaking the covenant bond. While God might use human instruments in some cases to fulfil his will, he was the ultimate source of the curses. These curses vary in type – some relate to diseases affecting humans, crops and animals, others relate to severe weather conditions such as drought and dust storms, while others envisage invasion by foreign armies. Several of the terms only occur here in the Old Testament and therefore their translation is doubtful, but the overall picture is clear. Ultimate destruction of Israel would ensue if there was disobedience to God's instructions (see verses 20-22, 24). In verse 25 Israel is depicted as suffering the very same devastating defeat in battle as her enemies would undergo if she was obedient (see verse 7). In covenant-making ceremonies it was common for animals to be cut in pieces as a sign of what would happen to those making the covenant if they did not keep its provisions (see Gen. 15:10-17). The disobedient would find that they themselves would become like those dismembered animals and their bodies would be food for the birds and animals (see Jer. 34:18-20; Ps. 79:1-4). The idea is also carried over to the fate of rebel sinners in the final eschatological judgment (Ezek. 37:4-17; Rev. 19:17-19).

27-37 The main description of these curses is also arranged in a chiastic pattern:

A   incurable disease (verse 27)
B   madness (verse 28)
C   continual oppression (verse 29)
D   frustration (verse 30-32)
C¹   continual oppression (verse 33)
B¹   madness (verse 34)
A¹   incurable disease (verse 35)

It is a frightening picture of a life of utter distress, leading even to loss of sanity. At every turn the efforts and plans of the people will be reversed, and there will be no prosperity resulting from all their labour. Even when blindness is mentioned (verse 29) it is caused by a psychological change, as the context makes it plain that physical blindness is not intended. It is as if the whole exodus from Egypt is to be reversed, and Israel to be brought back there to suffer many of the well-known Egyptian diseases (verse 27). Twice Moses repeats the sad phrase: 'and there is no saviour' (NIV 'and none to rescue you'). When these judgments come God will not intervene to deliver his people, because the judgments are from his hand. The final verses of the section (verses 36-37) point to exile, a fate already mentioned for the sons and daughters who will be carried off into slavery (verse 32). The people and even their king will be carried away, and in a foreign land they will worship idols. Instead of being a praise among the nations (26:19) Israel will be a thing of derision. All the promises to Abraham will in effect be reversed – the large nation reduced to a remnant, the promised land occupied by others, and instead of being a blessing to all the nations, Israel is to become the object of scorn and ridicule.

38-48 Further description is given of the reversal of fortunes for Israel if God's curses come upon them. Instead of being a land of plenty, there will be devastation caused by insect plagues (verses 38, 40, 42). The plagues of Egypt did not trouble the Israelites because God gave the assurance that his people would not be touched by them (Exod. 12:13). However, these ones will affect them deeply so that famine and ultimate destruction would befall them. They will lack food, clothes and money (verse 48). In this situation the families will lose their children to captivity, while the aliens, who normally occupied a lowly position in Israel will be so elevated in status that they will be in a superior position, even to the point of providing loans for Israelites. All these things were the very opposite of the promised blessings for obedience (see especially verses 11-13). The reason for the application of the curses is given in verses 45-48, along with further description of the nature of the captivity Israel is to undergo. The curses will pursue them relentlessly because of failure to keep God's commands. Covenant unfaithfulness will be followed by covenant sanctions. In Egypt God performed signs and wonders (Exod. 7:3; 10:1), but now his curses on Israel will be a testimony to the nations that God has dealt in judgment with his own people. The NIV translation suggests that they will be a sign and wonder *to Israel* but it is better to understand that the curses would be on Israel as a sign to other nations (cf. NKJV 'And they shall be upon you for a sign and a wonder'). It is possible to take the phrase 'for ever' at the end of verse 46 to refer to the devastation of the exile as the climactic judgment of God upon Israel. If the words are thought to point to an even more ultimate fulfilment, then Paul's words in 1 Thessalonians 2:16 need to be considered. He speaks of the hostility of the Jews to the early Christians and the fact that they are heaping up their sins to the limit. 'The wrath of God has come upon them fully' (NIV margin).

49-57 Preliminary references to siege and exile in the earlier part of the chapter are crystallised now with a vivid depiction of what the siege will mean for the people. It was a means of forcing cities to capitulate to an enemy by cutting off all supplies. Those who thought that high fortified walls were their safety (verse 52) would find that they had trusted in vain. The conquerors are described in terms of barbarian invaders, coming from a distant country and swooping as an eagle does on its prey. The picture of cannibalism was fulfilled during the Syrian siege of Samaria in the time of king Joram (2 Kings 6:28-29).

58-63 While the curses are not set out in chronological order in this chapter, there is a growing clarification of the reversal of the patriarchal promises. Disobedience to the ways of the LORD is going to lead to plagues of disease. This disobedience is linked here with failure to reverence the glorious and awesome name of their God. The description in this present section goes beyond the earlier ones in adding mention of plagues that are not written in this book of the law (verse 61). Unimaginable terrors await the rebels. The large family of Israel is going to be reduced to a remnant (NIV 'few in number' translates the Hebrew verb from which the noun 'remnant' comes), it will be uprooted out of the land into which it is about to enter as its possession, and instead of being a blessing to the nations Israel herself will be under the disfavour of God. It is in his sovereign pleasure either to bless or to curse (verse 63). Earlier references hinted at the exile but now it becomes so explicit (cf. verse 63 with verses 25, 32, 36, 37, 41, 52). Israel was a shoot that God took out of Egypt and transplanted in Canaan (Ps. 80:8-16), but turning from the ways of the LORD caused her to be plucked out of the ground (cf. Prov. 2:22 for the use of the same verb).

64-68 The impending doom of Israel is described in terms of a scattering among the nations, which was fulfilled for Israel after the fall of Samaria in 722 BC and for Judah at the fall of Jerusalem in 586 BC. Those initial scatterings were the precursors of many others for the Jewish people down through the centuries, even to the present day. Having departed from a true covenant relationship the Israelites will turn to the worship of gods previously unknown either to them or to their fathers (see the earlier reference to false worship in verse 36). The frustration and distress that has already been noted as part of God's judgment (see verses 28-29, 34) will culminate in the inability to find a secure place of rest (verses 65-67). One of the great emphases regarding the land of Canaan was that Israel would find rest there (see Deut. 3:20; 12:10; 25:19). But that privilege was going to be forfeited and the people of Israel would long for a genuine resting place. In oppressive fear they would desire evening when it was only morning and for morning when it was evening (the Hebrew idiom in verse 67, 'If only it were ...' is the same as in 5:29; see commentary). If God blessed them in the Promised Land the other nations would fear them (verse 10). Instead disobedience would make them objects of scorn and ridicule. Even if taken back to Egypt as slaves themselves, no one would want to buy them.

3. Covenant Renewal in Moab (29:1–30:20)
The book moves to its climax with the actual renewal of the covenant in these chapters. The people are called upon to confirm their adherence to the LORD and the words of his covenant. Life or death is the solemn choice, with strong encouragement being given to choose life, and to enter into possession of the blessings promised to Abraham, Isaac and Jacob.

(i) Introductory Words (29:1)
The words forming an introduction to Moses' last appeal to Israel are reminiscent of the opening words of the whole book. Some wish to take them as a subscription to the previous part (cf. the fact that in the Hebrew Bible they come as the last verse of chapter 28) rather than as a superscription to what follows. However, the context here and also the parallel with 1:1 suggests that it is best to take them as a preface to the covenant renewal ceremony. The connection made in this verse between the covenant made at Horeb and that in the plains of Moab is a fresh reminder of the significance of the whole book as a covenant renewal document.

(ii) Historical Reminder (29:2–8)
In common with the fuller historical treatment earlier in the book, Moses draws upon the past to reinforce the lessons for the present. As he speaks, his words become imperceptibly the words of God himself (cf. 'the LORD has not given' in verse 4 with 'that you might know that I am the LORD,' verse 6). Moses was the intermediary through whom God spoke, and though he commences by speaking of God in the third person ('the LORD' in verses 2, 4), in verse 5 he speaks in the first person ('that you might know that *I* am the LORD your God').

2-4 The events surrounding the Exodus were acts of God's power and grace, yet spiritual blindness prevented the people from viewing them with spiritual perception. The lack of insight is described in terms of not understanding with the heart, not seeing with the eyes, and not hearing with the ears. It is attributed to an act of God, who needed to grant such apprehension, even to those who actually were themselves eye-witnesses of the events. Paul later used verse 4 in combination with Isaiah 29:10 when speaking of the unbelieving Jews (Rom. 11:8), and the idea also lies behind his discussion in 2 Corinthians 3:12-15.

5-6 During the wilderness experiences God made special provision for Israel. They did not have access to the normal food of bread and wine, nor did they need to renew their clothing or their shoes. This miraculous provision by God in the wilderness was intended to meet a practical need. It was also to serve to bring them into closer personal acquaintance with him as their own God and redeemer.

7-8 Reference is made again to the defeat of Sihon and Og (cf. 2:26–3:11). Up to that point the battles involving them were the most notable victories that Israel had made, and they were a precursor of other victories yet to be fought in Canaan. Conquering their territory was a preliminary fulfilment of the promise to Abraham concerning the land, and the possession of the territory of these two kings by two and half of the tribes was part of the inheritance into which the rest were yet to enter.

(iii) Appeal to Israel (29:9-15)

The solemnity of the occasion is now brought home to Israel. They are standing in God's very presence to renew their allegiance to him. It is striking that those embraced within the covenant included wives, children and servants (verse 11) and even unborn generations (verses 14-15). All those within the sphere of authority of an individual were incorporated with him in the covenant relationship (see Gen. 17:23).

Several of the technical expressions regarding covenant making occur in this context. The covenant was to be made by the LORD (verses 1, 12, 15; Heb. *karat*, 'cut', reflecting the common practice of slaying animals in such a ceremony). Israel had to enter (Heb. *'avar*, 'pass through') the covenant and the curse. The whole expression is rare, and seems to be connected with the practice of passing through dismembered animals in oath-taking ceremonies (cf. Gen. 15:17-18; Jer. 34:18-19). In verse 12, English versions have 'oath'.

9 Prosperity in the land of Canaan was not to be automatic. Covenant commitment also entailed covenant responsibility, so Israel was told that total obedience to the words of the covenant is required. Their vision for the future would only come to pass if they were faithful to the stipulations of the Great King. Those stipulations have been set out in detail. Now formal adherence to them was required.

10-11 All those who were part of the assembled body of people (including the aliens) had to stand in the LORD's presence. The Hebrew verb translated 'standing' in verse 10 is not the usual verb, but connotes a more formal positioning of the people for the covenant ceremony. The NIV renders 'your leaders and chief men,' but this is an alteration of the Hebrew text which reads 'your leaders and your tribes' (as in the NKJV version). While as far back as the Greek Septuagint translation there was a desire to conform the expressions here to other lists of leaders (as in Deut. 16:18; 21:2; Jos. 8:33; 23:2; 24;1), yet the Hebrew textual tradition is uniform. The stress is on the comprehensive nature of the assembly. The wives and little children were present, along with the aliens. Two representative examples of the aliens are cited – wood cutters and water carriers – though doubtless the aliens were involved in many other activities as well. Because they came under the authority structures in Israel they were required to be present at the ceremony.

12-13 The purpose of the ceremony is stated explicitly in these verses. The gathered community is entering into a binding covenant with the LORD, which is also called 'a curse' (Heb. *'alah*). This

word (a different Hebrew word to those used in 28:15ff.) is virtually
a synonym for covenant, drawing attention to the solemnity of
the transaction and the penalty that would ensue for breach of
covenant law. The reference in verse 13 to the confirmation of
Israel as God's own people is important. The same Hebrew verb
is used of the confirmation of the original creation covenant in
the time of Noah (Gen. 6:18; 9:9, 11, 17). Its use here reinforces
the idea of the continuity of the covenant in that Israel, already
the people of God, is reaffirmed in that status by this ceremony.
This idea is further strengthened by the fact that the central core
of the covenant relationship is re-stated in terms that go back to
language God used in making his promises to the patriarchs: 'I
will be your God ... and you shall be my people'. The formal
aspect of the covenant was only the shell surrounding the kernel.

14-15 The continuity of the covenant in coming generations was
an important aspect. God had pledged that he was a faithful God,
keeping covenant and mercy to a thousand generations (Deut. 7:9).
Those entering into a solemn oath with God were committing
their families after them to continue the bond with the LORD. There
was no automatic application of grace to each child in the covenant
(see comment on next section), but the promise could certainly be
given to them and their children, and 'to as many as are far off',
i.e. of generations to come (Acts 2:39).

(iv) Warning against Apostasy (29:16-29)
Dangers of apostasy and spiritual pride were ever going to be real
for Israel. Care had to be taken lest there be turning to idolatry or
even falling into the danger of mere outward adherence to the
covenant. There is continuation of the technical language of
covenant making throughout this section.

16-18 Idols were not something new for Israel. They had seen
them in Egypt and in the countries through which they passed on
their way to the plains of Moab. They had even imitated them
with their own golden calf at Sinai (Exod. 32:1-35). No individual,
clan or tribe should be tempted to turn from the LORD and become

servants of alien gods. The Hebrew word for 'turn' used here
(*panah*) is frequently used of a deliberate forsaking of the LORD.
Care had to be taken lest there be any seed in them that could
ultimately become a poisonous plant. This metaphorical
description highlights both the insidious nature of a tendency
towards idolatry, along with its ruinous outcome. The ideas of
root and poisonous fruit are developed in the following verses
(verses 19-21, the root; verses 22-28, the fruit).

19 The danger of sheer nominalism would be very real. Some
would think that simply because they belonged to Israel all would
be well. They would invoke blessings on themselves when they
heard the words of the covenant (Heb. *'alah*, 'oath'; see comment
on verse 12). These people would not remember that in addition
to physical circumcision spiritual circumcision was also required
(Deut. 10:16; 30:6). Later in the Old Testament the principle is
asserted that a Jew could be circumcised yet uncircumcised (Jer.
9:25-26). Paul draws the fitting conclusion that a man is 'a Jew if
he is one inwardly; circumcision is circumcision of the heart by
the Spirit' (Rom. 2:29). Here Moses says that a feeling of safety
will prove false when God sends his judgment on the land.

20-21 All the outward conformity to covenant requirements
(including circumcision) would not save such persons. Those who
walk in the stubbornness of their own hearts would find that there
was no forgiveness. While the biblical teaching is that pardon is
available for the penitent (2 Pet. 3:9), yet it also declares that
those who deny the 'sovereign Lord' will bring 'swift destruction
on themselves' (2 Pet. 2:1). God's wrath will be manifest in
bringing to pass all the curses of the covenant, and blotting out
such a man's name altogether. Not only will he himself perish,
but he will have no descendants to carry on his name. An individual
could not hide among the tribes of Israel and think that he was
beyond detection. While corporate Israel was responsible to God,
so also was each individual within that collective whole.

22-23 The land stricken by God's judgments will be a silent testimony to future generations and also to foreigners. They will see the calamities (Heb. *makkot*, the same word as used in the curses section, 28:59, 61 [NIV 'fearful plagues', 'disaster']) and sicknesses that had been brought upon the land. The land of milk and honey will become a desolation – no planting of seeds, no early growth, no sign of vegetation. The nearest parallel will be what happened to Sodom and Gomorrah, Admah and Zeboiim. These four places are mentioned together in Genesis 10:19, while the destruction of Sodom and Gomorrah is recorded in Genesis 19:24-25. Just as that event was a demonstration of God's anger (verse 23) so will the ultimate destruction of the land be an exhibition of that same anger (verse 20). The curses will be real, not just vain threats. Even as Sodom, Gomorrah and the associated cities suffered, so Israel will know that it is a fearful thing to fall into the hands of the living God. The same warning holds true under the New Covenant (cf. Heb. 10:26-31).

24-28 The time will come when foreigners, viewing desolate Israel, will ask the question: 'Why has the LORD done this to this land? Why this fierce, burning anger?' Only one answer can be given: 'It is because this people abandoned the covenant of the LORD, the God of their fathers, the covenant he made with them when he brought them out of Egypt' (verses 24-25). The verb 'abandon' is another technical term, being used over a hundred times in the Old Testament in connection with the act of breaking God's covenant. It is also employed in paired statements describing what God did to Israel because they had abandoned him (see Deut. 31:16b-17a; Isa. 54:7-8; 2 Chron. 13:10-11). The covenant was not simply the one being confirmed at this time in the plains of Moab, but it was in direct continuity with the covenant with the patriarchs. Even when the final desolation came to the land with the fall of Jerusalem in 586 BC it was because of the breach of this covenant. Successive Old Testament covenants did not abrogate the preceding ones but supplemented them.

The sin of Israel is summarised in other words in verse 26. The people, in abandoning the living God, had followed, served and worshipped other gods. Idolatry was an abomination to the LORD for it was a repudiation of his lordship and an express violation of his instruction regarding not making idols. Hence the first two commandments focus attention directly on the centrality of sole worship of the LORD. The language ultimately used by the historian of Israel in describing the reason for the fall of the northern kingdom (2 Kings 17:7-18) bears an unmistakable likeness to that of this present passage. Once more the fact that desolation of the land and exile from it would be a sign of God's great anger is enforced in the following verses.

27-28 Just as God uprooted little Israel from Egypt (Ps. 80:8-9), so he will uproot them even from the land of promise because of their unfaithfulness (the Heb. verb is identical in Ps. 80 and here). The final words of verse 28 'as it is now' (Heb. *kayyom hazzeh*, 'as this day') are words that will be used in the future by those asking the question in verse 24. The question will be posed in the exilic period and hence the nations are depicted by Moses as referring back to the present uprooted existence of Israel.

29 It is possible to take this verse as part of the answer to the question asked in verse 24. However, it seems better to take it as a comment by Moses as he concludes this part of his address. In the Massoretic Hebrew text there are very unusual punctuation marks used with the words 'to us and to our children'. This is probably to call attention to the directness of Moses' appeal. The closest parallel is the opening of chapter 5 where Moses emphasises the fact that the covenant is being made 'with us – us – these here today – all of us – living' (5:3). These words contain the warning against trying to pry into God's secret counsel. Curious speculation is no substitute for obedience to God's will. Whatever things lay beyond the understanding of Israel (because God had not revealed them) their concern had to be with what he *had* revealed. His way for them had been declared in the book of the covenant, and let Israel now yield obedience. It forms a fitting prelude to what follows in chapter 30, especially the reference to God's word being near the people (see comment on 30:11-14).

(v) Future Return to the Lord (30:1-10)

The picture of the future history of Israel, begun in the previous chapter, is carried here beyond the threatened exile. Moses speaks of a change of heart of the banished people of Israel and of a restoration to the land that had belonged to their fathers.

1-2 The opening verses of the chapter set out the circumstances under which the consequences of both God's blessings and curses will become operative. At an unspecified time in the future the experience of both God's blessings and curses will then be behind them. In their exile they will remember the LORD, and with obedient hearts give themselves afresh to his ways. At that time they would be able to claim that they were loving the LORD their God with all their heart and with all their soul (cf. the use of the these expressions in the Shema, 6:5). The wholehearted nature of their spiritual change at that time is emphasised by the repetition of these phrases again in verses 6 and 10. This prophecy was fulfilled in the return from exile as described in the books of Ezra and Nehemiah.

3-10 The consequences of the change in heart and mind will essentially amount to four things.

1. There will be a restoration to the land promised to the fathers (verses 3, 4, 5). After enjoying its sabbaths of desolation (Lev. 26:43; 2 Chron. 36:21), the land would again be inhabited by the Jewish people. The Hebrew expression used in verse 3, 'turn the captivity' (NIV 'restore your fortunes'), occurs again in the same connection in Psalm 126:1. This will be an act of compassion on God's part, an assurance that God was later to give to exiled Israel through the prophet Isaiah (Isa. 54:7-8). A gathering will take place of scattered Israel from where they had been banished (verses 3-4). Clearly this is qualified already by verses 1-2, and need not be pressed to mean every individual believing Jew will return to Palestine.

2. The restoration will involve a spiritual change on the part of Israel and probably a new covenant relationship (verse 6). Just

as circumcision was the covenant sign from Abraham onwards (see Gen. 17), so it will be repeated in a new way. It will take the form of a spiritual change so that the circumcision is inward as well as outward (cf. the use of the expression previously in 10:16 and the comments on 29:19).

3. The nations whom God uses as his instruments will then become subject to his judgment (verse 7). The curse that disobedience had brought on God's people would be turned on their enemies. The pattern of a judgment exercised simultaneously with God's salvation will repeat itself in the future, even as it had been manifested in the past (cf. the Exodus).

4. The future prosperity would be even greater than in the past (verses 5-9). This prosperity is expressed in terms of the blessings set out in 28:3-6, and also in terms of the Abrahamic covenant. Israel again will be a large family, and possess once more the land of Canaan (verse 5). This is important because there they are pictured as the result of fully obeying the Lord. In this present context the blessings are again closely linked to obedience ('you obey him with all your heart', verse 2; 'if you obey the LORD your God and keep his commands and decrees that are written in this Book of the Law', verse 10).

There are many echoes of this passage in the words of the prophets (see as illustrative of this, Jer. 29:13-14; 30:2-3). Moreover, the description of future restoration and blessing underlies the prophetic description of a new covenant relationship (Jer. 31:31ff.; Ezek. 36:24ff.). The emphasis here in Deuteronomy is on God's power and initiative in performing this restoration (see especially verses 3-9). The same emphasis is carried over in the prophetic passages. This is consistent with all covenant descriptions in the Bible, for it is God who moves towards men and joins them with bonds of covenant love to himself.

(vi) The Moment of Decision – Life or Death (30:11-20)
For the third time in this book (for the previous occasions see 11:26ff. and 28:1ff.) the people are confronted with the need to respond to God's words to them. There is an immediacy about the

challenge. They have to declare themselves as the LORD's people, or else renounce allegiance to him. No one could pretend that they had to ascend to heaven or cross the seas to obtain God's words, for his words had already been given to them.

11-14 A possible objection by the people is answered by Moses. Some could claim that God's revelation was hidden from them, instead of being readily accessible. The answer was simply that it was not in heaven nor in some country across the sea (verses 12-13). Rather, the LORD's word was exceptionally near to them, even in their mouth and in their heart. Paul quotes this passage in Romans 10:6-8 in reference to the word of faith. While here in Deuteronomy the reference is to the law, Paul applies it to the accessibility of the Gospel. The word of faith (Rom. 10:8) meant that righteousness is achieved not by works of righteousness but by believing and confessing that Jesus is Lord.

15-16 The summons to the people contrasts life/prosperity with death/destruction. The use of the term prosperity (Heb. *tov*) is noteworthy because of its use elsewhere as a distinctively covenantal term (cf. its use at the conclusion of Ps. 23:6, 'goodness and steadfast love', and earlier in this book in 12:28). The positive side of the total covenant relationship is summarised in verse 16. Love and obedience to the LORD is linked with life and prosperity in the land of Canaan. This in effect restates the blessing element of chapter 28.

17-18 The negative element of the dual sanctions of the covenant is repeated once again. Disobedience and apostasy to the worship and service of other gods will result in total destruction. Entry into the land sworn to the fathers is no guarantee of perpetual occupancy. The Israelites will themselves become subject to the same kind of judgment that was to be meted out to the Canaanites – a dire warning indeed! Temporary occupation of the land only will be the penalty for renouncing their allegiance to the LORD.

19-20 The final segment forming part of this covenant renewal consists of an appeal to heaven and earth to witness that the blessings and curses have been set before the people, and an appeal by Moses to the people to choose life. In the extra-biblical treaties, the gods of the respective parties were regularly involved as witnesses, and sometimes heaven and earth as here (cf. 4:26; 32:1; for the appeal to heaven and earth in the prophets, see Isa. 1:2 and Jer. 2:12). They were third-party witnesses to all that had been said and done. While different terms are used compared with verse 15, the meaning is the same. There can be no doubt as to the alternatives facing the people. The climax of the whole ceremony is the urgent appeal, 'Choose life!' (verse 19), and the result will be that they will enjoy having the LORD as their life, and living for many years in Canaan. The closing reference to Abraham, Isaac and Jacob is a reminder of the fact that the people are in effect renewing a very ancient covenant relationship. It also served to draw attention to the fact that current blessings were the fulfilment of promises given long before.

E. COVENANT CONTINUATION (31:1–34:12)

1. A New Leader and Divine Witnesses (31:1–31:29)

The final part of the book of Deuteronomy commences with this chapter. Moses indicates his successor and makes provision for the periodic reading of the covenant document (chapter 31). He teaches Israel a song which shall be a witness against later apostasy (chapter 32) and pronounces a blessing over the twelve tribes (chapter 33). The book concludes with the brief chapter relating to Moses' death (chapter 34). Several of the features in these chapters are reminiscent of promises of extra-biblical treaties or of practices in connection with them. These include the succession arrangements regarding leadership, the deposition of the covenant document, the indictment against erring Israel, and the promise of the blessings.

(i) Joshua as Successor (31:1-8)

The time has now come for Moses to hand over the leadership to Joshua. Long before he had been made a military commander against Amalek when he was presumably thirty or forty years of age (Exod. 17:9-14). He had served as Moses' servant (Exod. 24:13) and had been invested with authority by Moses himself (Num. 27:18-23). Now he had to assume the full responsibility of leading the people in their invasion into the land of Canaan.

1-2 The text reverts at this point to narrative. The opening words indicate that there is an implied break between the end of the previous chapter and the beginning of this one. At some stage after concluding the appeal to the people to choose life, Moses went out again to address all Israel. The main text of the covenant has been given in chapters 5-28, along with the historical introduction in chapters 1-3 and the conclusion in chapters 29 and 30. There is a marked similarity between the opening of the book and the opening of this section, as almost identical words are used in both.

Deuteronomy 1:1

*These are the words Moses
spoke to all Israel in the
desert east of Jordan*

Deuteronomy 31:1

*Then Moses went out and
spoke these words to all
Israel*

Leaving out of account the intervening material, the opening of
this section can be viewed as resuming the narrative from the end
of 3:29. It is striking too how the subject of Joshua's role as Moses'
successor connects 3:28 and 31:1-2 together.

Moses' age was not the main factor involved in the transfer of
leadership. Though he was a hundred and twenty years old, he
was still in good health (34:7). The reason was not his inability to
continue to lead Israel because of advancing years or declining
health but because God's judgment had been spoken against him.
His punishment was that he would not enter Canaan (Num. 20:12;
and for references to this fact earlier in this book see 1:38 and
3:28). The fact that Moses' age is noted is important. Clearly his
life divides into three stages of forty years each – the period of
forty years before he fled into the desert of Midian (Acts 7:23),
forty years in Egypt before leading Israel out, and another forty
years to this time. The end of the first two periods marked escapes
into the desert, but now at the end of the third period of forty
years there is no escape for Moses. He must die according to God's
judgment and not enter Canaan with his people.

3-5 The promise of certain victory for the people is given in the
assurances that the LORD will cross over ahead of them, and that
he would give victory to them. The occupation of the land will be
a divine victory. The person of Israel's human leader was but a
secondary matter. What was most important was that they were
entering Canaan by divine appointment, at God's time (cf. the
incident recorded in 1:41-46), and with him as the great warrior
going before them. Recollection of the past was always a
significant factor in Israel's life. If they thought back to what had
happened to Sihon and Og they would be encouraged by God's
intervention on their behalf (see the commentary on 2:26–3:11).
The earlier instructions of 7:1-6 are summarised by the command

given in verse 5, with the verb 'destroy' (Heb. *hishmid*) occurring in both passages.

6 The appeal to the leader and people alike to be strong and courageous is based on the promise of the abiding presence of the LORD with them. The ark of the covenant would be a visible symbol of that presence as they crossed over the Jordan and went into battle. The same promise of the LORD's presence is reiterated to Joshua after Moses' death (Jos. 1:5), while Joshua is exalted as leader to demonstrate that the LORD is with him (Jos. 3:7; 4:14). The expression 'be strong and courageous' appears to have become a standard one, as it is later used again for Joshua (Deut. 31:23; Jos. 1:6-7, 9, 18), for the people of Israel (Jos. 10:25), for Solomon (1 Chron. 22:13; 28:20), and for Hezekiah's military leaders (2 Chron. 32:7). The concluding words of verse 6 give the reassurance that God will never fail nor abandon his people. Entry into Canaan and possession of the allotted territory will only come to pass because of the constancy of God's presence. The author of the epistle to the Hebrews utilises this verse as he teaches his readers to be content with what they have in life (Heb. 13:5). This was a promise that proved true over the centuries, and may well have become a regular part of the liturgy or homiletical usage in Greek-speaking synagogues.

7-8 What had already been said to the congregation of Israel (verse 6) is now directed to Joshua as the new leader. As he stands before the people, Moses challenges him with his new responsibilities. He has to exhibit strength and courage as he leads Israel into the land of promise. The link with the patriarchs is reaffirmed, for all the present events are in fulfilment of a solemn oath that God had made to them. Not only will Joshua lead the people into the land, but the allocation of territory as the inheritance of each of the tribes is also his responsibility. The words of verse 8 are virtually a repetition of those in verses 3 and 6. The renewed assurance of God's presence should banish fear, along with the repeated assertion that God will not leave or desert him as the leader.

(ii) Regular Reading of the Law (31:9-13)
The concern for instruction in the law is evident throughout this book, with emphasis particularly on parental responsibility (4:9-10; 6:7ff.; 6:20ff.; 11:19). This emphasis is maintained here with provision being made for the solemn public reading of the law every seventh year.

9 The requirements of God's covenant were not only oral instructions, but were committed to writing. In Exodus, in addition to the Ten Commandments written on stone by the finger of God, there was the Book of the Covenant (Exod. 24:7). This practice of committing the covenant laws to writing was well-known in connection with the extra-biblical treaties, as both parties to the treaty then had a copy. Moses wrote the law and committed it to the priests and elders. Later in this chapter provision is made for depositing the written code (called again 'the Book of the Law') beside the ark of the covenant so that it could be a witness against the people (31:24-26).

10-11 The representatives of the people to whom the Book of the Law was given were charged with the responsibility of seeing that it was read publicly in the year of cancellation of debts (Heb. *sheⁿnat sheᵐmittah*; see comment on 15:1ff.). The occasion for reading the law is significant. The time was at the Feast of Tabernacles in the year of release, a sabbatical year. That year was an extension of the basic principle of the sabbath, which marked out God's rule over his people and reminded them of the ultimate consummation he would bring. At the time of the harvest in the sabbatical year the people would be reminded of the need to consecrate themselves afresh to the LORD if they were to enjoy the fullness of covenant blessing. As the people gathered at the central sanctuary on that festive occasion the Book of the Law was to be read in their hearing. When Ezra read the law on the return from Babylon it took him from daybreak till noon (Neh. 8:3), which suggests that a large portion of Deuteronomy was read. To enable a large crowd to hear the law the people were probably divided into groups, with the Levites both reading the law and explaining it (see Neh. 8:7-8).

12-13 The intention of the instruction was to ensure that the present generation and the succeeding ones would learn to know the law and fear, with filial devotion, its giver. Stress is laid on the comprehensive nature of the assembly – men, women, children and aliens. The aliens, though underprivileged in other ways, had access to religious participation such as being present at this type of assembly, of bringing offerings, and coming under the regulations regarding purity (Lev. 17:8-16). The continuity of instruction generation after generation is brought to the fore again in verse 13. Israel had to pass on knowledge of the LORD to successive generations (see Ps. 78:1-8) both as an essential duty in itself and also because continued possession of Canaan depended upon a God-fearing nation.

No instruction is given as to who should read the law. Nor do we have sufficient evidence from the Old Testament historical books to know if the reading took place consistently over the years. The surprise at finding the Book of the Law in Josiah's time suggests strongly that this instruction was often disregarded (see 2 Chron. 34:14-33). There was certainly public reading of the law after the return from exile (Neh. 8), along with exposition of it. The later Jewish practice developed of reading set portions of the law each Sabbath in the synagogue, ending on the final day of the Feast of Tabernacles (called in Heb. *simchat torah*, 'rejoicing in the law').

(iii) Instructions from the LORD (31:14-29)
The remainder of this chapter contains three charges with specific instructions to Moses, Joshua and the priests. The time of Moses' death is drawing closer, and further instructions are given to guide Israel when he is no longer their leader.

14-15 With a view to his coming death, Moses is told to appear with Joshua before the LORD at the Tent of Meeting. 'The Tent of Meeting' was one of the names for the tabernacle (see its use in Exod. 27:21; 28:43), and it was a reminder that it served as a meeting place between the LORD and his people, and especially a meeting arranged by God. The appearance of God was in visible form, for the supernatural cloud that had accompanied the people out of Egypt had settled over the tabernacle (Exod. 40:34). Just as when Aaron and Miriam were summoned to meet the LORD, he came down in a pillar of cloud (Num. 12:5), so on this occasion also. The intention of the meeting was not only to give final instructions to Moses but also to instruct Joshua in his duties (verse 14, Heb. 'I will command him', NIV 'I will commission him').

16-18 To Moses God gives a certain picture of the future apostasy of Israel, when the people will prostitute themselves to other gods. This expression is used for a double reason. Marriage in Israel was regarded as a covenant (see Prov. 2:17; Mal. 2:14), and hence it was an easy transition to make use of terms relating to breach of marriage bonds to describe forsaking the LORD for heathen gods. To break covenant with the LORD was adultery. The other reason for the use of the expression is that worship of Canaanite gods often involved physical acts of immorality. If the people forsook God (verse 16), in his anger he would forsake them (verse 17). Used most commonly in the Psalms, 'hiding the face' is an expression describing God as being inaccessible. The phrase the NIV translates as 'and it will be destroyed' is awkward in Hebrew (lit. 'and he will be for eating'). Some manuscripts and the Samaritan text of the Pentateuch make it read 'and they [the people] will be for food'. It is best to refrain from emending the text, and take it as a reference to the nation of Israel mentioned in verse 16 (NIV makes it plural, 'these people'). There is no hope for Israel, which is going to be devoured by its enemies. In the day of calamity the people will recognise that all these things have come upon them because God is no longer in their midst (verse 17b). The action of God in hiding his face was not accidental, but a deliberate response to his rejection by Israel. The indefiniteness of the day of judgment mentioned already in verse 17 is confirmed in verse 18. That judgment will come suddenly and unexpectedly in that distant day of God's visitation.

19 In order to serve as a witness (Heb. *'ēd*) to later generations Moses and Aaron are given a song (the song itself is set out in chapter 32). Use of this song was intended as a reminder of covenant obligations and thus would serve as a witness to a wayward people. In keeping with Near Eastern practice what was important was immediately committed to writing. While Israel would have many different reminders of her obligations (such as reading of the law, festive occasions such as the Passover, the historical psalms) this song would serve as a special witness for the LORD (notice particularly the words 'for me').

20-22 The LORD spells out the future life of Israel, who will enter the promised land but become first complacent and then rebellious. In the land of milk and honey the people will enjoy the good products available, but forget the LORD who gave them and turn to other gods (cf. the warnings given earlier about this very sin of forgetfulness, 6:10-12; 8:6-20). The time will come when they will show disdain for the LORD and break the covenant bond. When ultimately judgment will come on them in the form of disasters and difficulties (the same phrase as already used in verse 17) the song will continue to serve as a testimony against them, because successive generations will remember it. Future events were not going to come as a surprise to the LORD, for he understood their attitude of heart and knew that their hearts will turn from him (cf. Gen. 6:5; 8:21). The Hebrew word used here for disposition (*yetser*) became part of a later rabbinic expression for the evil impulse in men (*yetser ra*). Moses complied with the LORD's direction, wrote down the song, and taught it to the people.

23 The second of the charges from the LORD is addressed to Joshua. Just as Moses was commissioned in Egypt (Exod. 3:1–4:17), so is Joshua commissioned as his successor. There is direct confirmation to Joshua, and this act, given in such a personal and intimate way (cf. Num. 12:5), sets him apart for the task of leading Israel into the promised land. Moses' words of encouragement to him (verses 7-8) are now given directly by the LORD himself. In leading the people into the promised land he can do so knowing that the LORD will be with him (the Heb. text emphasises '*I* will be with you'). What Moses had said to the people about God's presence with them (verse 6) is now turned into a personal promise for Joshua.

24-26 The third and final charge is from Moses to the priests concerning the book of the law. Moses had the task of writing 'in a book the words of this law from beginning to end'. It is best to understand this to mean that the central core of the covenant (represented by chapters 5–26, with the curses and blessings of chapters 27-28 added) was set out in writing. Later the expression 'the book of the law' may well be another term to refer to the whole content of Deuteronomy, including the prologue (chapters 1-4) and the epilogue (chapters 29-34). When the book of the law is found in the temple during Josiah's reformation it seems to be the whole scroll containing the text of Deuteronomy that is meant (2 Kings 22:8, 11). The function of the book of the law was to serve as a witness (Heb. *'ēd*) against the people. It was not to be placed within the ark of the covenant (which contained the two stone tablets of the law, Exod. 25:21; Deut. 10:5), but beside it. Presumably it was placed on the floor of the sanctuary beside the ark, though no details are given of the arrangement. Together with the song it was in part to serve as a witness against the people when they rebelled against the LORD. From another aspect the book of the law served to emphasise God's gracious redemption and the many blessings linked with it.

27 The rebelliousness of the people during Moses' lifetime was a precursor of even greater acts of covenant disobedience in the future. Israel had been accused of being stiff-necked when the rebellion took place while Moses was on the mount with God (Exod. 32:9), and earlier in this book the expression is used of the people's unwillingness to obey the LORD's commands (9:6, 13; 10:16). The absence of Moses would only exacerbate the tendency to rebellion.

28-29 The priests are given the task of arranging the formal assembly of Israel to hear Moses recite the song. In verse 28 reference is made to the elders and the officials, while in verse 30 it is to the whole assembly of Israel. Presumably the leaders had the task of organising the congregation as it met to hear Moses' formal recitation of the song. The call to heaven and earth (verse

28, and in the song itself, 32:1) formed a further witness to Israel (for appeal to the heaven and the earth see commentary on 30:19). Moses has no false expectations of the future. Israel will forsake the LORD, disaster will come upon them, and they will be objects of his wrath because of their idolatry (lit. 'what your hands have made').

2. The Song of Witness (31:30–32:52)

The last verse of chapter 31 gives an introductory comment, and then the complete song is given in chapter 32. It was delivered to Moses by the LORD (31:19), written down by him and taught to the Israelites (31:22). In this act Moses was joined by Joshua (32:44), so that the departing and the incoming representatives of the LORD were linked together in giving this song to Israel.

The song has to be seen in a wider context. It is part of a biblical pattern of response to God in which the Israelites, whether in private or in public, reaffirmed their commitment to the LORD of the covenant. A song such as this has much in common with the historical psalms (such as Pss. 78, 105, 106, 135, 136), in which the people not only magnified the deeds of the LORD but also confessed their sin and covenant breaking. The importance of this song is reflected in its inclusion as 'the song of Moses the servant of God and the song of the Lamb' in Revelation 15:3-4.

Furthermore, as a song it is poetic in form, a form that often aids the memory. This song and the blessings on the tribes in the following chapter are the only poetic parts of Deuteronomy. As such they have much in common with many of the Psalms and with later prophetic speeches. Usual Hebrew poetic features are present, such as parallelism, and the use of some vocabulary different from that in Hebrew narrative (see the comment on the use of name Jeshurun in 32:15 and 33:5, 26). There are at least fourteen Old Testament words that only occur in this song, and many others that are very uncommon.

More particularly this song should be seen in its setting in Deuteronomy as part of a covenant document, and it exemplifies a pattern that occurs in several prophetic writings. When bringing a formal charge against Israel for breach of covenant obligations, the prophets put it in the covenant lawsuit pattern (Heb. *riv*).

Examples can be seen in passages such as Isaiah 1:2-3, 10-20; Micah 6:1-8; and Jeremiah 2:4-13. Often there is a basic framework in which the charge opens with an appeal for witnesses to pay attention. Then rhetorical questions are presented, followed by a record of past favours, an account of the breaches of the covenant, and finally blessings and curses of the covenant. There are also many similarities between Deuteronomy 33 and these prophetical passages. While the pattern here in chapter 32 does not follow rigidly the covenant pattern of the whole book, it does bear a general resemblance to it. The general structure of the song is as follows:

(i) Introduction (31:30)
(ii) Appeal to witnesses (32:1-4)
(iii) Statement of Israel's rebellion (32:5-6)
(iv) Recital of past blessings (32:7-14)
(v) The sin of Israel (32:15-22)
(vi) The curses of the covenant (32:23-35)
(vii) The compassion of God (32:36-43)

(i) Introduction (31:30)

30 The instruction to write the song was given in 31:19, while the writing of it was noted in 31:22. Now the introductory note to the song itself records that it was recited by Moses in order that Israel would learn it.

(ii) Appeal to witnesses (32:1-4)
1-2 The opening verses appeal to heaven and earth to hear the accusations against Israel (cf. 4:26; 30:19; 31:28). The similes used in verse 2 are chosen to compare the teaching being given to the gentle fruitful rain which falls on young plants. Just as those plants are nourished by the rain and grow thereby, so may Israel respond to this teaching by bringing forth new spiritual life.

3-4 God's character (lit. 'name') as he had made it known is to be proclaimed, something that God himself had done for Israel (see

the use of the same phrase of God's own action in Exod. 34:5).
That proclamation makes known yet again that he is true and utterly
faithful to his covenant. Moreover, greatness is to be ascribed to
him. This term 'greatness', when used of God, refers particularly
to his actions in redeeming his people from Egypt (see in addition
to this verse Num. 14:19; Deut. 3:24; 5:24; 9:26; 11:2). The epithet
used here of God is 'rock', which occurs several times later in this
song (verses 15, 18, 30, 31). The parallel expressions such as 'God'
and 'LORD' show that it is a synonym, stressing the permanence
of the God of Israel and the security he provides for those who
trust in him. The cluster of terms describing the Rock stresses his
faithfulness and justice. Many of these terms are expanded further
in Psalm 89 which extols God's faithfulness especially in relation
to the covenant with David.

(iii) Statement of Israel's Rebellion (32:5-6)
5-6 A brief statement of Israel's folly is given in verse 5 followed
by accusing questions in verse 6. The Hebrew text of verse 5 is
difficult to translate, and probably the NIV marginal reading is best:
'Corrupt are they and not his children, a generation warped and
twisted in their shame'. Israel was regarded as God's son (Exod.
4:22; Deut. 8:5) but a perverse generation could not claim that
privilege. If, like the man already mentioned in 29:19, people
thought that physical connection with Israel was a safeguard, then
they needed to realise that unless there was moral purity, they
would be disowned as God's children. New Testament teaching
is similar, for children of God are to be blameless and pure,
'without fault in a crooked and depraved generation' (Phil. 2:15).
The questions in verse 6 press the point further. If God was their
father and the one who had acquired them (Heb. *qanah*, 'to buy',
'acquire'), then their actions were all the more worthy of
condemnation. Any of those acting as they had towards their father
could only be unwise and foolish children.

(iv) Recital of Past Blessings (32:7-14)
7-9 A call to remember introduces a recital of the many blessings
that the LORD had bestowed on his people. The fathers or elders

should know of past generations, either by oral tradition or by reference to written documents, and so be in a position to teach the younger generations. The allotment of territories for all the peoples of the world was made by God Most High (Heb. *'elyon*, the only occurrence of this name for God in Deut.). The table of the nations in Genesis 10 sets out the various nations and their territories following the flood. It was God's intention that the world should be inhabited (Isa. 45:18). As Paul declared when speaking to the Areopagus, God 'determined the times set for them [the nations] and the exact places they should live' (Acts 17:26). The reference to Israel in verses 8b-9 is most significant for it highlights the unique place of Israel in God's plan. Out of all the nations he had chosen Israel to be his special people (Exod. 19:4-6; Deut. 4:32-38), so that they became his 'portion', 'his allotted inheritance'. This special relationship between God and Israel was a strong reason why the nation's sins were so heinous in God's sight.

10 The contrast is drawn in verses 10-13 and verse 14 of the difference in the provisions for Israel in the wilderness compared with the rich fare of Canaan. The reference to 'desert' does not indicate that the origins of Israel with Abraham's family is in view. Rather the point is that with solicitous care God looked after Israel in the desert experiences after leaving Egypt. He surrounded her (NIV 'shielded') with his loving protection, and jealously guarded the 'apple of his eye'. This a reference to the pupil of the eye, which in Hebrew is called literally 'the little man of the eye'. Later David uses this expression to pray for God's protection of him: 'Keep me as the apple of your eye' (Ps. 17:8).

11-12 The imagery changes to that of an eagle watching over her young, and especially helping them when they are beginning to fly. This practice of the eagles and vultures (the Heb. word *nesher* is used in the OT of both) is well attested in the Near East. It seems, however, to be more than just a general reference, as it is probably intended to recall what Moses was told to tell Israel prior to the giving of the law: 'You yourselves have seen what I did to

Egypt, and how I carried you on eagles' wings and brought you to myself' (Exod. 19:4). This description expresses the power of God as well as his tender care. It links in with what is said in verse 12. No foreign or alien god had the power to do what the LORD had done for Israel. Delivering them from Egypt and keeping them during the wilderness years were his exclusive achievement.

13-14 These verses contain a description of the provision Israel had already found on the east bank of the Jordan (see the reference to Bashan in verse 14 and cf. 3:1-11). Compared with wilderness fare it was rich and abundant – agricultural products, curds and milk, fattened animals, honey, oil and wine. While they were still looking forward to all that was promised in Canaan, they had already in Transjordania more than just a foretaste of what was to come. All this was God's gracious provision ('*he* made ... *he* fed ... *he* nourished').

(v) The Sin of Israel (32:15-22)
15 In spite of all God's goodness and power demonstrated in these experiences, Israel grew self-satisfied and Israel spurned him. She rejected her Saviour! The term 'Jeshurun', which only occurs here and three other times in the Old Testament (Deut. 33:5, 26; Isa. 44:2), has often been explained as an affectionate pet-name for Israel. This is based on the Hebrew word *yashar*, 'upright', and taken as a diminutive, 'little upright one'. While the etymology is correct, there is no evidence that Hebrew had any diminutive forms ending in -*un*. It is better to take it as meaning 'law-keeping' or 'upholding justice'. The irony is that the nation which should have been *law-keeping* is the very one being accused of being *a law-breaker*. She spurned her maker and rejected her Rock (see comment on verse 4).

16-18 Foreign gods had taken the place of the LORD and such abominations provoked his anger (see 31:29). These so-called gods were not the God of the patriarchs but newly espoused gods. Israel even sacrificed to spirits in the wilderness (see Ps. 106:37), a known practice in the ancient world to help preserve people and places from harm. Thus they had forsaken their own father – God! Hosea uses the same illustration when he speaks of God leading Israel as a little child out of Egypt, but then Israel went further and further away from him (Hos. 11:1-7).

19-20 God took notice of the sins of his children and rejected them. The verb used here regarding God's actions (Heb. *na'ats*) only occurs twice elsewhere in the Old Testament. Jeremiah describes the destruction of Jerusalem as a spurning of priest and people (Lam. 2:6), the very thing he had prayed would not happen (Jer. 14:21). Because they were unfaithful sons and a perverse generation (verse 20) God's anger would be unleashed against them.

21-22 The people who trusted in a no-god (Heb. *lo-'el*) would find that God would use a no-people (Heb. *lo-'am*) to bring his judgment upon them. A non-covenant people will be used to display God's anger against his own people. Later, Hosea's message was to centre around the concept that though God would at that time call Israel 'not-my-people' (Heb. *lo-'ammi*), the day was coming when he would call them 'my people' (Heb. *'ammi*, Hos. 1:9; 2:23). Paul uses Hosea's message in Romans 9:22-26 and then Peter merges it with other Old Testament ideas in 1 Peter 2:9-10. The second part of verse 21 is quoted by Paul in Romans 10:19 as he speaks of Israel's failure to accept the gospel message about Jesus. In the Second Commandment (Exod. 20:5; Deut. 5:9) with its warning against idolatry God had asserted that as the covenant God of Israel he was a jealous God. He reacts to the unfaithfulness of Israel with the jealousy of a husband whose wife has been unfaithful to him. The threat for Israel was the usual penalty for adultery – death. His judgment fire will burn even to the grave (Heb. *she'ol*) and the land will fail to produce its crops (verse 22b).

(vi) The Curses of the Covenant (32:23-35)
In poetic form the song sets out the curses of the covenant. They would involve disease, destruction and invasion, culminating in

exile and dispersion. What was spelt out in narrative form earlier (28:15-68; 31:16-21) is now reinforced in this song.

23-24 Canaan, which Israel thought was going to be another Eden, would prove to be a place of disaster. What would appear to be natural calamities would really be visitations of divine judgment (the NKJV version reflects the Heb. verbs, 'I will heap ... I will spend ... I will also send ...', whereas NIV is a little freer in its translation). Various diseases would come upon them, and also attacks by wild animals and snakes. The use of the word 'arrow' to describe God's judgment is also found elsewhere in the Old Testament (see verse 42; Job 6:4; Pss. 7:13; 38:2; Ezek. 5:16).

25-27 Those who were left in the land would face other calamities. Invading armies would wield the sword, and terror would pervade the country. Where the people thought safety would be found (in their towns and homes) there would be death of old and young. The only escape for the people would come from God's desire to avoid a situation in which the Gentile nations would think that they had achieved this destruction (verses 26-27). If they claimed that it had been achieved by their hand and that the LORD had not done it all, then his name and power would be dishonoured. God is jealous for his own glory. The verb rendered 'scatter' in the NIV (verse 26) is not the usual Hebrew verb for that idea. It occurs only here in the Old Testament and probably means to dash in pieces (so NKJV) which fits in well with the parallel in the second part of the verse ('blot out their memory').

28-29 It is possible to take the nation in these verses to refer to Israel. In this case the LORD would be expressing an earnest desire that his people would change (cf. Ps. 81:13-16). But the context favours taking it as a reference to one of the nations which God was using as his instrument of judgment. That nation would be shown to be foolish for thinking they had conquered by their own power. If only they knew that they themselves were to be subjected to God's judgment as well (see verse 35)! Their 'end' would be a day of disaster as well.

30-33 The folly of the enemies is developed further in these verses. Whereas God at times enabled his people to conquer with only a few (Judg. 7:2ff.), here the picture is of God allowing the enemies with only a few to rout Israel. The real explanation of Israel's defeat was not the enemies' power, but the fact that God, their Rock (see comment on verse 4), had sold them (for the use of 'sell' in this connection, see also Isa. 50:1). It was not even the nations' gods who had done this. Here and in verse 37 the word 'rock' is used of heathen gods. This usage in the Near East is known from extra-biblical documents. Even if Israel used the same word on occasions for their deity, this does not imply that they borrowed with it the concepts which non-Israelite people attributed to their 'rock'. The heathen nations had to face the fact that Israel's God truly displayed his awesome power (see Exod. 14:4, 25; Num. 23 and 24: Josh. 2:9-10; 1 Sam. 4:8; 5:7ff.; Dan. 4:34ff.). The gods of the nations are described (verses 32-33) as vines, grapes and wine, which have their source in Sodom and Gomorrah. That is to say, the pagan worship of these gods found its source in the same kind of perversion as represented by Sodom and Gomorrah (Gen. 18:20; Isa. 3:8-9; Jer. 23:14; Ezek. 16:44-52). To take the fruit of this vine would first bring a bitter taste to the mouth, and in due course death.

34-35 God was permitting other nations to punish Israel but in due time he would discharge justice to them as well. His plans were not available for present scrutiny ('kept in reserve') but were certain in their outcome ('sealed'). The statement in verse 35 is very significant for a large group of Old Testament passages that use the same Hebrew root as here (*nqm*). Having used the nations to judge Israel, God will in turn judge them for their pride and arrogance. He will take vengeance on *his* adversaries (verses 35, 41b, 43). This vengeance will show both God's justice and the means by which he will deliver his people. It will be redemptive judgment, a principle which finds its fullest expression in the death of the Messiah on Calvary's cross. When their day of doom comes their foot will slip (a common Old Testament expression for calamity; see Pss. 38:16; 94:18; 2 Sam. 22:37) and they will be overtaken quickly by their doom. In Romans 12:19 Paul quotes the words, 'It is mine to avenge; I will repay', in application of the underlying principle that God is the supreme judge who executes vengeance.

(vii) The Compassion of God (32:36-43)
The closing section of the song depicts the ultimate compassion of God on his people. When he sees their extremity, he will challenge them in regard to the false gods whom they have worshipped. They will then turn to their God for salvation.

36-38 Looking further ahead beyond the punishment of exile, the song speaks of the mercy of God being extended to his covenant people. The parallelism in verse 36a suggests that the verb 'judge' be taken in the sense of 'vindicate', especially as the context deals with restoration after punishment. This part of the verse is quoted along with verse 35 in Hebrews 10:30, though verse 36a is identical with Psalm 135:14 so that the writer to the Hebrews could have been quoting either passage. The poetic forms in verse 36b are difficult. Literally it reads: 'when he sees that the hand has disappeared, and at an end bound and abandoned'. The early versions do not offer much help, as it has been explained in various ways. The reference to the 'hand' seems to imply that power is gone. 'Bound and free', which occurs as a fixed expression just five times in the Old Testament, could be a description of the whole of society – 'from slave to free person' (SO NIV, NKJV). Another possibility is that the phrase means 'helpless and destitute', which certainly fits the context well – 'when he sees their power has gone, and they are in extremity, helpless and destitute.' The song goes on to depict God taunting his people for their folly in deserting him (verses 37-38). Where now are the gods they turned to, the other 'rock' in whom they took refuge? They had participated in festal occasions of sacrifice to these gods. The challenge is given that if they exist, let these gods rise up to help and provide a hiding place for them. The thought and language here foreshadows the way in which Isaiah in particular mocks Israel for turning to worthless idols (Isa. 41:21-24; 44:6-20; 46:1-7).

39 As the song moves to its close, there is a declaration of God's incomparability, like to the one given earlier in 4:35. The form of words (Heb. *'ani 'ani hu'*, 'I, I [am] he)' may well be behind Isaiah's use of similar expressions, and ultimately be the Old Testament background for the assertions that Jesus makes, commencing with the words, 'I am ...' (Gk. *ego eimi*). He is the God with all power at his disposal, the destroyer and the life-giver. It is possible that verse 39b is a description both of the exilic judgment and restoration. God is able to make the dead bones live (Ezek. 37:1-14), and as he wounded Israel, so can he heal. The final expression, 'and no one can deliver out of my hand', ties in with the following verses, asserting the inevitability of judgment on his adversaries.

40-42 With solemn oath the LORD declares that ultimate deliverance will come when he judges the enemies of his people. While God's own word is sure, he confirms it with an oath (verse 40b) to show its irrevocable nature. This occurred with the promise to Abraham (see Heb. 6:13-20), and variations of the phrase 'as surely as I live forever' appear repeatedly in the Old Testament in connection with the LORD's assertion of what he was going to do (see Num. 14;21, 28; Isa. 49:18; Ezek. 5:11; Zeph. 2:9). Because there is no other by whom he can swear, the LORD swears by himself (Isa. 45:22-23). The judgment is to be against *his* enemies (not Israel's), and he will repay to the full those who hate him. 'To hate God' is another way of saying that someone was not in a covenant relationship with him (see 5:9; 7:10; 2 Chron. 19:2; Ps. 139:20-21). The poetic power of verse 42 is heightened by the fact that the third clause completes the idea of the first clause, and the fourth finishes the idea of the second.

43 The final call of the song is for the Gentile nations to join with Israel in rejoicing over God's judgmental work. This call points to the messianic age when the blessing of Abraham will come to its realisation in the work of Christ (Gal. 3:14). These words are quoted by Paul in Romans 15:10 in the form contained in the LXX: 'Rejoice, O Gentiles, with his people'. The certainty of the coming judgment is emphasised by the repetition of the idea of taking vengeance on the enemies (see verse 41). The phrase 'to avenge the blood of his servants' occurs also in 2 Kings 9:7 (Jehu to destroy the house of Ahab), while the idea appears twice in the book of Revelation (Rev. 6:10; 19:2). The concluding part of this verse claims that the day is coming when the guilt of the land and of the people will be removed. The greatest expression of God's compassion (verse 36) will be restoring his people to fellowship with himself and restoring them to the land of promise.

3. Moses' Appeal to the People (32:44-47)
44-47 Moses, accompanied by Joshua, completes his task of teaching the song to all the people. There is an unusual use of an older name for Joshua, Hoshea, in the Hebrew text of this verse (see NIV margin). Clearly Hoshea ('salvation') is the earlier form of the name, but Moses renamed him 'Joshua' ('the LORD saves'; Num. 13:8, 16). While Moses himself thereafter used the name Joshua, here the writer of the theocratic history reverts to the earlier name. Joshua is present while Moses teaches the people the song, appearing as Moses' successor at this act of witness and warning. Along with the recitation of the words of the song to all the people, Moses further encourages them. His concern is that they will see in the words of this song what will be life for them if they obey God's precepts. The ceremony of teaching this song thus forms a public commitment to the covenant and a renewed warning against departure from its demands. Life in the land of Canaan and the abiding right to be there will depend upon their response to God's law. Future generations are to be instructed to obey implicitly the demands of God's covenant, demands which Moses solemnly sets before them. This once more reaffirms the need for the education of each new generation in Israel in the covenant demands (cf. 4:9; 6:7; 11:19; 31:13).

4. Proclamation of Moses' Death (32:48-52)
48-52 On the very same day as the Song of Witness was delivered to the people, Moses received the command to go up to Mount Nebo, where he was to die. He had earlier been told this (see

Num. 27:12-14), though fuller details are given here. Moses and
Aaron were both guilty over the incident at Meribah Kadesh (see
Num. 20:2-13). Instead of simply speaking to the rock, Moses
struck it with his staff. God's holiness had not been upheld (verse
51) because the people should have been shown that water came
out of the rock by divine intervention, not human power. Whereas
Aaron died and was buried on Mount Hor (Num. 20:22-29), as an
act of grace Moses is permitted a glimpse of the promised land.
Having sung the song to Israel, the singer is now dismissed in
order to make way for the new representative of the LORD. The
account of Moses' death (34:1-8) follows his final blessing on the
Israelite tribes (33:1-29).

5. The Blessing of the Tribes (33:1-19)

(i) Introduction (33:1)

1 The final speech of Moses recorded in Deuteronomy comprises
his blessing of the tribes. In a manner similar to Isaac (Gen. 27:27-
29) and Jacob (Gen. 49:1-28), Moses blesses his 'children' before
his death. He had cared for them for forty years as though they
were his children (see Num. 11:11-15). He is not just one of the
patriarchs but he is also linked with the prophets through the
description 'man of God' (see its use in 1 Sam. 9:6, 10). In 34:5
he is called 'servant of God', a term which is also used to refer to
particular prophets. These descriptions help to set Moses apart as
the holder of a unique relationship with God.

Death-bed blessings had an important role in the Near East.
The bestowal of a blessing, though oral in form, could be upheld
in a court of law. Thus Isaac's blessing was irrevocable, as both
testaments emphasise (Gen. 27:30ff.; Heb. 12:16-17). These
biblical blessings also partake of the spirit of prophetic utterance.
Along with prediction they contain doxologies, prayers and
commands.

Like the other blessings (particularly Jacob's in Gen. 49), this
one is in poetic form. This creates translational problems and also
difficulties of interpretation. These two things are interconnected,
because a translator has to come to understand a passage before

rendering it into English. Because this is so, translations are in effect interpretations of the text of Scripture, especially of difficult parts. Comparison of modern translations of this passage (such as NASB, NIV, NKJV and NRSV) shows considerable variation, particularly in the opening verses. In spite of the differences (some of which will be noted), Moses' blessing has much in common with Genesis 49. The subject is the same, though the order of the tribes is different and to some extent also the content is different. It commences with a poetic description of God's appearance at Sinai, proceeds to delineate the tribal blessings, and concludes with an assertion of the absolute uniqueness of Israel's God.

(ii) A Majestic Appearance (33:2-5)

2 The coming of God to Sinai is depicted as if it had been a sunrise. The description has similarities to the theophanies (visible appearances of God) given in Psalm 68:7-18 and Habakkuk 3:2-15. Seir and Paran seem to be used here in poetry synonymously with Sinai, which only occurs here in Deuteronomy (elsewhere 'Horeb' is used). Divine appearances on mountain tops are striking in both Old and New Testaments. On Mount Moriah the angel of the LORD spoke to Abraham (Gen. 22:9-18), while it was at Horeb that God appeared to Moses (Exod. 3:1, 12) and where he later gave his covenant law (Exod. 19:11ff.; 24:16). The temple was built on Mount Moriah (2 Chron. 3:1), while prophets describe a pilgrimage of the Gentiles to the mountain of the LORD in the last days (Isa. 2:2; Mic. 4:2). In the New Testament the transfiguration takes place on a high mountain (Mark 9:2; cf. also Peter's comment on this event, 2 Pet. 1:16-18), while the final appearance of the risen and glorified Jesus took place on a mountain he had designated (Mt. 28:16). In the biblical revelation mountain tops seem to symbolise something of nearness to God.

God is the holy warrior who appears in majestic splendour (cf. the descriptions of what took place at Sinai in Exod. 20:18-19 and Deut. 5:22-27). This is in keeping with what is written in the Song of Moses about his deliverance of Israel from Egypt (Exod. 15:1-12). The second part of verse 2 contains several problems. While 'myriads of holy ones' is a possible translation, with some revocalisation of the Hebrew the translation becomes 'with the myriads of Kadesh' (i.e., Kadesh Barnea). 'From the south' (NIV) is possible, as the Hebrew word used (*yamin*) can have that meaning (cf. the use of the Arabic word *yemen* for the southern Arabic country of that name). The main alternative is to take the more literal meaning of the Hebrew ('right hand') and accept that it expresses the origin of the law: 'from His right hand, *came* a fiery law for them' (so NKJV). The difficulty with this is that the translation 'fiery law' is dubious, as is the NIV rendering 'from his mountain slopes'. The parallelism in the verse suggests that the LXX rendering 'messengers (or 'angels') with him' may well be based on knowledge which we do not possess today. This rendering would also fit in well with the New Testament references to the law coming by angels (see Acts 7:53; Gal. 3:19; Heb. 2:2). The translation of the second part of the verse would then be: 'He came with myriads from Kadesh, from the south angels came with him.'

3-5 These verses appear to be a response by the people to the introductory words by Moses. God's kingship was displayed in his redemption of Israel from Egypt, and his setting out their constitution as a nation in the form of covenant laws at Sinai. Before God they bow and they receive instruction from the law that had been mediated by Moses. It was at Sinai that God organised the nation as his visible kingdom, and his kingship was acknowledged by Israel's acceptance of his law. Over Jeshurun (for comment on this name for Israel see on 32:15) he reigned as king, and it was by his authority that assemblies of the people occurred (Exod. 19:7-8; 34:31-32; Deut. 29:10-14).

(iii) The Blessing of Moses (32:6-25)
The blessing given here is different in order from Genesis 49, which basically commences with Leah's sons, then proceeds with those of the handmaids Bilhah and Zilpah. There are two striking differences.

1. Simeon is omitted entirely, because this tribe was to lose its identity in accordance with Genesis 49:7, and eventually it

appears to have merged with Judah (see the allotment of
territory to Simeon within the territory of Judah, Jos. 19:1-9).
Also, it was the tribe so conspicuously associated with the sin
at Beth-peor (Num. 25:14).

The Blessing of Moses (32:6-24)

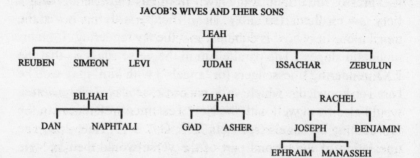

JACOB'S WIVES AND THEIR SONS

2. The order appears to be that following the firstborn Reuben
   (still given first place in spite of his loss of birthright) then
   come the tribes according to their role or function. Judah, the
   leader, precedes Levi, who had charge of sacred things, and
   Benjamin, 'the beloved of the Lord' (verse 12). Then after that
   come Joseph, Zebulun and Issachar, and finally the descendants
   of the maids. The lists can be compared as follows:

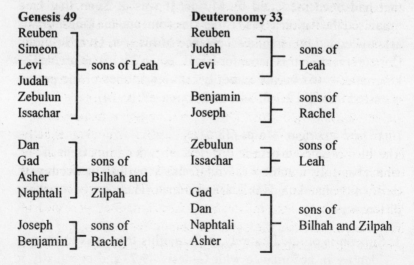

Genesis 49		Deuteronomy 33	
Reuben		Reuben	
Simeon		Judah	sons of
Levi	sons of Leah	Levi	Leah
Judah			
Zebulun		Benjamin	sons of
Issachar		Joseph	Rachel
Dan		Zebulun	sons of
Gad	sons of	Issachar	Leah
Asher	Bilhah and		
Naphtali	Zilpah	Gad	
		Dan	sons of
Joseph	sons of	Naphtali	Bilhah and Zilpah
Benjamin	Rachel	Asher	

(a) Reuben (33:6)

The prayer for Reuben the firstborn is that this tribe might continue to exist though reduced in numbers (this is following the NIV marginal note which reads verse 6b as 'but let his numbers be few'). It was never to play an important role in Israel's history, nor produce significant leaders. When judgment came on Israel the territory of Reuben was one of the areas to suffer (2 Kings 10:32-33) as the nation commenced to experience the covenant curses of Leviticus 26 and Deuteronomy 28.

(b) Judah (33:7)

The brevity of this prayer is remarkable, and also its military overtones. However, Genesis 49:8-12 sees Judah in a military role, and from Numbers 2:9 it is clear that Judah was to lead the people, at least in their wilderness experiences. There is no mention here of the messianic aspects already set out in Jacob's blessing (Gen. 49:10). Moses implores God to assist Judah in battle and to bring him back to his people in peace (according to the Aramaic Targum Onkelos, the authoritative Aramaic paraphrase for Babylonian Jews from about 400 AD).

(c) Levi (33:8-11)

By direct address and prayer to the LORD Moses seeks a blessing on the priestly tribe. In the persons of Moses and Aaron, Levi had been tested at Massah (Exod. 17:1-7) and at Meribah (Num. 20:1-13), and may have acted in a comparable way at Horeb (Exod. 32:26-29) and Shittim (Num. 25:1-9). Jacob's curse (Gen. 49:5-7) is turned into a blessing, as Levi is viewed as the recipient of special revelation when hard decisions were to be made by the use of stones called Urim ('curse' = a negative response) and Thummim ('perfect' = a positive response). It is unclear exactly how the messages were received. The other main functions of the tribe would be teaching (cf. Mal. 2:5-8) and the offering of sacrifices (verse 10). This is the charter for the Levites to act as the teachers and priests in Israel, and these functions were clearly interrelated. Material blessings are sought for Levi, as well as a prayer for divine intervention against his enemies. In verses 7, 11 and 17 there is mention of the ability of Judah, Levi, and Joseph to stand in the strength of the LORD against their enemies.

(d) Benjamin (32:12)

This is a cryptic statement regarding Benjamin, the LORD's beloved (Heb. $y^e did$; cf. the name for Solomon, Jedidiah, 'beloved of the LORD'). Benjamin as the youngest son of Jacob was particularly loved by his father (Gen. 44:20). In Jacob's blessing Benjamin is spoken of in very warlike terms (Gen. 49:27), and the same is true of the Song of Deborah (Judg. 5:14). Here Benjamin's safety is said to depend upon the constant protection which the LORD gives. The last line of the verse is difficult. The term 'shoulder' is used in the Hebrew text in Joshua 15:8 and 18:16 of the side of the mountain on which Jerusalem is situated. The best way to interpret this line is accept that the LORD is the one who dwells between Benjamin's shoulders, alluding to the fact that ultimately, in the visible form of the tabernacle, God would dwell there. Jerusalem was within Benjamin's territory.

(e) Joseph (33:13-17)

13-17 In language very similar to Genesis 49:22-26 Joseph receives his blessing. In size and importance of territory Joseph occupied a pre-eminent position among the tribes, especially as his sons' tribes of Ephraim and Manasseh were given separate allotments of territory (note the superiority of Ephraim in verse 17; cf. Gen. 48:8-20). The main blessings of Joseph were to be richness of the produce of the field and victory in battle. The repeated use of the Hebrew word *meged* ('yield of fruit') draws attention to the abundance of God's provision for Joseph. It occurs five times in verses 13-16, though many English versions obscure its presence by the variety of translations they employ. NKJV reflects the Hebrew text with its use of 'precious fruits', 'precious produce' and 'precious things'. The abundance of food for Joseph's descendants is a fitting blessing, seeing that Joseph was the one who in the time of famine had kept Egypt and the surrounding nations supplied with food (Gen. 41:35-57). Joseph would also have the most important blessing of the presence of the God of the covenant, who had revealed himself in the burning bush to Moses (verse 16; cf. Exod. 3:2ff.). Apart from Exodus 3, this is the only reference to the burning bush in the Old Testament.

(f) Zebulun and Issachar (33:18-19)
18-19 A conjoint blessing is expressed for the fifth and sixth sons of Leah. As the last two sons, Zebulun and Issachar had a close relationship within the family, and also their tribal territory was to be in close proximity. The contrast in the blessing in verse 18 suggests that in trade Zebulun will be successful, while Issachar will be fruitful in sedentary agricultural pursuits. It is unclear if verse 19 is referring jointly to these tribes or separating them from one another. Possibly Issachar is in view in verse 19a and Zebulun in verse 19b. If so, the reference to worship (including the offering of sacrifices) on the mountain may be to the existence of a shrine on Mount Tabor in the territory later occupied by Zebulun. While such a site is condemned in Hosea 5:1, it is quite possible that earlier on it was a legitimate place of worship. Zebulun was to occupy the sea-coast around the present site of modern Haifa. Drawing out from the seas and sand probably alludes to later maritime activity on the part of Zebulun, though the biblical text gives no later clues to the fulfilment of this prophecy.

(g) Gad (33:20-21)
When Transjordania had been conquered, Gad received a worthy reward. The Gadites saw the fertility of the pasture lands there and realised that they were very suitable for cattle (Num. 32:1-5). They were leaders in battle, and seemingly played a major part in overcoming Sihon. This showed their commitment to the LORD, for they carried out his judgments.

(h) Dan (33:22)
In this the shortest blessing, Dan is compared in strength and energy to a lion's cub. Jacob's blessing contains the same type of reference to the aggressive qualities of the tribe (Gen. 49:16-17). After the conquest the Danites needed further territory and following investigations, a new Danite settlement was made around the town

of Laish (called Leshem in Josh. 19:47; renamed Dan after their ancestor) in the upper Jordan valley (see Judg. 18). The phrase 'from Dan to Beersheba' became the standard expression for indicating the northernmost and southernmost extent of Israel. In the list of the tribes in Revelation 7:5-8, Dan is omitted without any indication of the reason, though it may be because of the connection with idolatry.

(i) Naphtali (33:23)
This word contains a prophecy of the rich blessing of God on Naphtali and an indication of the area bordering on the sea of Galilee which would be allotted to it. While the Hebrew word *yam* used here can mean 'west[wards]', the context suggests that it refers to the Sea of Galilee, while 'south' may imply the fertile area of the Jordan valley south of it. This whole area, from the Waters of Merom, north of the sea of Galilee, to the Jordan valley south of it, provided room for Naphtali to grow and prosper.

(j) Asher (33:24-25)
The final blessing is on Asher who will live up to his name ('blessed'). The blessing takes the form of a wish for the tribe: 'Most blessed of [Jacob's] sons is Asher. May he be favoured by his brothers and bathe his feet in oil'. The Galilean highlands were noted for their olives even in ancient times, and Asher is to share in the abundance of agricultural wealth. The territory he was to possess stretched along the coast from Acre north to Tyre. As this was situated on a coastal route for trade as well as invasion, verse 25 speaks of fortifications that would be taken over by Asher, with the assurance that it will remain constantly strong.

(iv) The Uniqueness of the God of Israel (33:26-29)
The blessing of the tribes is framed by the opening declaration of God's majesty (especially as revealed at Sinai) and this closing section extolling the uniqueness of Israel's God and the tenderness of his care over them. The conclusion of the blessing picks up the use of the name 'Jeshurun' from verse 5 (for the meaning of the name see the comment on 32:15). In language which lies behind

many prophetical passages (see in particular Isa. 40-45), Moses extols the incomparable God. The terms used here of God show a striking resemblance to those in Psalm 90, the one Mosaic song incorporated in the Psalter.

26-28 This final section does not start with a question but a declaration: 'There is no God who is like Jeshurun's God'. The description that is given of this unique God has its closest parallel in the closing verses of Psalm 68, which are probably based on this passage. God's majesty is displayed in his power in creation and providence, but also in his special relationship to Israel. He is a refuge to his people (cf. the opening of Ps. 90 which uses the same word 'refuge' in the Heb. text), and by his power he protects them. He is also the God who is going to deliver the land of Canaan into their hand as he expels the Canaanite inhabitants (verse 27b).

28-29 Israel's security in Canaan is assured. There the people will enjoy the rich fruits of the land (summarised here as 'grain and new wine'), while the heavy dew for which Palestine has always been noted will continue to water the ground. The reference to 'Jacob's spring' is an allusion to the fact that from Jacob came forth a large nation. As Stephen put it in his speech recorded in Acts 7, Jacob and his relatives numbered seventy-five when they went down into Egypt, but from that number 'the people grew and multiplied' (Acts 7:18, NJKV). Israel was a unique people, for no other nation could claim to have been redeemed by the LORD, or to have him as their shield, even as he assured Abraham long before (Gen. 15:1). What is said of Israel in verse 29 is dependent on what is said of the LORD in verse 26. The closing statements reaffirm that victory will come to Israel, as her enemies bow before her. The imagery of warfare should be maintained in the final clause, and therefore the NIV marginal reading is to be preferred: 'You will tread upon their bodies.'

6. The Death of Moses (34:1-12)
One of the characteristics of the Old Testament historical narratives is that one writer takes up where another left off. This can be

seen, for example, in the way in which the book of Ruth is tied in with the conclusion of the book of Judges. An even more striking case is the connection between 2 Chronicles and Ezra, for the opening words of Ezra repeat the closing words of the previous book. Most probably the inspired writer who continued the covenant history in Joshua, completed the account of the covenant renewal in the plains of Moab by recording the death of Moses. Quite likely the same writer has already given the blessing of Moses in the previous chapter, as is shown by the use of the third person in the introduction in 33:1 and in the ten-times repeated 'he said'.

(i) A Glimpse into the Promised Land (34:1-4)

1-3 Just as the LORD had said, Moses is given a glimpse of the entire land of promise from Dan in the north to the Negev in the south, from the Jordan valley to the Mediterranean. From Nebo the Mediterranean (Heb. 'the western sea') is not naturally visible. Pisgah was most probably the term for the entire range, Mount Nebo being the highest peak. It is significant that it was the LORD himself who showed him the land, including one of its northern mountains on which Moses would later appear with Elijah at the time of Jesus' transfiguration. A viewing of the land like this may have been part of a known legal process which was normal when acquiring possession (cf. Gen. 13:14-15).

4 The final declaration of God to Moses is in the form of a reassurance. The land he can now see is indeed the land pledged to the patriarchs so long before. What had been promised to them was on the verge of being fulfilled, but Moses has to die, knowing that for him entry into the land was forbidden.

(ii) Moses' Death and Burial (34:5-8)

The stress continues to the very end of the book on the distinctive position of Moses as 'the servant of the LORD'. Forty times in the Old Testament this name 'servant' is given to him. As the final verses of this chapter and this book point out (verses 10-12), he occupied a position to which no one else could aspire. He was a faithful servant over God's house (Heb. 3:5), and as such was faithful to death. The account given here of Moses' death has mysterious elements in it, in keeping with the fact that Moses did not die on Pisgah because of old age. 'His eyes were not weak nor his strength gone', is the testimony of the sacred historian (verse 7). Failure to enter Canaan was not caused by death through old age or sickness, but as a punishment by God. He was buried by God in an unmarked grave in the valley near Beth Peor (see the earlier references in 3:29 and 4:46). Probably this was a way of preventing the Israelites carrying his bones over into a new burial place in Canaan, which would have been a violation of God's instructions. The only other place in the Bible where the death of Moses is mentioned is in Jude verse 9. There was clearly a tradition carried through the centuries by the Jewish people that the devil wanted the body of Moses, and that Michael the archangel (see Dan. 10:13, 21; 12:1; Rev. 12:7) had had to contend with him. This appears in different forms in the Aramaic paraphrase of Deuteronomy (the Targum Jonathan) and in the apocryphal book, *The Assumption of Moses*. The death of Moses was followed by the customary period of mourning of thirty days (see the account of the mourning for Aaron in Num. 20:29).

(iii) Joshua as Successor (34:9)

The leadership of the people was not left to human choice but provided by God himself. The transition period of joint leadership by Moses and Joshua was now finished. The continuity of leadership was symbolised by the laying on of hands. Three times the biblical text describes this act of transferring authority to Joshua by mentioning the laying on of hands (Num. 27:18, 23; Deut. 34:9). The Hebrew verb used (*samach*) is a technical term used also of transference of guilt as on the Day of Atonement (Lev. 16:22). Joshua had been assistant to Moses for many years, and was now to lead Israel into the land which he himself had already visited as one of the spies (Num. 13:8, 16). Just as Moses' leadership of the people was attested by his victory over the host of Egypt and over the waters of the Red Sea, so Joshua would be attested by the crossing of the Jordan and the victory over the hosts of Canaan. The contrast is immediately drawn in the second part of verse 9 between the two men. While Israel listened to Joshua (thus signifying their acknowledgment of his leadership), yet their obedience was to what Moses had given them from the LORD. This stress on Moses' words as foundational continues to the very end of the Old Testament (see Mal. 4:4).

(iv) The Uniqueness of Moses (34:10-12)
The uniqueness of Moses' position is amplified in the concluding verses of the whole book. He did not receive revelation from the LORD as other prophets did, but spoke with him face to face (verse 10). This is made plain in Numbers 12:8, in a passage contrasting the manner in which the LORD communicated to Moses as distinct from other prophets. Joshua, though successor to Moses, had no such direct revelation but had to receive it from the priest (Num. 27:21). The final words of the book (verses 11-12) point to the wondrous deeds of God performed by Moses at the time of the exodus. When God redeemed his people, Moses was the instrument through whom his mighty power was displayed. God's revelation in words was the accompaniment of his mighty deeds of saving mercy.

The book of Deuteronomy ends on the note of redemption. When Moses next appears in the biblical record he is on the mount of transfiguration talking with Elijah and Christ about the exodus that Christ was to accomplish in Jerusalem (Luke 9:30-31). In spite of his greatness, his work is only preparatory. The period he inaugurated continued until another came, not a servant but one who was master over his house (Heb. 3:5-6). Moses had no memorial stone but his work and God's revelation through him paved the way for the coming of the prophet like Moses (18:18; Acts 3:22-23). This great prophet, Messiah himself, would declare God's word, and of him God would say: 'This is my son, whom I love. Listen to him!' (Mark 9:7).

Further Reading

The following literature will give great help to those who wish to pursue details in the book of Deuteronomy further.

P. C. Craigie, *The Book of Deuteronomy* (Grand Rapids: Eerdmans, 1976; NICOT series).

Raymond B. Dillard and Tremper Longman III, 'Deuteronomy', in *An Introduction to the Old Testament* (Grand Rapids: Zondervan, 1994), pp. 91-106.

Allan M. Harman, 'Decalogue (Ten Comandments)', *New International Dictionary of Old Testament Theology and Exegesis* (Grand Rapids: Zondervan, 1997), vol. 4, pp. 513-519.

Allan M. Harman, 'The Interpretation of the Third Commandment', *Reformed Theological Review* 47, 1 (January-April, 1988), pp. 1-7.

Allan M. Harman, 'The Structure of Deuteronomy with Special Reference to Chapters 5-26', *The Tyndale Paper (Australia)*, xxxii, 5 (November, 1987), pp. 1-7.

James Jordan, *The Law of the Covenant* (Tyler: Institute of Christian Economics, 1984), pp. 199-206.

W. C. Kaiser, Jr., *Towards an Old Testament Ethics* (Grand Rapids: Zondervan, 1983), pp. 127-137.

Earl S. Kalland, 'Deuteronomy', *The Expositor's Bible Commentary*, ed. Frank E. Gaebelein (Grand Rapids: Zondervan, 1992), Vol. 3, pp. 1-235.

Meredith G. Kline, *Treaty of the Great King* (Grand Rapids: Eerdmans, 1963). The commentary on Deuteronomy in this book can also be found in the *Wycliffe Bible Commentary* , eds. Charles F. Pfeiffer and Everett F. Harrison (London: Oliphants, 1963), pp. 155-204.

E. H. Merrill, *The Book of Deuteronomy* (Nashville: Broadman & Holman, 1994: New American Commentary series).

J. Gordon McConville, *Grace in the End: A Study of Deuteronomic Theology* (Carlisle: Paternoster Press, 1993).

J. Gordon McConville, *Law and Theology in Deuteronomy* (Sheffield: JSOT, 1984).

J. A. Thompson, *The Book of Deuteronomy* (Leicester: Inter-varsity, 1974; Tyndale series).

C. J. H. Wright, *The Book of Deuteronomy* (Peabody: Hendrikson Publishers, 1996; NIBC series).

Select Subject Index

The outline on pages 25–28 should be used for identifying where
a particular topic is dealt with in a more detailed manner